Henry Miller

Titles in the series Critical Lives present the work of leading cultural figures of the modern period. Each book explores the life of the artist, writer, philosopher or architect in question and relates it to their major works.

In the same series

Georges Bataille *Stuart Kendall* • Charles Baudelaire *Rosemary Lloyd* • Simone de Beauvoir *Ursula Tidd* • Samuel Beckett *Andrew Gibson* • Walter Benjamin *Esther Leslie* John Berger *Andy Merrifield* • Jorge Luis Borges *Jason Wilson* • Constantin Brancusi *Sanda Miller* • Bertolt Brecht *Philip Glahn* • Charles Bukowski *David Stephen Calonne* • William S. Burroughs *Phil Baker* • John Cage *Rob Haskins* • Fidel Castro *Nick Caistor* • Coco Chanel *Linda Simon* • Noam Chomsky *Wolfgang B. Sperlich* Jean Cocteau *James S. Williams* • Salvador Dalí *Mary Ann Caws* • Guy Debord *Andy Merrifield* • Claude Debussy *David J. Code* • Fyodr Dostoevsky *Robert Bird* • Marcel Duchamp *Caroline Cros* • Sergei Eisenstein *Mike O'Mahony* • Michel Foucault *David Macey* • Mahatma Gandhi *Douglas Allen* • Jean Genet *Stephen Barber* • Allen Ginsberg *Steve Finbow* • Derek Jarman *Michael Charlesworth* • Alfred Jarry *Jill Fell* • James Joyce *Andrew Gibson* • Carl Jung *Paul Bishop* • Franz Kafka *Sander L. Gilman* • Frida Kahlo *Gannit Ankori* • Yves Klein *Nuit Banai* • Lenin *Lars T. Lih* • Stéphane Mallarmé *Roger Pearson* • Gabriel García Márquez *Stephen M. Hart* • Karl Marx *Paul Thomas* Eadweard Muybridge *Marta Braun* • Vladimir Nabokov *Barbara Wyllie* • Pablo Neruda *Dominic Moran* • Octavio Paz *Nick Caistor* • Pablo Picasso *Mary Ann Caws* Edgar Allan Poe *Kevin J. Hayes* • Ezra Pound *Alec Marsh* • Marcel Proust *Adam Watt* Jean-Paul Sartre *Andrew Leak* • Erik Satie *Mary E. Davis* • Arthur Schopenhauer *Peter B. Lewis* • Susan Sontag *Jerome Boyd Maunsell* • Gertrude Stein *Lucy Daniel* Richard Wagner *Raymond Furness* • Simone Weil *Palle Yourgrau* • Ludwig Wittgenstein *Edward Kanterian* • Frank Lloyd Wright *Robert McCarter*

Henry Miller

David Stephen Calonne

REAKTION BOOKS

In memoriam
Mariam Galoostian
Armenian mystic
Magna Mater

Published by Reaktion Books Ltd
33 Great Sutton Street
London EC1V ODX, UK

www.reaktionbooks.co.uk

First published 2014

Printed and bound in Great Britain by Bell & Bain, Glasgow

A catalogue record for this book is available from the British Library

ISBN 978 1 78023 344 4

Contents

1 Paradise in the 14th Ward, 1891–1908 7

2 Go West, Young Man, 1909–19 21

3 Cosmodemonia, Mona, the Daimon of Writing, 1920–29 33

4 Finding his Genius: Paris, 1930–39 49

5 The Exile Returns: Air-Conditioned Nightmare and Big Sur
  Dream, 1940–51 78

6 Magus on the Mountain, Tropics Triumphant, 1952–62 109

7 Fame and Insomnia in Pacific Palisades, 1963–71 135

8 On the Way to Devachan, 1972–80 155

References 175
Select Bibliography 216
Acknowledgements 222
Photo Acknowledgements 224

Henry Miller, *Big Sur* (1957).

1

Paradise in the 14th Ward, 1891–1908

Henry Miller was born at approximately 12:17 p.m. on 26 December 1891 at 450 East 85th Street in Yorkville, Manhattan.[1] In his great 'autobiographical romance' *Tropic of Capricorn* (1939), he pondered the time:

> Slated for Christmas I was born a half hour too late. It always seemed to me that I was meant to be the sort of individual that one is destined to be by virtue of being born on the 25th day of December . . . But due to the fact that my mother had a clutching womb, that she held me in her grip like an octopus, I came out under another configuration – with a bad setup in other words . . . One thing seems clear, however – and this is a hangover from the 25th – that I was born with a crucifixion complex. That is, to be more precise, I was born a fanatic.[2]

In *The Nightmare Notebook* (written 1940–41, published 1975) he reflected further on his origins: 'Note: I was born just under the line – 1891, Dec. 26th. No wonder I have the "Equator" complex! Cancer, Capricorn, Draco and the Ecliptic, etc. "The Dark Night of the Soul!" The Grand Pralaya.'[3] These brief extracts contain in microcosm his psychological chart: his tendency towards self-mythologizing (he was actually born twelve-and-a-half hours too late), alienation from his mother, lifetime fascination with astrology and Eastern thought ('The Grand Pralaya' – in Hindu cosmology, 'dissolution'), the mystery of destiny and a sometime messianic complex due to the proximity of his own birthdate to that of Christ.[4]

In 1892, when Henry was one year old, the Miller family moved from Yorkville to Williamsburg – the north Brooklyn neighbourhood across the East River from the Lower East Side of Manhattan, about three miles from where Walt Whitman had lived, and which Miller always referred to as 'The 14th Ward'. The streets were cobblestone and automobiles were still a rarity.[5] Here the Millers would remain until they moved to Bushwick in 1901, to the 'Street of Early Sorrows'.[6] Williamsburg was a predominantly German enclave within New York and a gigantic centre of immigration. According to Kathleen Conzen, during the nineteenth century the population peaked in 1854 'at 215,009, and again in 1882, when over a quarter of a million Germans entered the United States', and it was New York City which contained the greatest concentration.[7] Indeed, by 1855 New York had one of the largest number of Germans in any city in the world – known as *Kleindeutschland* – surpassed only by Berlin and Vienna.[8] Not only did Germans move to America to prosper, they enriched its culture through creativity and imagination: American classical music was energized by the founding of Steinway & Sons by Heinrich Engelhard Steinweg in 1853, while the Brooklyn Bridge, designed by a German engineer, J. A. Roebling, and completed in May 1883, was then the world's longest suspension bridge.[9]

Both Miller's grandfathers were among those seeking a new life; and both were fleeing from military service in Germany.[10] His paternal grandfather, Heinrich Müller (the name was soon to be Americanized, a typical practice then), came from Minden am Weser in Hanover and married a Bavarian, Barbara Kropf. Miller's father, Heinrich, was born in 1895.[11] His mother's father, Valentin Nieting of Dortmund, worked as a tailor; from him Miller received his middle name, Valentine.[12] Nieting travelled to London at age sixteen and became involved with Syndicalism (which would later influence his grandson) and then to New York City, where he met Emilie Insel, whom he married on 1 April 1866.[13] Their second daughter, Miller's mother, Louise Marie, was born on 13 January 1869.[14] Miller's Lutheran parents met in 1889 and were married the following year: the Miller family would live in the building owned by his maternal grandfather.[15] Miller, however, often speculated that he was not of German–Lutheran ancestry but rather that some of his forebears might have been Mongolian, Jewish, Tibetan or, even more outlandishly, from Easter Island.[16] Miller thus attempted to account for his total alienation from American society and his turn towards 'non-rational', mystical, 'non-Western' traditions and cultures.[17]

Miller described his childhood in stark before-and-after terms: a pre- and post-lapsarian imaginative universe with Paradise located in Williamsburg, the 14th Ward. Miller's favourite areas to play in were North First Street, the block between Driggs and Bedford Avenues; and Fillmore Place, the block from Roebling Street to Driggs.[18] Miller often celebrated the free, joyous life of a boy in the streets, even though it was 'the worst neighborhood of all – in the worst possible area'.[19] He would return obsessively to these early memories in many of his works: *Black Spring*, *Tropic of Capricorn*, *The Books in My Life* and *The Book of Friends*. There is perhaps some irony in the fact that Miller became world famous for his supposedly 'obscene' and 'pornographic' works, while in fact one of his greatest subjects is the transcendence and joy of childhood.

One of his earliest memories at age four was seeing the corpse of a frozen cat in the gutter – his first encounter with death, and 'birds singing in the cage and I was in the high chair and I recited poems in German. I knew German before I knew English.'[20] Until he went to kindergarten, he spoke both languages.[21] It is possible that Miller's long struggle with language, with being able to express himself, has one source in this early bilingualism. In addition to his exposure to both the German language and its literature, his parents took him at age seven to the *Sängerbund* or Singing Society, where he experienced several hundred men and women singing ecstatically together in a chorus, followed by drinking large mugs of beer as a quasi-religious experience: these *Vereinwesen* or German cultural organizations were widely active in the New York of his youth.[22]

Yet these tender, nostalgic memories are balanced by the brutal discipline inflicted on children. In the nearby community of Ridgewood, where Miller would spend time with his cousin, he remembered the German Americans as 'a despicable lot – the kind who later made good Nazis'.[23] Both emotional and physical abuse were common. Once when Miller was four years old, his mother asked him what she should do about the warts on her hands: he replied that she should cut them off. Two days later the wounds became infected: his mother blamed, then cursed and beat him.[24] His mother's ignorance and cruelty were horrifying, but Miller claimed her neglect did not affect him greatly until he went to school and witnessed the ways normal mothers treated their sons: with love and kindness.[25] Later in life, having 'just finished the Kerkhoven book by Jakob Wasserman' (*Joseph Kerkhovens dritte Existenz*, 1934), Miller speculated: 'I was amazed and happy that he should have ended it on the mother note. I saw some correlations here with my own psychology. The inner fanaticism born out of the lack of parental affection.'[26]

Miller's cognitively impaired sister Lauretta, four years younger, was also the victim of her mother's rage when the child made mistakes in school lessons. He saw his sister as 'an angel in the real sense, and she's always stayed one. She has never known envy, hypocrisy, lies – none of that . . . She had a nature of the utmost goodness but, like angels, she was not made to live in this world.'[27] In 'The Old Neighborhood' he expanded this theme in connection with the French writer whose philosophical works would later

Miller as a child, 1895.

fascinate him: 'In *Louis Lambert,* Balzac talks about the angel in man. It is this I remember most about childhood, this angel business. I mean, of course, the sense of innocence . . . The criminals, or guilty ones, if you like, were our parents and teachers.'[28] This quest for the pure soul within would become a recurring theme in later books such as *The Smile at the Foot of the Ladder,* and Miller maintained throughout his life a Romantic sense of the inviolability of childhood in the tradition of Wordsworth: the child is father of the man.

Miller's relationship with his father was more affirmative. Heinrich was a wonderful storyteller, easy-going and beloved by his friends; however, he drank heavily and later his son would be compelled to act as a kind of caretaker for him. Miller claimed his father 'never read a book in his life' except for John Ruskin's *The Stones of Venice.*[29] His mismatched parents would frequently fight at the dinner table. When an argument commenced, Miller would gag and was hence unable to eat: this fractured relationship with food was a problem which recurred for many years.[30] During his many periods of unemployment, he would starve and beg in the streets and his hunger then developed into 'phagomania': he would eat yet his hunger was not assuaged and he remained famished.[31] His relations with his grandfather were also more congenial than those with his female relatives. In the tailor's shop as a boy of six or seven he was sung to by his grandfather and in return Miller enjoyed reading aloud.[32] As he recalled in *Tropic of Capricorn*: 'I remember him vividly in those moments when, pressing the hot iron against the seam of a coat, he would stand with one hand over the other and look out of the window dreamily.' *Dreamily* here suggests *Heimweh,* nostalgia for Germany, the *Heimatland.*[33]

In addition to the unloving ferocity of his mother, his father's drinking problem and his sister's mental disability, Miller's relatives also led lives on the edge. Back in the early 1880s his maternal grandmother went mad and was cared for by Miller's then thirteen-year-old mother prior to removal to an asylum.[34] Miller's 'crazy' Uncle George was the product of an incestuous relationship between one of his relatives named Maggie and her brother, which horrified and shamed his parents.[35] His mother's eldest sister, Tante Melia, descended into madness and Miller was charged with taking her to the asylum, which he movingly described in *Black Spring*: 'During the journey I wept – I couldn't help it. When people are too good for this world they have to be put under lock and key. There's something wrong with people who are too good . . . I don't think that Mele had any knowledge of sin or of guilt or remorse. I think that Mele was born a half-witted angel. I think Mele was a saint.'[36] Thus we again see the emergence of the angel theme, this time in relation to a doomed and fragile aunt, who like his sister Lauretta was 'too good for this world'. These familial strains of mental fragility, incest and alcoholism led Miller to speculate about his own psychological identity: 'Everything in me is exaggerated; my faults, my feelings, my tenderness, my life, all is extreme to a degree.'[37] This gargantu-anism – the strong manic, mantic, mystical tendency in Miller's character, this volcanic propulsion towards transcendence and illumination – is evident in his compulsive esoteric studies. His psychological make-up illustrates the complex relationship between madness, genius, creativity, mystical proclivities and what Richard M. Bucke, an author Miller admired, called 'cosmic consciousness'.

If his family matrix was full of 'skeletons in the closet', Miller would find a welcome relief in the simultaneously welcoming yet violent streets of his neighbourhood.[38] Across the way from his house, the veterinary would hold horses to the ground and castrate them in public; as a boy he was sent to get beer from the nearby saloon; the burlesque house 'The Bum' attracted lines of lusty sailors from the Navy Yard. Pete Hamill declared that 'the essential Brooklyn style is often an irresistible (for a writer) combination of toughness and lyricism'.[39] Miller retained throughout his life a distinctive Brooklyn accent, punctuated by frequent 'doncha knows': his voice had a mesmerizing quality. Between the ages of five and ten he moved out into the world of his fellow 'little rascals' and 'budding young gangsters', free to wander as he desired and out of the orbit of adults.[40] He bonded with other boys in a kind of primal recapitulation of the social order of humanity's beginnings: 'It wasn't just a transitional period leading to adolescence, but something complete in itself and of a duration analogous to that of a geological epoch. As the primitive lingers on despite all our efforts to annihilate him in one way or another, so we lasted – until our wings began to atrophy.'[41] Miller demonstrated great generosity to his fellow children, and as a boy he had no attachment to things: he distributed his presents among the poorer children in his class, but was then punished by his mother on his return home.[42]

Miller attended elementary school at Public School No. 17 on North 5th Street and Driggs Avenue; later he became friends with the boys of the streets, whom he frequently invoked in a roll-call of the immortals: Matt Owen, Bob Ramsey, Tony Marella, Harry Martin, Eddie Carney, Lester Reardon, Johnny Paul and Stanley Borowski or 'Stasiu'.[43] Thomas Carlyle's *On Heroes and Hero-Worship* would be an important text for Miller, and already as a boy he had 'a cult for my heroes': he clearly put his young friends in this category.[44] His panegyrics knew no bounds: for example, one of his friends, Johnny Paul, was lauded as the person who 'opened my eyes; not Jesus, not Socrates, not the Buddha.'[45] Miller was also close to Joey and Tony Imhof of Glendale, Long Island. Their father, a German émigré, was the first painter Miller had encountered; he made watercolours and created stained-glass windows for the churches in his neighbourhood.[46] This was an important moment, marking the beginnings of Miller's lifelong love of painting.

The Spanish-American War fascinated the young Miller. Thus another of his heroes was Emilio Aguinaldo (1869–1964), the courageous Filipino rebel who fought the American Admiral Dewey and defeated the Spanish forces on 17 February 1897. Miller confessed that he had 'worshipped' Aguinaldo, and that great fighter remained in his 'pantheon' for the rest of his life. Miller also included Aguinaldo in a list of his 'heroes' and 'idols' in the late essay 'A Nation of Lunatics', and in a letter to André Breton of 31 January 1950 he noted the similarities between photographs of two great 'public enemies' he adored: one of Arthur Rimbaud (about whom Miller had been writing his critical study *The Time of the Assassins*) in 'a sort of prisoner's garb on the banks of a river', the other of Aguinaldo.[47]

Miller now made his first sexual explorations: 'It was a hairless world I gazed upon. The very absence of hair, so I now think, served to stimulate the imagination, helped populate the arid region which surrounded the place of mystery.'[48] He also reported that at this time that he and his friends would pay a girl a penny and attempt intercourse with her.[49] In 1898, at age seven, Miller joined a military brigade at the Presbyterian church in his neighbourhood, the Battery A Coast Artillery. The boys wore uniforms and drilled according to a set pattern prescribed by the manuals.[50] At the age of ten in 1901, he with his family moved to 1063 Decatur Street in the presumably 'better' Bushwick section of Brooklyn, which Miller would subsequently call 'the street of early sorrows': his 'golden' period, the ages between five and ten, had come to an end.[51] In Bushwick, uprooted from his beloved Williamsburg into 'a Lutheran cemetery, where the tombstones were always in order and the wreaths never faded', Miller remained until he was twenty-one.[52] He was unhappy now in this 'bourgeois' environment and faced with a new set of boys, who challenged him.[53] He did well in school and also took piano lessons, yet he was not only intellectual: he practised the Roman ideal celebrated in Juvenal's *Satire* x, *mens sana in corpore sano*, and went on long bike rides, ran, and played ping-pong.[54]

Miller appears to have inhabited a 'liminal' realm between sanity and insanity, genius and madness, and he later became notorious for conflating truth and fiction, reality and imagination. For example, he once claimed that at age twelve in 1903, when Miller was visiting a cousin in Manhattan, he and a group of boys during a rock fight accidentally killed a child with a blow to his head. In later accounts of the incident he leaves the reader in some doubt whether the boy was actually killed, since he and the rest of the gang ran away swiftly before the police arrived.[55] What is striking, however, is that Miller evinced not a shred of guilt over the event. Yet as we shall see, he would often purposely alter facts to make them 'more interesting', and he reserved the right to shape the narrative of his own life in such a way that separating myth from reality is sometimes a challenging task.

In 1904 Miller graduated from Brooklyn's Public School No. 85 on Covert Street and Evergreen Avenue.[56] The artist Emil Schnellock, who was to be a lifelong friend with whom Miller conducted an extensive correspondence, recounts meeting him at this time and being impressed by 'the quality of his interest. It communicated intense enthusiasm, and made what I was doing take on a greater importance to me.'[57] Miller was thus already demonstrating the charismatic qualities which many would find so attractive throughout his life: he had a gift for friendship, and for making people feel that their lives mattered to him.

At the age of fourteen he met Miriam Painter, who was three or four years older, with 'the smile of an angel', the first in a long series of women he put on the proverbial pedestal.[58] This introduction to the mysteries of women, sexuality and love coincided with the metaphysical anguish of adolescence: he began to wonder about God's existence and why the world was such a tragic place.[59] As he began his studies at Eastern District High School on Wythe Avenue in 1907, he encountered his 'first love', Cora Seward, who lived at 181 Devoe Street in Brooklyn: after dinner each night he

Miller with his family, *c.* 1900.

would take the seven-mile walk to her house to see if she was at her window. For three years he was in the grip of this obsessive behaviour.[60] The relationship remained totally idealized, and he frequently returned to the central theme of elusive 'unrequited love' later in life, even claiming that Cora's face would most likely be the final image he would recall on his deathbed.[61]

Although Miller did well in high school, he was in many ways an autodidact and undertook most of his reading outside the classroom, a pattern he would follow for the rest of his life. He chose the books he loved to read, and his fare during childhood and adolescence was variegated. He habitually requested books for Christmas, and would wake on Christmas morning unable to wait and so sit reading in his nightclothes shivering with cold. When he would go places, he would customarily carry a book under his arm in case he got bored.[62] An important volume for him at the age of ten was Edmondo de Amicis's *Cuòre* (*The Heart of a Boy*); he wondered later in life whether the way Amicis portrayed a variety of boys in the classroom existing in a kind of socialistic harmony with one another influenced his development in his own anarchist beliefs.[63]

A significant figure for the young Miller was the British novelist George A. Henty (1832–1902), whom he declared taught him more about history than conventional historians.[64] One of Henty's books became especially important due to its significance in Miller's later intellectual evolution: it was in *The Lion of the North* that he first encountered the word *astrology*, in the description of Wallenstein in chapter XXII, 'The Conspiracy': 'the blind faith which the otherwise intelligent and capable general placed in the science of astrology was well known to the world.'[65] Miller had a lifelong fascination with occult and esoteric philosophy because, as he once declared, 'I cannot accept this world. I know there is another world behind it which is the real world.' He came to see his own life as influenced by the stars: he placed Jupiter 'high above the Christian cross – and he will be there long after the cross is forgotten. Jupiter is my benevolent reigning deity', the planet which always came to his aid.[66] Never believing in an anthropomorphic god, he sought order in the patterns of the starry heavens. Henty and the subject of astrology were strongly associated in his mind throughout his lifetime: he alludes to both in a letter to his friend the French scholar Wallace Fowlie when Miller was 56 years old and again when he was 80 in his interview with Christian de Bartillat. He would be

Xerxes Society, 1910. Miller is in the front row, on the left.

powerfully attracted to other British writers of the Victorian period with 'spiritual' themes, such as H. Rider Haggard (1856–1925) and Marie Corelli (1855–1924). He read *She* at age fourteen, and the novel's Ayesha would become a significant female presence in his later relationship to his *femme fatale* June Mansfield. In addition to these British writers, at sixteen his Polish friend Stanley Borowski loaned him Balzac's *The Wild Ass's Skin* (*La Peau de chagrin*) and Miller's father, thinking that 'anything by a Frenchman, by Balzac particularly, was immoral', took the novel from him.[67]

Miller's bookish interests were balanced by more mundane pleasures, for at sixteen he also discovered burlesk. He would go with an older male friend to Manhattan, Hoboken and to 'The Star' near Borough Hall and the Houston Street Burlesk on 2nd Avenue. He enjoyed the comedians, while the fabulously erotic women were irresistible. Yet the laughter was equally important. Rabelais had famously said 'For all your ills I give you laughter', an apothegm Miller never tired of quoting. And this aspect of the burlesk he found to be life-bringing: 'I could easily have ended up a neurotic like most youngsters today. Thanks to the filth, the vulgarity, and the humor of burlesk I was saved.'[68] His equally dominating intellectual interests found a focus when the following year he joined the Deep Thinkers club, which merged with another group from Brooklyn's Greenpoint and had twelve members called the Xerxes Society. Many of the boys had musical interests and spent time in music-making and discussion.[69] Miller was an excellent student, but found his intellectual sustenance outside formal institutions: he firmly believed that 'all schools should be blown up'.[70]

As Miller prepared to graduate from high school, the students were each asked what they planned to do in life: he responded that he wanted to be a clown in the circus.[71] His anarchistic, rebellious character was formed from the beginning. Like Rimbaud, he was in total revolt against the status quo, against 'society', against the whole 'American way of life'. An 'internal émigré' and anarchist, he early on identified with misfits, outsiders and artists. Yet being a clown also had a spiritual side, for the clown was 'a symbol of man's suffering on earth . . . and of his conquest over it, too'. And returning to the 'schizophrenia' theme, Miller would tell Robert Snyder that 'at bottom I think there is a great deal of the clown in me. I'm kind of a schizoid type, who laughs and cries at the same time.'[72] He wanted to be a clown and an angel; but to communicate his message to the world he would need to be an author. From the age of sixteen to twenty he would pray: Dear God, please make me a writer.[73]

2

Go West, Young Man, 1909–19

Miller matriculated at the City College of New York, which he considered a 'madhouse', dropping out after one month because he could not abide studying Edmund Spenser's *The Faerie Queene*: 'if books like this (or 'Hermann und Dorothea' or 'John Gilpin's Ride') had to be read and digested in order to be educated, then I wanted to remain uneducated. I have never changed my opinion on this score.'[1] In addition to formal education, he would ultimately reject traditional marriage (although he married five times), country, patriotism, organized religion and employment. Like Groucho Marx, a fellow New Yorker, he did not care to belong to any club that would have him as a member. But for now he worked: he found his first job as a clerk at the Atlas Portland Cement Co. on Broad Street in lower Manhattan's financial district, where he remained for three years.[2]

Now age eighteen, he continued his voracious, heterodox reading. When he asked the librarian at the Brooklyn Public Library for A. P. Sinnett's *Esoteric Buddhism* (1884) – one of W. B. Yeats's favourite books – she exclaimed, 'Yes . . . but do you know what you're asking for?'[3] Miller also plunged into Maurice Maeterlinck, Strindberg's *Le Plaidoyer d'un fou* (The Defence of a Fool, 1895), William Lecky's *History of European Morals from Augustus to Charlemagne* as well as Marie Corelli's *Vendetta*, *Thelma* and *Wormwood*, the last of which he read secretly in bed; by the age of 21 he had read most of her work.[4] He would rediscover Corelli in

Paris 25 years later and again in his eighties. During this period he was also fascinated by the Chinese philosophers and immersed himself in Lao-Tzu's *Tao Te Ching*.[5] Already in his adolescence he had embraced the *Tao*: the 'way' towards spiritual liberation and enlightenment through living in accord with the cyclical rhythms of Nature, with the seeming opposites of experience, which reveal on deeper thought their paradoxical unity.[6]

In 1910 Miller began an affair with his first mistress, Pauline Chouteau, originally from Phoebus, Virginia. His musical talents led him to give piano lessons, and he met Pauline at the house of her friend Louise when he was teaching Louise's daughter.[7] He remembered the relationship later in Oedipal terms, noting that Pauline was the same age as his mother and that she had a consumptive son named George who was about the same age as Henry.[8] George had been sent to a sanitarium, where he died.[9] Pauline was fifteen years older, in her mid-thirties, which Miller considered 'the best period in a woman's life', and he acknowledged later in his career that Pauline had played the role of mother to him: 'The psychologist might say that I had been weaned too young, that I longed for the mother's breast. And what is wrong with that? The breast of a beautiful woman is always a comforting thing, whether one drinks from it or not. What is woman, after all, if not the comforter?'[10] He moved into Pauline's place at 366 Decatur Street, not far from his parents' home.[11] Yet he soon sought to flee and would also later claim that his love had been based primarily on pity for her.[12] Furthermore, less savoury memories of their relationship were revealed decades later when, in *The Nightmare Notebook*, the notes Miller took during his trans-American auto trip, he recalled: 'Pauline having baby in outhouse . . . George, her son, dying in next room while we fuck on floor. The landlady objecting to abortions being thrown down the toilet. Squeamish soul!'[13] Pauline had indeed become pregnant, and in another version of the crisis, Henry returned home one day to find Pauline in a heap on the bed and the five-month-old fetus in a drawer.[14]

Perhaps in honour of the Chinese philosophy of yin and yang, to balance an intensifying sexual life he now began a vigorous athletic programme. He exercised regularly, swam, ran, played tennis and rode his special racing bicycle made in Chemnitz, Bohemia, down the six-mile race path from Prospect Park to Coney Island. He enrolled in Sargent's School of Arms, located on Columbus Circle, with the intention of becoming a physical education instructor. It was a four-year course of study, but he had to quit after a few months because his mother asked him to care for his increasingly drunken father.[15] He admired the boxer Jack Johnson (whom he would meet later in Paris), and one of his great heroes was the wrestler Jim Londos, known as 'little Hercules' (later celebrated by Miller in *Plexus*), as well as Earl Caddock, 'the man of a thousand holds'.[16] During this period he was also a fan of the great cyclists Frank Kramer, Oscar Egg, Walter Rutt, Jimmy Folger and Eddie Root.[17]

While living with Pauline, he made unsuccessful efforts to write with a tiny broken pencil, but quit after composing only a few lines.[18] Miller felt severely split between his literary ambitions and his physical self.[19] He was leading two lives: one spiritual and metaphysical, the other manic and sexual, and the overwhelming tension led him at 21 to despair.[20] He consulted a phrenologist near Union Square, who told him he could become a corporation lawyer.[21] Indeed, Miller would confess to Lawrence Durrell in 1937 that he was unable to write during this period and felt he might go mad, even though he knew himself to be possessed of tremendous powers: 'Every move I made I burned my bridges behind me. Despair, desperation, megalomania . . . I saw what few men have seen without losing their faith or their balance.'[22] He found a way out of his impasse at the close of 1912 when his friend William Dewar (who would become 'MacGregor' in *The Rosy Crucifixion* series), introduced him to his half-brother Robert Hamilton

Challacombe ('Roy Hamilton' in *Tropic of Capricorn*), who belonged to the Theosophical Society, founded in New York in 1875 by Madame Blavatsky and Colonel H. S. Olcott.[23] In his essay 'To Read or Not to Read' from *Stand Still Like the Hummingbird* (1962), he recalled that Challacombe instructed him 'in the art of reading'.[24] It was from him that Miller first heard the name of Swami Vivekananda, and Challacombe is lyrically described in *Tropic of Capricorn* as a kind of guru, the first in a long line of wisdom figures Miller will praise throughout his life, encountered just at the moment of greatest crisis: 'I felt that I was in the presence of a being such as I had never known before . . . He was indeed strange, but so sharply sane that I at once felt exalted. For the first time I was talking to a man who got behind the meaning of words and went to the very essence of things.'[25] Challacombe also took Miller with him to hear the evangelist Benjamin Fay Mills, a popularizer of 'New Thought', which further electrified Miller's spiritual aspirations.[26]

In a recently published letter Miller claimed that he applied for a position out West as a gymnasium instructor in Colorado Springs: he got the job, but did not remain long and returned to New York.[27] Soon after he decided to make a journey to California to break from Pauline's grip, urged on by Challacombe, who had himself lived in Point Loma, California, before moving to New York. Miller wanted to live the simple, active, healthy life of a 'cowboy' in the great outdoors – Theodore Roosevelt's 'strenuous life'.[28] Miller hoped that this robust regimen would cure his near-sightedness (he had been treated for a year by a 'quack' doctor whom he claimed had nearly ruined his eyes), and accordingly he discarded his eyeglasses and made his way to New Mexico, arriving in March 1913, but found to his dismay that the days of the cowboy had faded into the past; he then continued towards the coast.[29] His first stop was Barstow, California, and he then worked on a cattle ranch near San Pedro.[30] He laboured as a ranch-hand in a grove in

Chula Vista near San Diego, where he burned pruned branches from the lemon trees. He was christened 'Yorkie' by the ranch-hands, who were astonished by his tales of skyscrapers, subways and fast living in New York. The work was hard: a jackass pulled the sled he drove and by nightfall his face had been roasted to a crisp through constant exposure to the fires.[31] One day, he had time off so he took a trip to National City, attracted by the name of the place. He suddenly experienced his first 'blackout': he had no memory of who or where he was: 'The 'I' was simply a dim, approximate awareness of an ego, a consciousness temporarily held in leash during a crucial planetary conjunction in which my proper destiny was being worked out for me', as he later wrote in his essay 'The Brooklyn Bridge'. The experience lasted just a few moments but seemed like an eternity and Miller was thoroughly terrorized when he came out of it, fearing that this was the first sign of a serious mental illness which might recur later in a more exacerbated form.[32]

A later traveller out West, Jack Kerouac, on a spiritual journey from the East Coast, described Sal Paradise in *On the Road* undergoing a very similar identity loss in Des Moines, Iowa, as he awoke in a hotel room:

and that was the one distinct time in my life, the strangest moment of all, when I didn't know who I was – I was far away from home . . . and I looked at the cracked high ceiling and really didn't know who I was for about fifteen strange seconds. I wasn't scared; I was just somebody else, some stranger, and my whole life was a haunted life, the life of a ghost. I was halfway across America, at the dividing line between the East of my youth and the East of my future, and maybe that's why it happened right there and then, that strange red afternoon.[33]

Kerouac, like Miller, was in his twenties leaving New York for the West in search of nirvana, in a transition period between youth and adulthood, looking for America and himself: here again is 'schizophrenia', loss of self and mystic proclivities which edge into madness. Later in life Miller had a second loss of identity experience, which lasted several minutes, while in Toulouse, France. He also experienced a recurring nightmare: he looks into the mirror and sees instead of his own face that of another person; he is then incarcerated in an insane asylum, escapes, but when he tries to speak to people, no one can understand what he says.[34]

Miller became friends with Bill Parr from Montana who was affiliated with the Industrial Workers of the World, known as the 'Wobblies'.[35] One evening, instead of a planned outing to a bordello, Miller and Parr decided to take the Toonerville Trolley from Chula Vista to San Diego to hear a lecture by Emma Goldman.[36] The great anarchist, who had travelled to San Diego with Ben Reitman, lectured on sexual freedom, birth control and modern drama.[37] Goldman had last been in San Diego a year earlier, in May 1912, to support the IWW in their opposition to a city ordinance restricting meetings in the street, and raging crowds had gathered to oppose her. Now, the following May, mobs once more threatened violence; Goldman and Reitman were taken away under police protection, so she was unable to speak. Miller may somehow have met and spoken to Goldman, but she never delivered the lecture on Nietzsche, Dostoevsky and Ibsen Miller said he had attended at that time.[38] We have yet another example of Miller shaping and dramatizing the narrative of his life for maximum effect. Miller's memory, however, was often faulty. For example, he said the loss of identity described earlier took place in National City, yet he would later write on the wall of his home in Pacific Palisades that it took place in Imperial City.[39] Yet Goldman's influence was significant: Miller would remain an anarchist with a small 'a' for the rest of his life, never joining organizations of any kind or voting in an election. In addition to Goldman, the Russian anarchist Prince Kropotkin, author of *Bread*, was also a strong influence.[40] Curiously, it was Goldman's fiery idealism which led Miller to abandon his life as an energetic cowboy in the Roosevelt mould and return to New York to be an urban intellectual again and work in his father's shop.[41]

When Valentin Nieting died in 1912 he had left money for Heinrich to co-own a tailor's shop at 5 West 31st Street in Manhattan.[42] Miller would work for his father from approximately 1913 to 1917: his role was to 'keep tabs' on him for his mother to see that he did not drink. Here he learned about silks and woollens, how to fit a suit and develop an appreciation of fine fabrics, knowledge which stayed with him throughout his life.[43] His father would have his first drink of the day about noon at the bar of the Wolcott Hotel, which was directly opposite his shop.[44] George Wickes observed that Miller's 'father moved in a comfortable, masculine atmosphere of bars and good eating, with the easy comradeship of actors, salesmen, and other sporting types'.[45] Miller would preserve this model of gregarious male camaraderie: Alfred Perlès, with whom he would live in Paris; Emil White, his factotum at Big Sur; Vincent Birge, who would pilot him across Europe during the early Sixties; and Joe Gray, an actor he met in Pacific Palisades who doubled for Dean Martin. Once during this period Henry opened his father's safe and discovered a drawer filled with pornographic playing cards and condoms bathed in talcum powder. But he was a very protective son: he once got into a violent fight with a man who insulted his father, flinging him vigorously to the floor before being restrained from choking him to death.[46]

Miller was sustained by elite intellectual nourishment during this period. During one phase he and Henri Bergson's *Creative Evolution* (1907) were inseparable: Miller carried the volume with him everywhere. The incongruity of reading such an abstruse text while working among his illiterate but lovable colleagues in the tailor's shop is described in *Black Spring*: 'He [Paul Dexter] frowned when he saw me sitting on the bench with the midgets trying to expound the meaning of *Creative Evolution*.'[47] And in *Tropic of Capricorn*: 'With *Creative Evolution* under my arm I board the elevated line at the Brooklyn Bridge after work and I commence the journey homeward toward the cemetery . . . I am the most unique individual down there . . . My language, my world, is under my arm. I am the guardian of a great secret; if I were to open my mouth and talk I would tie up traffic.'[48] The intuitive, instinctive and anti-materialist Miller would naturally gravitate towards a philosophy which celebrated the *élan vital* (one of his most beloved critical works later in life was Pandelis Prevelakis's *Nikos Kazantzakis and his Odyssey*; Kazantzakis had been a student of Bergson) and he refused a mechanistic reduction of reality. Leszek Kolakowski describes the book as 'the boldest attempt to assimilate the theory of evolution to a world view which implied a Great Mind at the steering-wheel of the universe and the absolute irreducibility of the human soul to its material conditions.'[49] Miller also became enthralled by Elie Faure's *The History of Art*, which was translated by Walter Pach, one of his father's customers.[50] Indeed, Miller would develop a penchant for synoptic works of encyclopaedic scope and ambition, such as *The History of Art*, Spengler's *The Decline of the West*, Keyserling's *Creative Understanding* and Blavatsky's *The Secret Doctrine*. He read Nietzsche's *The Antichrist*, which would inspire him to write his first essay at the age of 23.[51] He also read in German, as he revealed in a late letter to the Vietnamese Buddhist monk Phong Cong Thien: 'To me it is like the sound of distant music, the music I heard as a child and later, after leaving High School, on the long elevated train rides back and forth to work, when, to keep up my German I always took with me (holding on to a strap to read) Goethe, Schiller, Heine, but not Hölderlin, unfortunately.'[52]

Miller had by now taught himself to type: in addition to his essay on Nietzsche, he began to compose long letters to his friends.[53] Yet he still struggled with expressing himself and continued to lack self-confidence in his ability to write. Much of the time, as he went on his long walks to and from the tailor's shop – through the Bowery, Madison Square Garden, Union Square – he was an ambulatory volcano, composing in his head, thinking to himself about phrases, characters, plots, ideas, scenes, dialogue but never writing anything down on paper. Becoming an author was a quest for salvation, like becoming a 'saint, a martyr, a god'.[54] Yet he was encouraged by his first important literary encounter: Frank Harris was a customer at the shop and Miller would listen as Harris held forth in his booming voice on Shakespeare and Jesus as Miller helped him with his clothing.[55] Ultimately, one of Miller's essays would appear in *Pearson's*, which Harris edited from 1916 to 1922.[56]

Miller's relationship with Pauline continued its downward trajectory. He had made his trip West to escape her, and things had not improved. His friends Joe O'Reagan and Bill Woodruff stayed with the couple and Miller didn't mind that O'Reagan made passes at Pauline.[57] Before he had left for California, his friend Dewar introduced him to an attractive 22-year-old pianist named Beatrice Sylvas Wickens (1891–1984), who had received her education in a convent, earned a scholarship to the Metropolitan School of Music and taught piano to 25 private students.[58] However, he did not spend much time with Beatrice until the fall of 1914, when he began piano lessons at her home on 9th street: one of her favourite composers was Liszt.[59] An index of the Lisztian bombastic style Miller was churning out at the time can be gauged by the letter of 27 October 1915 with which he began his courtship of Miss Wickens: 'Got up and practiced this morning and . . . there I sat. Just me and the piano, wringing sweet agonies of sound from each other and sat in the halo of the rising sun as seen through an Indian summer's fog.'[60] Several months later, on 13 June 1916, he was confiding to her his literary ambitions and wondering if 'something will come of all this vain talk and we shall see if I be of such stuff as the gods are made'.[61] Miller comically describes in his novels the love affair which ensued. Beatrice was puritanical and felt guilty about sex so Miller launched a variety of inventive stratagems to lure her into the act.

Miller's father stopped drinking in 1916, which finally released the son from the role of guardian, so Miller now exited the tailor's shop. America had entered World War I and during the spring of 1917 the Government was seeking office workers in preparation for war: Miller went to Washington, DC, to work as a clerk sorting mail in the War Department.[62] He was apparently partially motivated to make this move by his desire to escape again from Pauline. Miller was a pacifist (as he would be throughout his life) and discovered that he could avoid the draft were he to marry. He therefore proposed to Beatrice and the couple wed on 15 June, moving to a brownstone apartment at 244 Sixth Avenue, in the Park Slope district of Brooklyn.[63]

A major event in his intellectual life occurred in the same year when Miller met John Cowper Powys – the Anglo-Welsh writer was touring America at the time – following one of his lectures on 2nd Avenue at the Labour Temple.[64] Powys, like Miller, would publish his first novel at age 43 (*Wood and Stone*, 1915) and Miller would become an enthusiastic advocate of Powys, praising his *Glastonbury Romance* (1933) as well as his *Autobiography* (1934). Powys is little read today, although he has been championed by no less a figure than George Steiner, who has reckoned him to be the equal of Tolstoy and Dostoevsky.[65] He read the work of W. E. Burghardt Du Bois at this time, who along with Powys were the first 'great figures – men of culture' whom he encountered in America.[66] This intellectual ferment was matched by Miller's engagement with the anarchist movement. As the Russian Revolution broke out, the topics of Lenin and Trotsky were in the air: Miller stood at 14th Street, Union Square, listening to Emma Goldman, the longshoreman Jim Larkin, and, as we have seen, immersed himself in Kropotkin, whose book

Hubert Harrison.

Bread Miller considered to be the work of a 'saint'. Miller also was enraptured by brilliant soap-box speeches in Madison Square given by a supremely gifted Socialist, Hubert Harrison: in *Plexus* (1953) he movingly recalled Harrison's profound dignity, self-possession and electric, poetic power, which made the white men around him seem to Miller to be like cultural and spiritual 'pygmies'.[67]

While literature and anarchism fed Miller's spiritual and intellectual hungers, matrimony was proving more challenging. He and Beatrice battled continually and had financial difficulties: to help with the rent, they had boarders live with them, including Harold Orvis Ross, a gifted pianist from Minnesota.[68] In addition to these travails – although he had retrieved a large roll-top pigeonhole desk from the tailor's shop – his efforts at writing were unsuccessful.[69] The new couple now travelled in the summer of 1918 to visit his mother-in law, and Miller would later claim that he engaged in intercourse with her, but Beatrice denied this could possibly have occurred, declaring that she had never let Miller out her sight during the whole trip.[70]

A turning point for Miller's literary morale occurred in January 1919 when he learned about *The Black Cat: Clever Short Stories* magazine, which offered subscribers the chance to submit critiques, for as the magazine's policy statement claimed: 'There is no better way to learn to write than by analysing the work of other writers.'[71] He submitted his 486-word essay on Carl Clausen's 'The Unbidden Guest', which was published in the May 1919 issue, and received a cheque for $4.86 (writers received a penny per word).[72] Miller went on to contribute to the June, August and October issues of the same year, so at 27 he was finally a published writer.[73] In his review of 'When the Red Snow Falls', which appeared in June, he found fault with the fact that 'the story is merely an adventure story of no particular interest'. There is a 'sterility' in the work of American short story writers which the great Russian and French writers avoid. They seek 'to stir one to his philosophical depths', as Miller put it in his review of 'The Unbidden Guest'.[74] He had already revealed in a letter of 9 December 1915 to his friend Charles Keeler his 'disgust' and 'pessimism' about life in America: 'Do you know where I have had to turn for any satisfaction for my disgust? To the Russian authors. There is a grim reality about their writings that appeals to me.'[75]

Miller was a published author and now he was also a father: on 30 September his daughter Barbara was born, named after Miller's grandmother.[76] This did nothing to bring about domestic tranquility, and the couple's fights escalated into total warfare. His essay on the story 'The Graven Image' for the June issue of *The Black Cat* seemed composed with one eye on his own situation: 'The single truth about marriage is that it is a disillusioner'. In his description of 'the wife absolutely devoid of character' and his sarcasm concerning 'ideal marriage', he appeared to be voicing his despair at his own horribly mismatched, destructive and ill-conceived marriage to Beatrice.[77]

3

Cosmodemonia, Mona, the Daimon of Writing, 1920–29

Now a husband and father as well as aspiring writer, it was time
for Miller to face reality. Early in 1920 he walked down to 22nd
Street and applied for a job as a messenger at the Western Union
Telegraph Co., was rejected and in anger went directly the next day
to the boss at 33 Park Place: he delivered an impassioned rhetorical
speech detailing his qualifications and was surprisingly offered a
higher position at $240 a month.[1] His official title was Employment
Manager, Messenger Department, and his duties included going
from office to office observing the messengers to make sure they
were fulfilling their responsibilities and ascertaining whether items
were stolen or money taken from the cash registers. Miller would
work eight to ten hours a day and return home at two or three in
the morning.[2] His own office was in the Fuller Building, located at
22nd Street and Broadway, later known as the Flatiron Building. He
and Mike Rivise, Chief Messenger Dispatcher, whom Miller was to
meet in 1922, had neighbouring desks on the ground floor.[3] Here he
would remain for four-and-a-half years, until September 1924.[4]

Miller's Cosmodemonic Telegraph Office (the name he gave
Western Union in *Tropic of Capricorn*) was a frenetic inferno of
demonic, insane, ceaseless and absurd activity. The company employed more than 2,000 messengers.[5] Telephones were constantly
ringing, and when Miller arrived at work early in the morning
there was already a mob of desperate men seeking employment.
This becomes for Miller the madness of American capitalism in

microcosm. He attempted to help the men he encountered, loaning them money, bringing them home to sleep at his place, and they would later populate his fiction: Mike Rivise became 'Spivak' in *Tropic of Capricorn*, while his switchboard man Sam Sattenstein was 'Hymie Laubscher'.[6] Miller customarily wore an old, worn, brown felt hat at an angle.[7] He confided to Rivise his literary dreams and asked him to read his manuscripts. The two would go on long walks together, Miller erupting in monologues; one of his favourite routes was Broadway to Delancy Street on the Lower East Side of Manhattan, then east about six blocks to the Williamsburg Bridge.[8]

The arrival of Barbara did nothing to improve his marriage, and Miller pursued women in the office, including Muriel Maurer (who later became the wife of the literary critic Malcolm Cowley) and her sister, Ethel.[9] Miller also made friends with Emil Conason, who was doing a research project at Columbia University. He contacted Miller in order to ask questions of the messengers to assess their IQs, since Emil was attempting to determine the intelligence levels of various professions.[10] Another friend was Harold Orvis Ross, the young musician from Minnesota studying at Juilliard who had come to live with Miller and Beatrice: the three got on well together and Miller hoped Harold would take Beatrice off his hands.[11] But the most important encounter was in 1921 when Miller met Emil Schnellock, a painter he had known in P.S.85 and with whom he greatly enjoyed discussing art.[12] Schnellock had been to Paris, and he ignited Miller's interest in watercolours, becoming 'Ulric' in *The Rosy Crucifixion*. Miller sent his first letter to Schnellock in 1921 (they would correspond until 1960), many of which were composed on violet-tinted paper.[13] Miller never kept a journal, so letters – many of them tremendous outpourings from 20 to 30 pages in length – were his method of recording striking events and impressions, of experimenting with ideas and perfecting his literary technique.[14] Schnellock became one of his closest friends and left a memorable account of Miller during this period, describing how when they dined together, people would inevitably be drawn to his ebullient energy. Yet he would also sometimes give 'the illusion of being completely out of the body, a man rapt to another world. These trances came upon him now and then, often at the most unusual, unexpected moments. Suddenly he was "gone".'[15] When he visited Schnellock, Miller would typically ask how he might help him, rather than ask for help for himself.[16]

In January 1921 Beatrice took Barbara with her to Rochester, New York, to live with her aunt. Miller then found an apartment at 179 Cumberland Street, Brooklyn, with Joe O'Regan (Ted O'Mara in *Tropic of Capricorn*), a friend whom he had drafted as his assistant at Western Union.[17] Miller wrote Beatrice a series of letters imploring a reconciliation. On 22 February he confided: 'I am still swimming along the surface and have a very fine grip on myself. In fact, I seem to possess an unusual sense of well-being and poise and all that sort of thing, attributable doubtless to the calm which unusually follows the storm (in this instance you represent the storm).' Beatrice was convinced to make another go of it and after visiting each other several times they were reunited in the spring of 1921.[18]

In April 1921 Miller conceived the idea of writing a novel to be called *Twelve Messengers*, based on Theodore Dreiser's *Twelve Men*, which would depict the eccentric characters he had encountered during his work at Western Union. During a three-week vacation a year later, Miller finally sat down to work on the book, writing to Schnellock on 20 March 1922 that he wrote eight hours a day, composing 5,000 words each session.[19] The vice-president of Western Union, a Mr Willever, had shared with Miller his concept of a Horatio Alger-style book about the messengers.[20] Miller decided to take this idea and turn it upside down: he now altered the original conception of his novel – which was merely to be a series of character portraits – changed the title to *Clipped Wings*, and focused on undermining the American myth of 'success' for the 'common man.' As he recalled in *Tropic of Capricorn*: 'I saw the

Horatio Alger hero, the dream of a sick America, mounting higher and higher . . . You shits, I said to myself, I will give you a picture of twelve little men, zeros, without decimals, ciphers, digits, the twelve uncrushable worms who are hollowing out the base of your rotten edifice. I will give you Horatio Alger as he looks the day after the Apocalypse, when all the stink has cleared away.'[21] Miller hammered away at a typewriter, completing a script of 75,000 words. He would acknowledge that it was a failure, but he would recycle some of the material a few years later in his next book, *Moloch*.[22]

The reconciliation with Beatrice, however, did not seem to quell Miller's volatile romantic urges. Miller and O'Regan hired the attractive Camilla Euphrosnia Fedrant (Valeska in *Tropic of Capricorn*), who could not take shorthand or type, but nevertheless came with him during his tour of the company offices. He took Camilla to clubs in the Village and apparently indulged in a rather torrid affair with her; but she was fired when the Company discovered Camilla was a 'mulatto'.[23] He also pursued a girl named Gladys, who studied Greek and Latin, was interested in Nietzsche and worked in a Greek restaurant. This fantasy quickly vaporized.[24]

During this period Miller made one of his greatest literary discoveries – the Norwegian Nobel Prizewinner, Knut Hamsun. On leaving Rochester after his visit with Beatrice, he boarded the train back to New York, reached for his coat pocket and discovered that his wife had given him a copy of Hamsun's *Hunger*: 'I started reading and mountains moved. And I who had thought she couldn't read! He made me realize that what I wanted to do was to tell what I was seeing.'[25] He fell in love with Hamsun's style and would struggle mightily to imitate him. And of course Hamsun's obsessions with romantic love spoke deeply to him. As Isaac Bashevis Singer (later one of Miller's favourite authors) would declare: 'The war of love was Hamsun's topic.'[26]

During the summer of 1923 Miller frequented the 'taxi-dance' halls near Times Square where male customers would pay ten cents to dance with a girl; he was also fond of Harlem's Roseland, where Maxwell Bodenheim was a regular.[27] One evening he headed to Wilson's Dance Hall at the corner of 46th Street.[28] He danced with the 21-year-old Juliet Edith Smerth, who went by the name June Edith Smith (or by her stage name Mansfield after she had been accepted as an actress in Lee Simonson's Theatre Guild), and his life was changed forever.[29] June was mysterious, dark, lulling, perfumed, exotic, seemingly drugged, incoherent, jumping spasmodically from one thing to the next, and the two established an immediate common ground in their excited discussions of Pirandello, Strindberg, Hamsun and Dostoevsky.[30] She was the third of five children, born on 28 January 1902 of Jewish parents in Bukovina in the Carpathian Mountains, her name Anglicized from Smerth when the family moved to America from Czernowitz in northern Romania (now Chernivtsi, Ukraine).[31] In *Tropic of Capricorn* Miller recalled: 'I remember distinctly now the fullness of her body, and that her hair was fine and straight, parted on the side, like a man's', thus foreshadowing her bisexuality, which would later torment him.[32]

As with his other inamoratas – Beatrice, Gladys, Camilla – Miller began to compose a constant barrage of letters to June.[33] And as always, life began to imitate art: June saw herself as Filipovna in Dostoevsky's *The Idiot*; Victoria in Hamsun's eponymous novel; Ayesha in H. Rider Haggard's *She*.[34] Miller was aware that he was crossing over into a liminal realm, into a *vita nuova*, as he wrote in *Sexus*: 'I was approaching my thirty-third year, the age of Christ crucified. A wholly new life lay before me, had I the courage to risk all. Actually, there was nothing to risk: I was at the bottom rung of the ladder, a failure in every sense of the word.'[35] As at his physical birth, for which his mother was to be indicted for bearing him the day after Jesus's birthday, so now on the eve of his second birth through June's love he turns again to Christian imagery. He had spent seven years with Pauline, seven with Beatrice, and he felt himself on the cusp of another cycle of seven.[36] And he had found his double: June also lived on the dangerous edge between reality and fantasy, often having difficulty separating one from the other. One night he told Beatrice about June: she understandably became furious.[37] A few weeks later in August, Beatrice caught them in bed together and the marriage was finally over: the divorce was granted on 21 December 1923, with Judge Harry Lewis officiating. Beatrice was granted sole custody of Barbara, and the alimony was calculated at $25 a week, with Miller insisting on paying $30.[38]

Miller and June struggled financially, and late in 1923 the couple stayed first with Emil Schnellock and then moved to 524 Riverside Drive, where they shared an apartment with Emil and Cele Conason.[39] June supported Miller's literary dreams and continued to earn money through her various liaisons (platonic or not was always a question) with men as a 'hostess' at dance clubs. Her husband meanwhile achieved a notable literary success with the publication of his essay 'Black and White' (a portrait of the Hindu messenger Tawde from the unpublished *Clipped Wings*) in W.E.B. Dubois's *The Crisis*, the official monthly of the National Association for the Advancement of Colored People (NAACP), in May 1924 under the pseudonym 'Valentine Nieting', his grandfather. This was a double satisfaction for Miller, since he admired the African-American author and scholar Dubois profoundly.[40]

If his literary work gave him a relatively stable source of psychological equilibrium, June's personality might best be diagnosed as labile, and Miller later described her during this period in his 'Notes on June' under the heading 'Destructiveness': 'clothes, towels, shoes, socks, hats, expensive gowns, worn to shreds in no time, or ruined by cigarette holes, by spillt [sic] wine or gravy, or paint. Habit of doing what she likes regardless of what she has on – because it would cramp her style. Allowing others to wear her things and ruin them for her: fur coat, beautiful slippers, evening wraps, mantillas, scarves, etc.'[41] 'Love is blind', says the

June in the 1920s.

cliché, and Miller fell completely into her web – a Jungian might say entranced by the pure female *anima* answering to his body and soul, a dark electric sexual socket leading to ecstasy but also to madness and death. The couple had to borrow money to pay for a marriage licence and became husband and wife on 1 June 1924 in Hoboken, New Jersey, at 11:30 a.m.[42] They asked Emil and Cele Conason to be witnesses but neither appeared, so they drafted a few people off the street to be witnesses. Miller tried to convince June to be married by a Rabbi and wanted to convert to Judaism, but he was apparently unsuccessful in this effort.[43]

They moved into a sumptuous brownstone at 91 Remsen Street in Brooklyn Heights where the rent was $90 a month, about double what Miller considered affordable given the alimony payments to Beatrice and the now four-year-old Barbara, whom he would visit on Sundays.[44] The apartment had lovely wooden floors, walnut wall panels, large bookcases, high ceilings and a stained-glass window. In *Plexus* (1953), the second novel in *The Rosy Crucifixion* trilogy, Miller would call it their 'Japanese love nest'.[45] Yet in September, according to his co-worker Mike Rivise, just three months after their marriage, he was fired from his job and given a pink slip indicating he had just two weeks more of employment.[46] Miller however proudly told the story of how he bravely quit, walking up Broadway around ten in the morning with his small briefcase saying to himself that he would never work for anyone again, feeling sorry for all the men caught up like insects in the relentless American capitalist business machine.[47] It seems very likely that Rivise has in fact given us the true version, for Miller was completely impractical, a dreamer, and the farthest thing from an 'organization man'. As Rivise declared in his book *Inside Western Union*: 'Miller was always up in the clouds – he couldn't hold his job as a Western Union employee.'[48] What is perhaps remarkable is that he lasted as long as he did.

Psychologically, this was a key moment, for Miller was now in a virtually totally financially passive role of dependency on June. He had been earning about $65 a week at Western Union: his income was now zero.[49] Again, it would seem unlikely with a wife, an ex-wife and a child to support that he would have quit Western Union voluntarily, however impetuous he was during this period. Miller believed he had genius and could indeed become a writer, but he had nothing to show for his ambition except his 'megalomania'. June took a job working as a hostess at the speakeasy Raymo's in the Village, which lasted only a short period, while Miller borrowed money from old friends.[50] The couple then decided to sell candy. In a typed notice addressed to 'Friends and Givers of Alms' and signed by Henry V. Miller and June Edith Mansfield (her stage name), Miller announced that their appeal is 'occasioned by deep distress and fathered by humiliation . . . Frankly, it is a form of high-class begging.' He asks that every week the recipients buy from them one box of 'choice imported candies'. The couple even had stationery printed with 'June E. Mansfield, 91 Remsen Street, Brooklyn' at the masthead with a catchy saying at the top: 'Candies for the sweet tooth, the critical tooth, the decayed tooth.'[51]

June was more successful than Miller in door-to-door sales – she was after all practised in the arts of seduction; however, this scheme (rather understandably) fell through. Miller had been writing various sketches and articles, informing Emil Schnellock that he had made contact with '*Colliers*, *Sat. Eve. Post, Sunday Tribune*, *NY Journal*', but little had come of these efforts.[52] Thus when Miller's friend Joe O'Regan reappeared (he even lived with the Millers for a few months) after a trip to the Caribbean and hatched a new money-making plan, suggesting Miller print his writings himself and offering to defray expenses, Miller immediately took him up on his offer, calling his project *Mezzotints*, after the American artist James Whistler and recycling some of his earlier writings under this new rubric.[53] Each instalment was to be about 350 words, printed on one side of 6 x 9 coloured paper. The impressionistic sketches sometimes had fanciful titles, such as 'If You're Dying, Choose a Mausoleum' (on modern funerals); 'Papa Moskowitz' (the owner of a restaurant Miller frequented); 'June the Peripatetic'; 'Cynara' (this had been a letter sent to June). One *Mezzotint*, 'The Awakening', deals with the dramatic night Miller considered eloping with Gladys.[54] Miller must have felt he was in an august tradition: after all, fellow Brooklynite Walt Whitman had also peddled his work door-to-door.

Again, he and O'Regan were less adept than June, so it was decided to print June's name rather than Henry's on every *Mezzotint*: the exception was 'Dawn Travellers', which was signed 'Henry V. Miller'. June now would easily sell a sheaf of *Mezzotints* for $70 or $80 during her peregrinations through the haunts of Greenwich Village.[55] June again raised the suspicion that she was selling more than just literature during these transactions, introducing the theme of sexuality, jealousy and a kind of covert pimping on Miller's part into the relationship. But within a few months this moneymaking scheme played itself out. Perhaps the most striking aspect of the episode is that in having the *Mezzotints* signed with her name, June continued the dramatic identity-theft/swapping psychological game between herself and Henry. He needs her to sell his work (and most likely her body as well); she needs him to pretend to be a writer or *artiste* in the Greenwich Village crowd. June even met a banker named Howell French who said he would support her as a writer, but this scheme fell through and appeared to be yet another disguise for a sexual *quid pro quo*.[56]

Their financial problems mounted and they were finally evicted in the spring of 1925 from Remsen Street and moved successively to Garden Place in Brooklyn Heights, to their friend Stanley's, to Karl Karsten, an old statistician friend of Henry's in Long Beach (who would become 'Karen Lundgren' in *Plexus*), and to Clinton Avenue.[57] June conceived the idea of opening a speakeasy selling bootleg gin in Greenwich Village in a small basement apartment which they rented at 106 Perry Street with money Miller borrowed from his uncle.[58] In *Plexus* Miller was less than flattering about the Village: 'The Village had indeed deteriorated. There were nothing but dives and joints, nothing but pederasts, lesbians, pimps, tarts, fakes and phonies of all description.'[59] Yet again, Miller had to pretend not to be June's husband so she could entertain her male suitors: he stayed in the background preparing drinks and washing dishes, enduring further humiliation in his inferior role as sexually passive husband, which provoked him to jealous rages.[60]

To escape, Miller decided to go to Florida with Joe O'Regan and Ned Schnellock, Emil's brother, to try and cash in on the real estate boom. On Thanksgiving 1925 they began hitchhiking and arrived in Jacksonville, Florida.[61] Miller wrote an account of the trip entitled 'Gliding into the Everglades' after returning to New York a few months later: 'Florida, Florida, Florida! It had been dinned into our ears for so long that I quite expected every fifth man in America to be hitting the long, long trail to the Everglades, to the land of perennial sunshine and orange-blossom fragrance. Florida: the workers' Paradise and the playground for the plutocrats!'[62] However, just as would happen more than 50 years later in the United States in 2008 during the financial crisis, the housing boom went to bust and Miller had to borrow $100 from his father in order to return to New York in December.[63]

Upon his return, Miller discovered that June had gone to live with her mother in Bensonhurst while he, at age 35, went back to live with his parents at 1063 Decatur Street, hiding in the closet when visitors came since his mother did not want them to know her son was a writer.[64] Some small literary balm for what must have been by now a monstrously wounded ego came when Miller sent an article on Theodore Dreiser to the *New Republic*: it was rejected, but a brief excerpt was published as a letter to the editor in the April 1926 issue.[65] One T. K. Whipple had criticized the style of Dreiser's *American Tragedy* and Miller responded: 'it becomes evident that Mr Dreiser's effects are not achieved in spite of but because of his style. The 'cheap, trite and tawdry' enable him to present a world which a more elegant and precise style could only hint at.'[66] And Ronald Millar, editor of *Liberty* magazine, asked him to write an article on 'words', which was based on an interview with Dr Vizetelly, editor of *Funk and Wagnall's*; Vizetelly wrote to Miller's father declaring his son a genius. Miller was paid $250 for his article but it was considered 'too good' for the magazine and was not published.[67]

In the spring of 1926 the couple moved to Hancock Street in Brooklyn, whereupon one lunatic scheme followed another: June decided to offer driving lessons to men; June, Henry and Joe

O'Regan headed to Asheville, North Carolina, in quest of another real estate boom; June got jobs at several speakeasies, including the Perroquet on East 61st Street, The Pepper Pot at 146 West 4th Street and the Catacomb, former haunt of Dreiser and O'Neill; Henry tried his hand at selling encyclopaedias. Then they moved back to Remsen Street, but to much less palatial digs. Miller became accustomed to begging in the streets, walking uptown to panhandle from people coming out of the theatres. Once he even stole from a blind newsvendor, but did not take all of his change, only what he needed. In 'choosing' this life of begging and poverty, Miller seemed to be unconsciously imitating the life of a *sannyasin*, the Hindu wandering mendicant, renouncing like the hero of Knut Hamsun's *Hunger* the life of materialism to live the uncompromising and spiritually dedicated life of the artist.[68]

June was now emulating the Greenwich Village bohemian style: she walked with a swing and wore heavy make-up, a black velvet suit, cream-white blouse, a scarf trailing around her neck, dispensed with panties and removed the centres of her bra cups allowing her nipples to be exposed. When she and Henry were at home, she wore a loose kimono, leaving herself open for Henry's pleasure, crossing and uncrossing her legs as he looked up from his typewriter. In *Intellectual Follies*, Lionel Abel composed a tart portrait of June, who 'at twenty-three was much too beautiful to think of doing anything whatever . . . She felt that just to exhibit her beauty was quite sufficient; by showing herself she was giving others far more than they deserved.'[69]

But this new immersion in *la vie bohème* would have unforeseen consequences. By October 1926, while working at The Pepper Pot, June became involved in a passionate relationship with Jean Kronski, a young, half-mad, drug-addicted sculptor who admired Rimbaud and carried with her a pet puppet named Count Bruga, a character in a Ben Hecht novel based on Maxwell Bodenheim.[70] The trio then relocated to a cellar apartment on the coincidentally named Henry

Street: she and June slept together in the twin bed. Miller described in his posthumously published novel *Crazy Cock* how Jean ('Vanya') began redecorating the place: 'The green walls were converted to pitchblende, the ceiling ripened into a violet shudder, the electric bulbs were tinted a Venetian pink and etched with obscene designs. Then came the frescoes.'[71] The apartment was soon wrecked: there were unmade beds; stopped-up sinks; dishes were washed in the bathtub; the shades were always drawn down over unwashed windows; the floor amassed paints, books, cigarette butts; Jean wore overalls, June was half-naked. When it got too cold, they smashed up furniture to burn in the fireplace.[72] This chaos seemed to offend Miller's orderly German sensibility. The situation devolved into a drama resembling Jean-Paul Sartre's play *Huis-clos*: three people torturing each other for eternity. Henry sought an exit and got some pills from Conason in order to commit suicide: he swallowed them, opened all the windows, and let the snow drift in. But he woke the next morning in fine fettle: Conason had given him an opiate.[73] He would have to suffer some more injuries to his male ego at the hands of the two women who were now apparently in league against him.

He took odd jobs as a dishwasher and elevator operator, slept over at his friend Emil's on the couch and went with June and Jean on Christmas Day 1926 to his parents, but a jolly time was not had by all.[74] Henry then tried various ruses to reawaken June's interest in him, such as leaving for Philadelphia and Atlantic City; but when he returned, these absences had failed to make June's heart grow fonder.[75] By March 1927 Jean and June had become obsessed with going to Paris. Without a job and in despair, Henry ran into his old friend Jimmy Pasta, who offered him a position with the Queens County Park Commission.[76] He returned home one day to find that June and Jean had left a note beneath a small statue of which Miller was particularly fond, explaining they were sailing on the ss *Suffren* for Europe; he proceeded to smash the statue against the mirror, tear up the furniture and weep like a child. Within a week he was back at his parents' house on Decatur Street.[77] Henry soon began to receive cables from June requesting money. Miller was now past despair, even considering going back to Beatrice, but he sent June a good part of his paycheck.[78] Yet it took this crisis finally to fire the spark which would lead to his creativity as a writer: he had found his subject. On 21 May 1927 he sat down at his job at the Parks Department in Queens and over the next 24 hours compiled about 30 pages of notes concerning his tumultuous life with June and her liaison with Jean.[79]

Meanwhile in Europe, the stars were in alignment: June and Jean quarrelled and Jean disappeared to Algiers with an eccentric Austrian named Alfred Perlès. At the beginning of July, June cabled Miller to report that she would be arriving on the *Berengaria*: Miller patiently waited for her but she did not appear until a week later.[80] June regaled Henry with stories about art and culture in Paris and they moved to another fancy place at 180 Clinton Avenue.[81] June opened a new dive she named The Roman Tavern on Macdougal and Third streets in Greenwich Village, where she encountered an affluent admirer named Ronald Freedman (or 'Pop'), so the cash-flow problem for now was solved. Furthermore, 'Pop' wanted to support her writing – he had been impressed with 'her' *Mezzotints*. If she could produce a novel, he would come up with the money to send her to Europe to live as an *artiste*.[82]

Miller now began writing, under June's name, the novel *This Gentile World*, which he later named *Moloch*, the Canaanites' and Phoenicians' god who demanded bloody sacrifice – 'the cringing submission of the slave', as Bertrand Russell put it in *A Free Man's Worship*. Moloch's name is chanted in the second section of Allen Ginsberg's *Howl*: 'What sphinx of cement and aluminum bashed open their skulls and ate up their brains and imagination?'[83] *This Gentile World* describes Miller's life during the early Twenties, his first marriage and employment at Western Union (he becomes

Dion Moloch while Beatrice is Blanche) and recycles episodes from the unpublished *Clipped Wings*. Miller struggled with the text and the stilted and derivative style may be gauged by the opening line: 'Dion Moloch walked with the dreamy stride of the noctambulo among the apparitions of the Bowery.'[84] In the spring of 1928 he and June took an enjoyable vacation to Montreal, experiencing its food and wine as a foretaste of their move to Paris.[85] When they returned, June delivered the manuscript to 'Pop': he was well pleased, the money for June's trip to Paris arrived and the couple sailed for Europe in July.[86]

In the recently published (2012) *Paris 1928: Nexus II*, Miller described their arrival: 'So this is it, said I to myself, coming down the gangplank at Le Havre ready to set foot on French soil. *Europe!* Though I had been preparing for it for seven days, and before that for seventy-seven years or centuries, I could scarcely believe my eyes. No child could welcome its mother with more eagerness than I welcomed the sight of Europe.'[87] Miller loved bicycle riding, so he and June bought bikes and set off on a tour suggested to them by the sculptor Osip Zadkine, whom June had met during her earlier trip to Paris: Auxerre, Vézelay, Lyon, Éze, Monte Carlo, Nice, the château of Beaucaire, through the Rhone Valley to Avignon. One town, Tarascon, particularly fascinated Miller because of Alphonse Daudet's *Tartarin*, so he made a special visit there, which he thoroughly enjoyed.[88] They journeyed across Europe, to Belgium, Germany, Hungary, Austria, Poland, and even made a special trip to June's birthplace in Czernowitz, Romania, on the Russian border, which Miller recalled five decades later: 'the flies so thick at meal time that two sons with fans kept brushing the flies away from our food.'[89]

Miller also made a significant literary contact in Paris: the American writer Walter Lowenfels and his wife, Lillian, to whom he showed his novels; they were unimpressed. But 'a year or two later Henry started on an entirely new tack and we began receiving carbons of chapters that eventually turned into *Tropic of Cancer* and *Black Spring*. With the chapters came letters – and sometimes letters without chapters.'[90] After their money ran out, the couple returned to New York on 8 November 1928 on the ss *Leviathan* and rented an apartment at 7 Clinton Street. June now fell into heavy drug use while Miller continued his career as *sannyasin*.[91]

Miller began a new book about himself and June which he at first titled *Lovely Lesbians*, and later *Crazy Cock*. Since his return from Europe, Jean had come back to New York, was put in an asylum and then committed suicide, while Beatrice married a man 25 years older than herself.[92] Miller again tried to make sense on paper of his chaotic life, taking as subject-matter the traumatic triangle starring three deranged protagonists of 1926–7: he is Tony Bring in the novel, while June and Jean are Hildred and Vanya. Published posthumously, as was *Moloch*, *Crazy Cock* is narrated in the third-person and the prose is again burdened by a nineteenth-century style: Miller would not break out into his original, first-person barbaric yawp until *Tropic of Cancer* (1934). June found another sugar daddy in Stratford Corbett, an insurance man who worked at New York Life, while Miller began making watercolours.[93] June now invented her final stratagem: Roland Freedman, alias 'Pop', continued to be in her clutches and she was ready to squeeze from him whatever she could. She told Henry that it would be best if he returned alone to Europe to work on his writing, while she remained in New York. Meanwhile, other cataclysms were rocking the world: Black Thursday fell on 24 October 1929, the Wall Street Crash which led to the Great Depression.

4

Finding his Genius: Paris, 1930–39

In February 1930, Miller boarded the ss *Bremen*, borrowing $10 from Emil Schnellock as he did so, and set sail for Europe.[1] He had intended to head for Spain, but June had supplied only enough money for a trip to Paris. He arrived in London on 25 February, continuing on to France on 4 March, first staying at the Hôtel de Paris (where he had been previously with June), then at the Hôtel St Germain des Pres, 36 rue Bonaparte.[2] An inveterate walker in New York City, he now tirelessly enjoyed the streets of Paris, at one point passing by the house at 147 Boulevard Saint-Germain of his hero Elie Faure, author of *The History of Art*, but was too shy to knock.[3] Miller was stupefied by the glories of Paris, admired the Seine (its quiet movement would provide the serene closing image of *Tropic of Cancer*) and made periodic trips to American Express to determine whether June had wired any funds: the answer was usually negative and Miller starved. To pay for the first hotels, he sold the suitcases and clothes given him by his father, but he also slept several times under bridges. His poverty was extreme: his possessions amounted to a toothbrush, a raincoat, a Mexican cane and a single pen.[4]

He encountered Alfred Perlès, the Austrian whom he had met during his trip with June in 1928. 'Alf' wrote fine English, composed novels in French and arrived just in the nick of time, for Miller described himself picturesquely: 'The ass was out of my breeches and my tongue was hanging out.'[5] Perlès worked at the

Chicago Tribune (Paris Edition), so he had a small but dependable salary: the two stayed for a time at the Hôtel Central located on rue du Maine.[6] Perlès helped him learn French, and with the aid of a dictionary Miller translated *Moravagine* by Blaise Cendrars. As Cendrars' daughter Miriam recalled, this was 'one of his first attempts at reading the French language'.[7] Miller would never become a master at controlling the pure, nuanced registers of written or spoken French, as did other expatriate authors such as Samuel Beckett or the Romanian E. M. Cioran. But France became his real spiritual mother, as opposed to his German mother, whom he hated, and Paris, the muse of artists for centuries, afforded him the freedom to express himself openly and to invent the poetic language with which to transcribe his feverish inner life.

Miller arrived in Paris after the heyday of America's 'Lost Generation' – Hemingway, Fitzgerald, Stein and Dos Passos. His was the Paris of the Depression and mass unemployment, yet Miller retained his *joie de vivre* and fully shared the French love of superb food and wine. He would write hymns of praise to the city's urinals as well as the great essay 'The Staff of Life', which unfavourably compared tasteless, vapid American bread to the glorious baguette.[8] The 'picturesque quarters' of Paris reminded him of his paradisal time in Brooklyn's 14th Ward, yet their many blandishments could not assuage his heartache when he failed to receive any letters from June.[9] He remained celibate for a few months, then indulged in *filles de joie*, becoming particularly fond of one Germaine Daugeard, about whom he would compose his first successful story, 'Mademoiselle Claude'.[10] However, in late September he finally received word from June, who announced she would arrive soon on the *Majestic.* The couple then moved from hotel to hotel, fighting constantly, and by the beginning of November June had returned to America.[11]

He had always made friends easily, and soon he encountered the Russian Eugene Pachoutinsky, who came to his aid, as well as the photographer Gyula Halász, son of an Armenian mother and Hungarian father, who would become known as Brassaï. When they met in December 1930 through his friend the painter Louis Tihanyi, Brassaï was making a poor living composing articles for Hungarian newspapers.[12] Miller would become fascinated by the photographs in *Paris by Night* (1932) and composed an admiring essay about his work entitled 'The Eye of Paris' (from *Wisdom of the Heart*). Brassaï later recalled Miller's

> sonorous bass voice – warm and virile, punctuated by 'yeses' and 'hmms', and accompanied by a deep, gentle rumble of pleasure . . . he was slender and gnarled, and without so much as one ounce of excess body fat. He reminded me of an ascetic, a mandarin, a Tibetan holy man.[13]

Miller also met Fred Kann, a painter interested in theosophy, whom Miller would visit a decade later during his 'air-conditioned

Blaise Cendrars, *c*. 1950.

nightmare' trip across America and who introduced Miller to Richard Galen Osborn, a Yale graduate who worked as a lawyer at the National City Bank in Paris, later depicted as the mentally unbalanced 'Fillmore' in *Tropic of Cancer*.[14] Miller seemed to attract neurotics; they found his warm, buoyant, energetic, affirmative charisma to be life-giving, and during the winter of 1930 Osborn put Miller up at his place at 2 rue Auguste-Bartholdi and helped him financially; in return Miller shined his shoes and kept house.[15] Miller also met Wambly Bald, who wrote a column in the *Tribune* entitled 'La Vie de Bohème (As Lived on the Left Bank)'.[16]

It did not take long for Miller's protean genius to begin igniting in multiple directions: he read Céline's *Voyage au bout de la nuit*, which he had obtained in proof before publication, D. H. Lawrence, Miguel de Unamuno, Jung, Spengler, Elie Faure, Blavatsky, Hermann Keyserling and Proust.[17] Indeed, Miller was doubtless the most widely read twentieth-century American author. Faulkner, Steinbeck, Fitzgerald, Hemingway, none come remotely close to the range and depth of Miller's vast intellectual curiosity. And he also differed from his compatriots in another crucial way: he did not see himself as a 'writer' who attempted to produce technically refined stories or novels, but was rather in the ravenous, philosophically striving tradition of Henry David Thoreau and Ralph Waldo Emerson. He immersed himself in everything from ancient Chinese and Indian texts to theosophical, esoteric, historical and philosophical tomes, and the writings of Dadaists and Surrealists. He began covering the walls with charts and complex diagrams, mapping out his ideas for writing projects.[18] Indeed, what became abundantly clear during this period was that Miller had never been a lazy, bohemian *poseur*, but rather possessed a hard-working, disciplined, unyielding will.

Miller's earliest writings published while he was in Paris include an essay on the 'Cirque Medrano', which he had attended with Osborn and been deeply impressed by the clowns. It was published in early 1931, as well as 'Six Day Bike Race', which appeared in the

Miller in Paris, 1930s.

Tribune.[19] Clowns and angels would coalesce into a double symbol for Miller of humanity's spiritual estrangement and yearning for plenitude. In April 1931 Miller again met Walter Lowenfels (whom he had encountered during his earlier trip with June), who in turn introduced him to Michael Fraenkel, a writer obsessed with the concept of death, then living at, and landlord of, 18 Villa Seurat. Miller briefly stayed here and returned three years later; Fraenkel and Miller would conduct a spirited exchange of letters published in two volumes entitled *Hamlet*.[20]

Miller created a scheme to have various friends feed him every day, and in this fashion he met Bertha and Joseph Schrank. During the summer of 1931 he fell for Bertha, who would appear in *Tropic of Cancer* as 'Tania'.[21] In July 1931 Perlès brought Miller to Ralph Jules Frantz at the *Tribune* office, who employed him as a proof-reader of stock exchange quotations for $12 a week. Miller soon disappeared for about ten days without informing anyone, so Frantz gave the position to someone else.[22] He had split for Belgium, apparently in the company of Bertha, who ended up breaking off their affair when her husband returned in September.

Miller took his dismissal easily, but of course he was never crestfallen when he lost a job.[23]

After the lease on 2 rue Auguste Bartholdi ran out, Osborn and Miller parted; Miller stayed at the Hôtel Central, where Perlès also lived. He now began to gain some notoriety, since Wambly Bald wrote a column about him.[24] He sent his essay on Luis Buñuel's *L'Age d'or* (the Spanish filmmaker's Surrealistic attack on bourgeois hypocrisy appealed greatly to him) and 'Mademoiselle Claude' to Samuel Putnam, who published the tale in the Fall 1931 issue of *The New Review*.[25] (Putnam would appear as 'Marlow' in *Tropic of Cancer*.) This was a breakthrough, for Miller had now begun to loosen his stilted, imitative prose style and created an affecting portrait of a prostitute with a heart of gold. The story was noticed by the editor Pat Covici in New York, who asked Miller to submit work: Miller sent his novel *Crazy Cock*, but it was rejected.[26] Peter Neagoe also published 'Mademoiselle Claude' in his *Americans Abroad*, a 1932 anthology which included Hemingway, Dos Passos and Ezra Pound.

In early September 1931 June was scheduled to arrive again. When she did, her appearance was ghoulish: she carried with her Count Bruga, which put Miller in a less than happy mood.[27] He now began writing *Tropic of Cancer*. Wambly Bald, with whom Miller went on long bike rides through the Bois de Boulogne on Sundays, recalled his ambition: 'What I want to do is write stuff that has real guts, not just the phony sentimental stuff that's called realism today but something that gets right down to the bone, hard, honest realism.' He was now writing 'from the top of his head' and had initiated a new form: autobiography as novel.[28] Miller's social circle began to expand. Richard Osborn had become Anaïs Nin's lawyer; she was the wife of his boss at the bank, Hugo Guiler. The couple lived about 45 minutes from Paris in a fancy house in Louveciennes. One day Osborn showed Miller a manuscript on D. H. Lawrence by Nin and shared with her the essay by

Miller on Buñuel's *L'Age d'or*. Nin was impressed: she compared the impact of his primal, atavistic style to hearing drums beating in the Tuileries gardens.[29] He in turn was entranced by the perceptive, nuanced delicacy of Nin's insight into Lawrence's mystic genius.

Nin had been born in Neuilly and was of Spanish, French and Danish descent. Her father, Joaquin, was a pianist and composer, with whom Nin had had an incestuous relationship. In 1913 Joaquin abandoned his family in France. Miller met the 28-year-old Nin at Louveciennes in October 1931, the start of a tempestuous, creative and fruitful relationship which would continue with several ruptures for the rest of her life.[30] Nin wrote in her diary after the first encounter with Miller that he was, like herself, a person who was intoxicated by life.[31]

June appeared wearing Rachel No. 2 face powder, was dyeing her hair in succession in mauve, purple and rust red, peppered her conversation with words like 'succubus' and 'necrophilian', continued to identify herself with Dostoevsky's Stavrogin, and swam naked in the Seine. She went to meet Anaïs Nin dressed in her flamboyant costume, and drama swiftly ensued, mirroring the earlier triangle with Jean. Nin was struck by her beauty.[32] And she wrote in her diary that she did not believe June and Jean were involved sexually; also that although June was just three years older than she, Nin saw her as the wiser one.[33] Miller would come to see the diaries (later published) as a masterpiece, but he also objected to Nin's refusal to live life fully by taking refuge in neurotic fantasy and psychoanalysis. Nin became friends with the Viennese psychoanalyst Otto Rank, author of *Art and Artist*, a book Miller admired for its insights into creativity, although he would often jeer at psychoanalysis. Rather like Vladimir Nabokov, who saw Freud as the 'Viennese quack' and found his own private ecstasy in butterflies, chess and complex intellectual games, Miller abjured shrinks and would seek other esoteric escape routes from his inner conflicts.[34]

Anaïs Nin, New York, *c.* 1950.

He again needed a job and at the end of December was offered a position at the Lycée Carnot in Dijon as a *répétiteur d'anglais*.[35] Before he left, a few weeks later in early 1932, Nin gave Miller a copy of *A la recherche du temps perdu*, which he read closely and annotated over the next several months, becoming mesmerized by the jealousy theme in 'Albertine Disparu' and 'La Prisonnière', which he experienced as an exact description of the psychological inferno he had endured with June. In one passage Miller marked next to Proust's text: 'This almost hurts too much to read.' [36] He found Dijon horrible and later hilariously recounted his experiences as a teacher in *Tropic of Cancer*: he had lectured his young students about the sex lives of elephants. One positive thing to come out of the trip was his friendship with Lawrence Clark Powell, who would later (1948) become librarian at UCLA, where he would establish the Henry Miller Archive.[37] He remained intellectually active in Dijon, writing Nin a constant stream of letters packed with his latest discoveries and ambitious plans. In a letter of 4 February 1932, he reported that he was translating Georges Duhamel's *Journal de Salavin*.[38] Nin also helped Miller financially and began reading his manuscripts, suggesting improvements to *Moloch*.[39]

In late February Perlès informed Miller of a job opening at the *Tribune* for a proofreader: Miller escaped from the Lycée Carnot without telling anyone.[40] At the end of March he and Perlès moved to a small apartment with two rooms, a kitchen and bathroom at 4 avenue Anatole-France in Clichy, a working-class neighbourhood which may have attracted Miller because Louis-Ferdinand Céline had lived at 36 rue d'Alsace.[41] He was swiftly terminated from the *Tribune* on 25 March because he did not have a work permit.[42] Miller was fond of the Café Wepler, which became his home away from home for two years, and where he observed and met various ladies of the night, while also relishing his visits to the Zeyer, Sélect, Dôme and Bouquet d'Alésia.[43] Meanwhile in April Nin began analysis with Dr René Allendy and by the end of the summer she was supporting Miller financially, thus replacing June in the role of fairy godmother.[44]

June returned in October, and the two women apparently became close intimates (indulging in some kissing) but not lovers, although as with June's relationship with Jean, these distinctions are perhaps very fine. Nin devoted her story 'Alraune' to the developing triangle, and Miller and Nin consulted Otto Rank in an attempt to disentangle the enveloping web. On Rank's suggestion, Miller wrote down his dreams and during 1933 transcribed 247 pages of his notes and analyses: many of his night-time visitations were very bizarre indeed.[45] June and Miller were essentially driving each other crazy, or crazier, and Nin and Perlès became concerned that Miller was headed towards a breakdown, so at Christmas they sent him away to London, while June sailed back to America at the end of December, a fiasco recorded in Miller's story 'Via Dieppe–Newhaven'.[46]

He continued his peripatetic labour on a work initially titled 'The Last Book', then 'The Tropic of Capricorn' and finally 'Tropic of Cancer', composed 'on the wing, as it were, between my twenty-five addresses'.[47] The title reflects his fascination with astrology – the book is steeped in references to the planets, zodiacs and horoscopes – and alludes to a sentence from one of his favourite books, Petronius' *Satyricon*: 'I was born myself under Cancer, and therefore stand on my feet, as having large possessions both by Sea and Land!'[48] As he often explained, 'the crab is the only creature to move sideways, to have ability to move in every direction, even backwards', suggesting his later absorption in the 'stand still like the hummingbird' philosophy of Zen.[49] As we have seen, *Tropic of Cancer* was thoroughly autobiographical, containing portraits of Osborne, Samuel Putnam, Wambly Bald, Bertha Schrank and even Michael Fraenkel, who becomes the death-obsessed 'Boris' in the famous opening, bursting with sexual and apocalyptic energy.

Miller had shifted finally from the third-person, almost Victorian, artificiality of his earlier writings to a rambunctious celebration of the first-person 'I', revelling in the spontaneous free style he had honed in his letters to his painter friend Emil Schnellock, such as one dated April 1930 from the Hôtel Central entitled 'Bistre and Pigeon Dung', while the passage on Burgundy derived from a letter he had written to Nin from Dijon.[50] The original manuscript was over 900 pages in length and Nin helped to cut the text considerably, rather like Pound performing his maieutic duties in pruning T. S. Eliot's *The Waste Land*.[51]

Miller gave the text to William A. Bradley, a well-known American literary agent based in Paris. Bradley submitted it to Jack Kahane, who exclaimed in his *Memoirs of a Booklegger* that he had read 'the most terrible, the most sordid, the most magnificent manuscript that had ever fallen into my hands'.[52] Kahane asked Miller to write a long essay on D. H. Lawrence to give him respectable literary credentials before bringing out the incendiary *Cancer*, and Miller began work on the project, at first finding much to object to in Lawrence. By April 1933 he began the third version of his manuscript, becoming thoroughly immersed in the English novelist's life and work. Nin helped. To provide Miller with a steady supply of paper she gave him the discarded New York Stock Exchange sheets from her husband's bank and Miller composed on the backs of them. He also posted gigantic sheets of wrapping-paper on his walls to use as charts when mapping out his ideas, but he eventually got lost in the labyrinth of Lawrence's genius and the project stalled. The book was never completed, but sections were published later as 'The Universe of Death' and other essays. The whole text appeared posthumously in an edited version as *The World of Lawrence: A Passionate Appreciation* (1980). Miller took a break by going for a bicycle tour of Luxembourg with Perlès.[53]

In March 1933 Nin met Antonin Artaud, who was also being treated by her analyst, René Allendy, and Miller would soon move into Artaud's apartment at Villa Seurat.[54] In the 'Preface' to his booklet on watercolours, *The Waters Reglitterized*, Miller praised Artaud's *Van Gogh, the Man Suicided by Society*. Artaud was a genius who was mad, like Van Gogh, Nerval, Swift and Nijinsky, and 'tinged with the vitriol of scorn, hatred, contempt and disdain for the "sane", for the bourgeois spirits, for the aesthetes, the patrons and the patronizers of art. Ditto for the whole breed of psychiatric quacks into whose hands men like Van Gogh and Artaud inevitably fall.'[55] Meanwhile, Kahane kept delaying publishing *Tropic of Cancer* for both financial reasons and fears of censorship.[56] Even in the midst of this frenetic activity, Miller had time in April 1934 to write Emil Schnellock a long letter about one of his favourite contemporary artists, Maurice Utrillo: he was overcome by Francis Carco's *La Légende et la vie d'Utrillo* (1928), which he read weeping in the rain while sitting on a public bench. In June Nin decided to provide 5,000 francs for Kahane to publish *Tropic of Cancer*.[57] Also with Nin's help, at the end of September, Miller began moving into 18 Villa Seurat, in the centre of a working-class neighbourhood in the 14th arrondissement near the Alésia metro.[58]

Miller completed the move to Villa Seurat on 24 September, the same day *Tropic of Cancer* was delivered to his door, 1,000 copies in paper covers printed by the Obelisk Press at 16 place Vendome.[59] The artistically crude cover was due to the fact that Kahane did not want to pay an artist for the illustration, so he had his adolescent son Maurice draw a crab clutching a nude woman in its claws (Maurice Girodias would continue the Obelisk firm of his father under the name of Olympia Press, which would publish works by Samuel Beckett and Nabokov's *Lolita*).[60] Miller expended prodigious energy making *Tropic of Cancer* known, sending copies to Aldous Huxley, Pound, Eliot, Cendrars, L.-F. Céline, Paul Valéry, André Breton and Tristan Tzara.[61]

Although *Tropic of Cancer* would make Miller famous due to its explosive sexual language, the book is the first in his long autobiographical sequence about the struggle for spiritual evolution. As he said, 'Liberally larded with the sexual as was that work, the concern of its author was not with sex, nor with religion, but with the problem of self-liberation.'[62] He gets pushed down to the bottom, and when this happens he waits patiently and floats back to the top. As in the mystical tradition, there is a death of the old self and a rebirth of the new. He learns to be free of hope and therefore of illusion, to take life in the moment as it is, no expectations, detached: the lessons of Zen Buddhism – chop wood, carry water. Miller is writing confession in the tradition of St Augustine and Rousseau and paving the way for the Beat movement. The opening – 'I have no money, no resources, no hopes. I am the happiest man alive' – prefigures *Howl*, the same *cri de coeur* as Ginsberg's barbaric yawp, but Miller is defiant, lusty and affirmative, even (or especially) in the face of apocalypse. Two other figures significant to the Beats influenced the composition of *Tropic of Cancer*. Hamsun's *Hunger* provided Miller with the model of a poetic, starving writer wandering the city, while *The Decline of the West* by Spengler (whom William S. Burroughs counselled Ginsberg and Kerouac to study) furnished him with a threnody to the demise of Late City Man. As Mario Praz observed, Miller described 'the carcass of a civilization in decay, represented by the horror of this squalid and sprawling city and the emptiness of a mechanized life'.[63] Even at the age of 87 Miller would declare that 'the whole damn civilization, to my mind, could blow up tomorrow and it would be all to the good'.[64] However, the angry and strident sections of the book are balanced by lyrical evocations of the beauty of Paris and a magnificent homage to Henri Matisse.

'Chap named Miller has writ a bawdy which will be very useful to put Wyndham [Lewis] and J.J. [Joyce] in to their proper cubbyholes; cause Miller is sane and without kinks', wrote Pound to Olga Rudge on 1 December 1934.[65] The following November, George

Orwell reviewed *Tropic of Cancer* in the *New English Weekly*, Herbert Read and Ernst Jünger responded appreciatively and Aldous Huxley confessed the book 'made him feel swallowed to an extent that no El Greco could ever do'.[66] Perhaps the review which mattered most to Miller was by Blaise Cendrars: 'Unto us is born an American writer . . . a noble book, a frightful book, just the kind of book I like best.'[67] Cendrars came to visit Miller on 14 December 1934, arriving at three in the afternoon. That day, as usual, Miller was without funds, so Cendrars took him to a wine merchant friend of his at place des Abbesses in Montmartre, where they had a splendid meal, drank, laughed and conversed until late that night. Miller would always praise Cendrars to the skies, declaring that with the exception of John Cowper Powys and Céline, 'no other contemporary writer made as great an impression on me'.[68]

The making of *Tropic of Cancer* was the death of Miller's relationship with June: without their tragic love he would never have become a writer.[69] In December he learned that June had divorced him by proxy in Mexico City.[70] Anaïs Nin went to New York with Otto Rank and Miller followed in January 1935.[71] He wrote to Cendrars (12 January): 'Everything seems more monstrously colossal and cruel and callous than ever. A detestable place!' The painter Hilaire Hiler arranged for him to meet several American writers, including William Carlos Williams, Nathaniel West, James Farrell and William Saroyan.[72] Miller also met Frances Steloff, who in 1920 founded the Gotham Book Mart at 51 West 47th Street and who would become his staunch champion.[73] And in a curious twist on Miller's relationship to psychiatry, he began practising analysis: by February Miller (as a 'lay analyst') was seeing four patients a day. Nin and her husband returned to Paris in May 1935, with Miller following soon after.[74]

He made another significant literary contact in James Laughlin, a young Harvard graduate who lived in Rapallo, Italy, where he had become a disciple of Ezra Pound. One day, Laughlin recalled,

Pound had a copy of *Tropic of Cancer* 'and he threw it across the table to me: "Waal, Jas, here's a dirty book that's really good. You'd better read that if your morals can stand it." So I read it and I thought it was wonderful.'[75] Thus would begin Miller's long relationship with Laughlin's publishing firm, New Directions. Miller had written a text about his just-completed trip back to America, which contained strong language, entitled *Aller retour New York* and an excerpt was printed as 'Glittering Pie' in the Harvard *Advocate* in September 1935. The editors were put in gaol overnight and threatened with a severe sentence, the copies of the issue destroyed by the Boston police, the first in Miller's long line of skirmishes over 'obscenity' with the legal system.[76]

Over the summer Miller wrote *What are You Going to Do about Alf?*, a humorous appeal to raise money for Alfred Perlès so that he could continue his writing projects, and Kahane also agreed to publish the book Miller was now completing, *Black Spring*.[77] In August, the 23-year-old Lawrence Durrell wrote him from Corfu, initiating a close literary friendship that continued for the next 45 years: 'It's a howling triumph from the word go . . . it really gets down on paper the blood and bowels of our time. I have never read anything like it.' Miller responded: 'Your letter rocks me a bit too. You're the first Britisher who's written me an intelligent letter about the book. For that matter, you're the first anybody who's hit the nail on the head.'[78] Miller became editor of the 'Siana Series', Anaïs spelled backwards, the intention of which was to publish members of the Villa Seurat circle; *Aller retour New York* was the first title, appearing in October 1935.[79]

During this period Anaïs Nin objected to Perlès' influence on Miller, so Perlès was ejected from Villa Seurat and moved nearby.[80] Perlès and Miller became acquainted with the German painter Hans Reichel, the spiritualist David Edgar and Betty Ryan. This 'Villa Seurat group' would expand to include Raymond Queneau, David Gascoyne, Grégoire Michonze, Brassaï, Abe Rattner and, in

1937, Durrell.[81] In April, 1936 Nin journeyed to Morocco and shortly therafter became involved with Gonzalo More, a Peruvian musician.[82] In the fall, Nin introduced Miller to the astrologer Conrad Moricand, who made Miller's chart, just as he had those of Picasso, Cocteau and Modigliani. It was Nin who awakened in Miller his interest in astrology, which had lain dormant since his childhood reading of Henty's *The Lion of the North*: Miller chalked his own chart on the walls at Villa Seurat. He also began to correspond with the astrologer Dane Rudhyar: Count Keyserling, whose *Travel Diary of a Philosopher* Miller enjoyed, advised him to read Rudhyar's *Astrology of Personality*, which became one of Miller's favourites.[83]

Black Spring (originally titled *Self-Portrait*) was published in June 1936 by Obelisk Press in an edition of 1,000 copies.[84] Miller returned to Petronius' *Satyricon* for the epigraph to 'The Third or Fourth Day of Spring': 'To piss warm and drink cold, as Trimalchio says, because our mother the earth is in the middle, made round like an egg, and has all good things in herself, like a honeycomb.' Petronius would also influence Fitzgerald's *The Great Gatsby* and Eliot's *The Waste Land*; Miller later became wildly enthusiastic about Fellini's film *Satyricon* (1969).[85] Petronius returns in 'A Saturday Afternoon': 'When I read Petronius or Apuleius or Rabelais, how close they seem! That salty tang! That odor of the menagerie! . . . Trimalchio tickles his own throat, pukes up his own guts, wallows in his own swill.'[86] One can see the influence of Petronius and Rabelais in the marvellous descriptions of food in Miller's memories of his Germanic childhood in 'The Tailor Shop': 'A merry crew and the table loaded with good things – with red cabbage and green spinach, with roast pork and turkey and sauerkraut, with kartoffelklosze and sour black gravy, with radishes and celery, with beautiful white cauliflower, with apple sauce and figs from Smyrna'.[87] In 'The Fourteenth Ward' Miller delights in his typically highly charged metaphoric breaking and soaring lyricism as he describes his first encounter with Dostoevsky: 'And then one day, as if suddenly the flesh came undone and the blood beneath the flesh had coalesced with the air, suddenly the whole world roars again and the very skeleton of the body melts like wax. Such a day it may be when first you encounter Dostoevsky.'[88] Raymond Queneau, with whom Miller would establish a significant relationship, wrote in his review in *La Nouvelle Revue Française*: '*Black Spring*, however, marks an advance on *Tropic of Cancer*: now the verbal mastery of Henry Miller affirms itself without weakness, his language has again grown in beauty, precise and strong, powerful.'[89]

Miller's lunatic dreambook notes found their way into *Black Spring* as 'Into the Night Life' (the title derives from Freud, 'into the night life seems to be exiled what once ruled during the day', from *The Interpretation of Dreams*), a kind of *écriture automatique* chronicling the volcanic creative energies of the unconscious. The chaotic, symbolic and intense flow of images illustrates Miller's fascination with Surrealism, which, he told Herbert Read, began practically on his first arrival in France. Yet in many ways, he would prefer the outrageous humour of the Dadaists.[90] Lawrence Ferlinghetti would take from Miller's text the epigraph 'A Coney Island of the Mind' for his book of poems. A Lewis Carroll-inspired form of surrealistic wordplay can also be seen in the story 'Jabberwhorl Cronstadt', a humorous character portrait of Walter Lowenfels. In an August 1936 letter to Durrell, Miller identified Carroll, Jonathan Swift and even Shakespeare as proto-Surrealists and declared that Surrealism attempted to rediscover the primal creative source in the solar plexus or unconscious.[91]

George Orwell and Miller met in Paris during Christmas 1936. Orwell was passing through to pick up his travel documents on his way to join the Loyalist / Republican cause in the Spanish Civil War, but Miller reasserted his pacifism. Miller gave Orwell his corduroy jacket, telling him that it would not protect him from bullets, but it would keep him warm. Orwell saw Miller's refusal to take sides as an abdication of moral responsibility, but he would write in 1940 the seminal essay on *Tropic of Cancer*, 'Inside the Whale' (the title is from *Tropic of Cancer*: 'The heroic descent to the very bowels of the earth, the dark and fearsome sojourn in the belly of the whale').[92] Miller himself now felt full of energy and at the peak of his powers, writing to Durrell in December 1936: 'I can hardly sleep at night for the ideas that are surging in my brain.'[93]

Tropic of Cancer now began to sell, so Kahane brought out a second printing and paid Miller 1,000 francs (about $50 today) a month in royalties.[94] Alfred A. Knopf made Miller a gift of $100, asking only that he show him his next three books, while Blanche Knopf showed an interest in publishing his letters to Emil.[95] Miller meanwhile began to immerse himself in Lao-Tzu and in Chuang Tzu's *The Musings of a Chinese Mystic*.[96] As Miller ascended (or retreated) into his increasingly private, esoteric universe, it is understandable that he became exasperated with what he saw as the insularity of the literary world: 'One enters a new dimension, certainly non-English, non-American, non-European. That world belongs to the past, to infancy – it gets sloughed off, like a snake's skin. So how to talk to Eliot, Mairet, Orwell, Connolly – all these bloody, bleeding blokes with their navel-strings uncut.'[97]

Durrell mailed Miller the manuscript of his *The Black Book* in March 1937 (Miller was wildly enthusiastic), which was inspired by *Tropic of Cancer*, and in early August, Durrell and his wife, Nancy, arrived in Paris. Durrell was born in 1912 in Jullundur, India, disliked England and had gone to Corfu in 1935, working for the British Consul and as an English teacher.[98] Miller and Durrell, the latter sporting a tan acquired from the island sun of Corfu, laughed loudly, their cigarette smoke filling the room: manuscripts, books, empty bottles and glasses were scattered everywhere. Alfred Perlès noted that Miller treated Durrell 'with the sort of reverence one might have for a beloved child, a wonder child'.[99] The two went to see *Lost Horizon*, a film which reflected Miller's fascination with

Shambhalla ('Shangri-La') and Miller began to speak of moving to Tibet and joining a monastery there.[100] On the more earthly, practical level, Nancy financed the Villa Seurat series in order to publish Durrell's *The Black Book*, Miller's *Max and the White Phagocytes* and Nin's *Winter of Artifice*.[101] But back home in America there was little opportunity for his parents to pursue the higher things of life, for, like their son, they were hounded by financial difficulties. Miller received a heartrending letter from his father on 6 December 1937 asking for help; he responded on the 15th that he himself possessed only one pair of corduroy pants, broken shoes and a worn hand-me-down coat, and had been reduced to begging, borrowing and sometimes robbing Michael Fraenkel.[102]

Miller's interest in movies continued with the publication of *Scenario*, a surrealistic 'film with sound' treatment of Nin's *House of Incest*.[103] But Miller had never seen himself just as a man of 'arts and culture'; rather, he was a pilgrim on the quest for spiritual illumination. He met Frederick Carter, the artist, writer and friend of D. H. Lawrence, in London and wrote him on 27 April 1938: 'And I am seeking now with all my heart and soul. Have been for the last six or seven years, I might say, ever since I passed what I call somewhere the inner Equator.' Miller compiled a list in 1938 which he had printed on a card 4 x 7 inches announcing that he wanted his 'friends and admirers' to know about these twelve books: Nijinsky's *Diary*, Balzac's *Seraphita*, *The Tibetan Book of the Dead*, Giono's *Song of the World*, Gutkind's *The Absolute Collective*, Blavatsky's *The Voice of the Silence*, E. Graham Howe's *War Dance*, Suzuki's *Introduction to Zen Buddhism*, Benjamin Tucker's *Instead of a Book by a Man too Busy to Write One*, Whitman's *Democratic Vistas*, Chesterton's *St Francis of Assisi* and *Obratnik Raka* (the Czech translation of *Tropic of Cancer*).[104] Nin began to observe his entrance into a 'mystic stage': he turned inwards, meditating, reading, listening to music, painting watercolours, limiting his social contacts and composing small texts written by hand in notebooks for his friends, including Nin, Schnellock, Durrell, Reichel, David Edgar and later George Seferis, as if to share more intimately and directly his inner life. He took up again A. P. Sinnett's *Esoteric Buddhism*, beginning on the page where he had left off on his last reading as an adolescent. And Conrad Moricand gave Miller a manuscript compilation of several hundred pages entitled 'Pages curieuses des grandes occultistes', including Hermes Trismegistus, Paracelsus, Jacob Boehme and Swedenborg.[105]

But Miller never became so disembodied that he abdicated the pleasures of the flesh. He smoked Camels or Lucky Strikes, never quite getting used to the more powerful Gauloise Bleue, though according to Perlès when low on funds he had to smoke

Lawrence Durrell in the 1930s.

the French variety of cigarettes (1F. 70 for a pack of twenty), for American brands cost 6 francs. He delighted in the variety and excellence of French wines, reciting their names in an euphoric litany – Nuits-Saint-Georges, Montrachet, Haut-Brion, Château d'Yquem – and he also kept his sense of humour – a characteristic often lacking in those spiritually inclined – as is demonstrated by his long essay 'Money and How it Gets that Way' of 1938.[106] Disbelieving in money's existence entirely, he could not respond in any way but comically to Pound's Social Credit economic theories. In November 1938 his 'Tribute to Blaise Cendrars' appeared in *Tien Hsia Monthly* in Shanghai. Another significant essay from this period, 'Open Letter to Surrealists Everywhere', was included in *Cosmological Eye* (1939). Miller also became involved as editor (1937–9) with *Volontés*, cofounded by Queneau, Le Corbusier, Jean-Frédéric Joliot-Curie and Georges Pelorson (later Georges Belmont), *The Phoenix* and *The Booster*.[107]

As we have seen, one of the most important books for Miller during this phase was Balzac's *Seraphita*.[108] He also pored over *Louis Lambert* and Ernst Robert Curtius's biography of Balzac, which resulted in two of his most profound essays, 'Balzac and his Double' and 'Seraphita', which would appear in *The Wisdom of the Heart* (1941). Balzac's inner struggle mirrored Miller's own 'life-long obsession' to reveal his essential 'innocence': the liberation of the angel within is the ultimate purpose of human life.[109] Furthermore, as Curtius pointed out in *European Literature and the Latin Middle Ages*, Balzac had read deeply in theosophy and mysticism, which precisely overlapped with Miller's devotion to the inner *daimon*, the divine spark occluded within the material body.[110] Along with *Seraphita*, one of the entries on the list of twelve favourite texts was Madame Blavatsky's *The Voice of the Silence*. Blavatsky entered European intellectual life during the great debates following Darwin's introduction of the theory of evolution. In *Isis Unveiled* – a book both W. B. Yeats and D. H. Lawrence studied – she wrote: 'Between these two conflicting Titans – Science and Theology – is a bewildered public fast losing all belief in Man's personal immortality, in a deity of any kind, and rapidly descending to the level of a mere animal existence. Such is the picture of the hour, illumined by the bright noon-day sun of this Christian and scientific era!' During this period, Miller reported having a preternatural experience when, after looking at a photograph of Blavatsky – whom he thought 'had the face of a pig' – she seemed to appear in the room with him. He now experienced an epiphany: he no longer blamed anyone, he alone was existentially responsible for all that befell him and was overcome by an immense sense of relief and freedom: it was 'a kind of awakening'.[111] Later, when he lived in Big Sur, Miller had yet another visitation by Blavatsky, who this time warned him that his friend the Jungian scholar Maud Oakes, then planning a trip to Peru, was in imminent danger. He admonished Oakes not to take the trip. However, she went, and was then involved in a terrible car accident in the mountains.

Miller discovered Jean Giono in a bookshop on rue d'Alésia when *Que ma joie demeure* was recommended to him by the owner's daughter. He travelled to Manosque with Henri Fluchère, the boyhood friend of Giono, but there they discovered that Giono was away on a promenade through the countryside. Miller saw Giono as a man

who accepts the blessings of creation and responds with hymns of joy. Passionate hymns they are, for he is a man of feeling, a man who senses everything first with the organs of the flesh. Being is what he worships, and the result is beauty expressed in terms of love.[112]

In September 1938 *Max and the White Phagocytes*, a collection of stories and essays, appeared. The title story concerns a poor,

Jean Giono.

neurotic, suicidal Polish-Jewish tailor whom Miller had befriended in July 1933, and the book also contains the excellent 'Via Dieppe–Newhaven', in which Miller alters what actually happened when he left for London to escape June: here he gives her the money and they drink merrily together.[113] During Christmas 1938 he went to London and met Dylan Thomas, whom he liked immensely, and T. S. Eliot.[114]

Hamlet, his correspondence with Michael Fraenkel, originally intended to be a 1,000-page tome on the 'death theme' which obsessed Fraenkel, was published in two volumes in 1939 and 1941. Miller's first letter dates from 2 November 1935, followed by 21 others until October 1938. *Hamlet* would influence Deleuze and Guattari's *Anti-Oedipus,* in which a long extract was featured.[115] Miller elaborates here his concept of 'China' as a symbolic autonomous realm of spiritual equilibrium: he had been moved by Havelock Ellis's *The Dance of Life* (1923) and its disquisitions on China.[116] He also explores the struggle for selfhood, which is the confrontation with the 'dragon', a symbol he derived from both Lawrence (*Apocalypse*, chapter 16) and Frederick Carter (*The Dragon of the Apocalypse*): 'Every man who is uniquely himself comes face to face eventually with the true dragon, which is the Self, and which must be slain in order to make the final reconciliation. This supreme acceptance, of life as a life-and-death process, saves one for the world eternally.'[117] The magisterial, 99 pages-long letter of 17 October 1938 demonstrates Miller's immersion in Jacob Boehme, Hermes Trismegistus, *The Tibetan Book of the Dead* and Theosophical texts: he refers to *Kalpa*, *Pravritti*, *Navritti* and allusions to *Samsara*, *Avitchi*, *Samadhi*, *Satori*, *Pralaya*, *Bodhisattva*, *Tathagata*, *Nirvana*, *Samvritti*, *Myalba*, *Bardo* and *Devachan* began increasingly to appear in his fiction, letters and essays. He wrote excitedly to Durrell about Tibetan Yoga, the poet–saint Milarepa (*c.* 1052–1135) and confessed 'I am a Zen addict through and through . . . No intelligent person, no sensitive person, can help but be a Buddhist. It's clear as a bell to me.'[118]

Tropic of Capricorn, appearing on 10 May 1939, chronicles his time at the 'Cosmodemonic Telegraph Company' during 1920–24.[119] Miller devotes some of the loveliest passages to his epochal meeting with June: 'One can wait a whole lifetime for a moment like this. The woman whom you never hoped to meet now sits before you, and she talks and looks exactly like the person you dreamed about.'[120] The physical description of June emphasizes her 'long, columnar neck', 'blue-black hair', 'large white face', as well as her brilliant, shining eyes, full body, and a mysterious smile 'borne aloft on a long white neck, the sturdy, swanlike neck of the medium – and of the lost and the damned.'[121] As we know, her hair was 'parted on the side, like a man's', hinting at Miller's later discovery of her apparent bisexuality. In *She*, H. Rider Haggard's novel Miller so much admired, we behold Ayesha's 'great changing eyes of deepest, softest black, of the tinted face, of the broad and noble brow, on which the hair grew low, and the delicate, straight features.' Haggard's concentration on Ayesha's neck, eyes, hair, face, and the sense of 'being in the presence of something that was not canny' and 'evil' and June as a 'medium', as well as the additional comparison of her to 'the lost and the damned', illustrate the probable subliminal influence of *She* on *Tropic of Capricorn*.[122] June is 'Mona', the unique and only one, but she also is named elsewhere 'Mara', a name Miller derived from his reading of Blavatsky's *The Voice of The Silence*: '*Mara* is in exoteric religions a demon, an *Asura*, but in esoteric philosophy it is personified temptation through men's vices, and translated literally means "that which kills" the Soul.' Frederick Carter's *Symbols of Revelation* supplied imagery depicting the drama of his experiences with June as a cosmic allegory: 'I saw the Dragon shaking itself free of dharma and karma . . . We were the twin snakes of Paradise, lucid in heat and cool as chaos . . . Leo fornicating with Draco . . . '.[123]

The book is notable for its extended surrealistic sequences, such as the 'Land of Fuck' section, which Miller says was written by 'dictation': forced against his will, he took down one inspired mad sentence after another as they were delivered by the cosmic Muse: 'What's that? I cried, never dreaming of what I was being led into . . . '.[124] The distinguished critic Gilbert Highet singled out a passage which described Miller's first sexual experience with his piano teacher. The section, 'both in language and in content is revolting . . . Some obscenity is normal. Much of Miller's is abnormal: the kind of thing that goes on only among the lowest . . . He has genius. Why does he want to show himself as a swine?'[125] The reaction is typical and will mark much of the criticism of Miller in the decades to come. In 1978 Miller remarked: 'The sex wasn't too pretty . . . But I played up the scoundrel in myself, don't you know, because he was more interesting than the angel.' And he emphasized his duality in his 'autobiographical romances':

'It's as if there are two Henry Millers . . . I created a monstrous character in my books and I gave him my name.'[126] As readers of Milton's *Paradise Lost*, such as William Blake, acknowledged, the most interesting character in the poem is Satan.

The Cosmological Eye was the first book of Miller's published in America by James Laughlin's New Directions in Norfolk, Connecticut, and he was given a $200 advance. It contains many of the same texts as *Max and the White Phagocytes*, with selections from *Black Spring* and other essays from magazines. Miller's 'New Age' one-world philosophy becomes prominent in an essay such as 'Peace, It's Wonderful!':

> A man is made out of the whole cloth, by a change of heart which alters every living cell of the body. Anything less than a change of heart is sure catastrophe. Which, if you follow the reasoning, explains why the times are always bad. For, unless there be a change of heart there can be no act of will.[127]

With the threat of war looming, in September 1938 Miller had given Jack Kahane the manuscript of *Capricorn* to put in his bank vault.[128] He wrote to Frances Steloff in April 1939 of his intention to leave Villa Seurat, and on 25 May he headed southwest for Rocamadour and then via Domme to Sarlat in the Dordogne, a place he adored (a photograph of the town is included in *Remember to Remember*).[129] A bookseller in Sarlat invited him to dinner and gave him a book on Michel de Nostradamus, which thrilled him.[130] He read Max Heindel's *The Rosicrucian Cosmo-Conception* (1911), writing on the first page of the text: 'Sacred Property of Henry Miller, 18 Villa Seurat, Paris (xiv) who has just discovered that he has been a Rosicrucian all his life . . . Paris, 3/5/39'. *The Rosy Crucifixion* trilogy would allude to these Rosicrucian studies, to 'the doctrine of the heart' he would celebrate in E. Graham Howe. Indeed, his increasing immersion in theosophy, astrology and now Nostradamus would impel Brassai to wonder whether Miller himself had ambitions to be a kind of shaman or magus.[131]

Durrell had already begun to coax Miller to come to Corfu in July 1938: Miller would have his own room with two windows overlooking the sea, colourful rugs brightening the floor, an encyclopaedia, a dictionary, a desk. He advised him to pack his portable typewriter, the manuscript of *Tropic of Capricorn* and also to bring a woman who would help the days pass by pleasurably. More tantalizing enticements were the blue sea where they could swim and sail, lunch with wine beneath the sun, a siesta, another swim, a cup of tea and 'then four hours' work in a slow rich evening'. Miller, naturally, set off for Corfu, his first real vacation since arriving in France.[132] On 14 July Miller took the *Théophile Gautier* from Marseilles to the port of Piraeus on the Greek mainland, reading Giono's loving tribute to his primal, sensual father, *Jean le Bleu* (the book given him by Henri Fluchère), on the voyage. He then sailed to Corfu and stayed with Durrell in Kalami, where he devoured Blavatsky's *The Secret Doctrine*. He also received a letter from Leonie Ungern-Sternberg, the sister of Count Keyserling, asking for an essay to celebrate her brother's sixtieth birthday and Miller composed 'The Philosopher who Philosophizes', which appeared two years later in *The Wisdom of the Heart*.[133] He had no money as usual; his posterior showed through his threadbare corduroys. He let his beard grow and swam naked: he loved the *nero* (water) in Greece and retreated blissfully into the archaic Greek elemental: water, earth, air, fire. Miller met George Seferis (Seferiades), George Katsimbalis, the painter Ghika and composed 'Reflections on Writing', which was published in *Ta Nea Grammata* in 1940, translated by Katsimbalis. He went with Ghika to his home on the island of Hydra and then for two months he travelled with Katsimbalis to Poros, Nauplia, Epidaurus, Mycenae, Knossos. In addition to his spiritual and cultural explorations, Miller also indulged in more earthly pleasures with 'a bright, naughty little red-headed girl with the sassiest-looking figure you could hope to behold', as Katsimbalis would later recall.[134]

Seferis liked Miller's approach to travel: he had not read the classical Greek authors before he arrived and thus his experiences in Greece were burdened by no preconceptions: 'I suppose I was the first man to give him a text of Aeschylus, when he decided to go to Mycenae. But of course he doesn't see anything from Aeschylus; he sees, in the plain of Argos, *redskins* while he hears a jazz trumpeter. That is spontaneous behaviour. And I admire it.'[135] In Hydra and Athens in November 1939, Seferis composed a masterpiece about Miller, the poem 'Les Anges sont blanc'. They had been discussing angels and the scene in Balzac's *Louis Lambert* when Lambert – the alienated genius who attempts to castrate himself – becomes paralyzed, speechless, and makes only one statement, 'les anges sont blanc', the angels are white. The poem describes Miller splendidly:

> . . . that man, the teethmarks
>   of the tropics in his skin,
> putting on his dark glasses as if he were going to work with
>   a blowlamp,
> said humbly, pausing at every word:
> "The angels are white flaming white and the eye that would
>   confront them shrivels
> and there's no other way you've got to become like stone if
>   you want their company
> and when you look for the miracle you've got to scatter your
>   blood to the eight points of the wind
> because the miracle is nowhere else but circulating in the veins
>   of man."[136]

In *Tropic of Capricorn* Miller had described Mona: 'She was double barreled, like a shotgun, a female bull with an acetylene torch in her womb', which perhaps suggested Seferis's marvelous image of the 'man . . . of the tropics' who may need his 'dark glasses' to protect him as he experiences an incandescent ecstatic vision of the visiting angels.[137] Miller did not want to return to America, and of course would have preferred to stay in Greece, a country he deeply loved and which he would later praise in *The Colossus of Maroussi* (his own favourite among his books), but he wrote to Steloff from Athens that his time was at an end: on 5 December American civilians had been ordered by Washington to leave Greece because of the escalating conflict in Europe.[138] Miller travelled to Eleusis with Ghika, to Sparta and the Peloponnese with the Durrells and said farewell to immortal Hellas on 27 December from the deck of the *Exochorda*.

Miller in Hydra, 1939, photographed by George Seferis.

5

The Exile Returns: Air-Conditioned Nightmare and Big Sur Dream, 1940–51

In mid-January 1940 the *Exochorda* approached Boston's harbour, and as Miller glimpsed the skyline he began to weep. After Paris and Greece, the total horror of America overwhelmed him. He went on to New York, where he arrived as penniless as he had left ten years previously, and after delaying the inevitable meeting with his parents he finally went to visit them, which he recounted in his heart-rending essay 'Reunion in Brooklyn'.[1] Again he now relied on female helpers: he stayed at Caresse Crosby's apartment at 137 East 54th Street and wrote to Frances Steloff to thank her: she had sent a cheque, and Miller was also extremely grateful for some cast-off clothes: '*Honestly*. I've walked around in other people's things nearly all my life – I fit into most any sized outfit – sounds incredible but it's so.'[2] But he wasted no time in self-pity: he quickly turned his attention to writing his book about Greece, *The Colossus of Maroussi*, which he composed in New York sitting at the back of a synagogue, where he was inspired by the music (he adored Cantor Sirota) as well as at Bowling Green, Virginia, where he had been invited in July by Caresse Crosby to stay at her estate, Hampton Manor. There he met Salvador Dalí (whom he disliked) and his wife, Gala.[3] During May and June he composed two texts, 'Quiet Days in Clichy' and 'Mara-Marignan', which he revised and published in 1956 as the small masterpiece *Quiet Days in Clichy*; here his narrative skill, humour and finely modulated prose are on full display, returning us to his happy days in Paris. He also received major critical attention this year in George Orwell's influential essay 'Inside the Whale': 'Here in my opinion is the only imaginative prose writer of the slightest value who has appeared among the English-speaking races for some years past.'[4]

Miller completed a manuscript titled 'The World of Sex', which would be privately published in a limited edition by Ben Abramson's Argus Book Shop in Chicago in 1941, then revised and reprinted in 1956, in which he attempted to uncover the role that love, sexuality and women had played in his life and work. H. L. Mencken ordered a copy and wrote to Abramson in June of that year: 'It seems to me that Miller's writing improves steadily. He has acquired a style that is really first rate – and he gets his effects with great precision.'[5] Miller had had the idea since the late Thirties of taking a trip across America and recording his impressions, and asked his painter friend Abraham Rattner to join him: they bought a 1932 Buick, a four-door sedan, for $100 (Miller quickly took several lessons at a driving school), and set off from New York on 24 October 1940 on what turned out to be an 'air-conditioned nightmare' journey, during which Rattner would create nearly 500 drawings to accompany Miller's text.[6] They went *to look for America*, in the words of Simon and Garfunkel, years before Jack Kerouac (Sal Paradise) and Neal Cassady (Dean Moriarty) did in *On the Road* or Peter Fonda (Wyatt) and Dennis Hopper (Billy) in *Easy Rider*. Miller's quest prefiguring that of the Beats and hippies was to uncover a 'true America' opposed to the dominant, destructive, materialist and life-denying White-Anglo-Saxon-Protestant culture.

Their travels took them to Fredericksburg, Virginia, where Emil Schnellock was teaching art, Washington, DC, Asheville, Atlanta, Charleston, Jacksonville, Mobile, New Orleans and on to Mississippi, where Miller visited the ancient mounds created by the Natchez Native American people.[7] He then learned his father was dying and took a ten-hour flight back to New York,

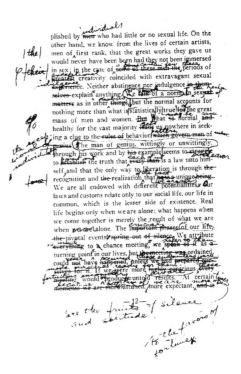

arriving just two hours after his father had peacefully passed away in his sleep. The undertaker clothed his father's body in woollen underwear Miller had brought from Greece. Nin described him in grief as 'resigned, mystical, quiet'. While in New York, he met Swami Nikhilananda (1895–1973), who gave him Romain Rolland's biographies of Ramakrishna and Vivekananda, and during his travels he wrote a series of fascinating letters to the Swami. When he and Rattner arrived in Pittsburgh, Miller reported his excitement:

Ramakrishna appeals to me tremendously – because he was the incarnation of joyousness, of wisdom, of tolerance, and is then that things happen, as we say. But things do not just happen. I doubt if in any realm things merely happen. The man who is wide awake makes ... happening a significant event. Not only is he himself altered but the whole world is eventually affected. If remote worlds appear to us to be following an ordered pattern, so certainly are human beings. Now and then a man arises who is able to penetrate the seeming confusion of our ... pattern and detect an order. these are the men we bow down before him. In the individual pattern the role of sex varies greatly with each individual. There are limits ... to the variations, as we realize when we study the subject so that It is possible to think of a greater pattern which includes the widest variations. When I think of sex I think of it as a universe ... which has been explored but the greater part unknown, mysterious, possibly forever unknowable. The same ... know a little, or ... but the further we push the more the horizon recedes. We are surrounded by mysteries. Until we accept the fact that life is a grand mystery, we shall know nothing. Sex, then, like everything is largely a mystery. That is what I am trying to say. I don't pretend to be a great explorer in this realm. My own personal adventures are as nothing compared to those of any ordinary Don Juan. For a city man I think my record is comparatively normal. For an artist it is in no way singular or remarkable. And yet it seems to me that in my timid explorations I have made certain discoveries which may bear fruit. Let us say, if you like, that I have charted certain

— 13 —

above all because he found God everywhere, because he raised man beyond belief and devotion to a realization of his own divinity, his own creativeness . . . I do believe Ramakrishna went further than Christ – in his conception of man's relation to man and to God. Ramakrishna corresponds to my own secret ideal of what man should be on earth.[8]

Miller's interior, spiritual quest for enlightenment (he also had begun reading the *Bhagavad Gita*) formed a stark contrast to his outrage at what he was finding in his native land. He and Rattner went on to Cleveland, Detroit and Chicago (where he met another wise man, Brother Vishwananda), but he found the industrial regions of America 'barbarous to the nth degree. I have the impression of being with weird insects who are masquerading for some diabolic purpose as men. I can see only disaster ahead – there is no way out of this!' In Detroit he was reminded of Céline's descriptions in *Voyage au bout de la nuit*, and was appalled by the infernal Ford automobile factory, 'a symphony of insane sounds'. He found the city to be a horrible preview of the Spenglerian apocalypse: 'The Duraluminium City! A nightmare in stone & steel. Terrifyingly new, bright, hard – hard as tungsten. Glitter of cruelty. Tough to be a beggar here in winter. The city of the future! But what a future! . . . *Bomb Detroit out of existence!!*'[9]

But the pair had loved Charleston, New Orleans and Biloxi, Mississippi, cities where, as Rattner put it, they could feel 'they were again becoming civilized beings' because the art of living was still practised there. They headed on to Des Moines and to Kansas City, where Miller met his painter friend from Paris, Frederick Kann, who was teaching at the Art Institute there; they discussed the 'Masters' and Blavatsky, and Kann loaned him Manly P. Hall's *The Phoenix: An Illustrated Review of Occultism and Philosophy* (1932), which he 'devoured'.[10] They then went to Memphis and Arkansas (from Little Rock, Miller wrote Swami Nikhilananda on 3 April 1941 that he broke down twice weeping as he read the *Life of Vivekananda*), Santa Fe, Albuquerque and the Grand Canyon, and then headed to Hollywood in May, where Miller met Aldous Huxley (with whom he had corresponded and who was now on a very similar spiritual path), the astrologer Dane Rudhyar, and in June the composer John Cage, whom he found to be a 'very fine young man'.[11] Although he completed the manuscript of *The Air-Conditioned Nightmare* by December 1941, now that the United States had entered the World War, an anti-American polemic was not welcome and the book did not appear until 1945.

Miller also went to visit Lawrence Clark Powell, who recalled that he 'came to my desk and said 'I am Henry Miller. My publisher said when I reached LA to go out to UCLA and see Larry Powell . . . Do you have any books by Jacob Boehme?' When Powell returned two-and-a-half hours later, he found Miller sitting Buddha-like on the cold library floor, rapt and joyously reading Boehme's *Aurora: Or the Morning Rednesse in the Sky*. Powell was struck by Miller's kindness and intuitive rapport with his two small sons on this visit, and noted his typical garb: a green corduroy jacket, a black-and-white checked cap, and leather sandals.[12] In October 1941, *The Colossus of Maroussi* – which would become Miller's own favourite book –was published by Colt Press of San Francisco (after being turned down by many publishers) in a signed limited edition of 100 copies printed on special paper.[13] Edmund Wilson declared it was 'unlike anything else ever written about Greece before' and the angelic theme returns throughout: 'Man is made to walk the earth and sail the seas; the conquest of the air is reserved for a later stage of his evolution when he will have sprouted real wings and assumed the form of the angel which he is in essence.'[14] Katsimbalis is the Colossus whose gargantuan, Rabelaisian, life-affirming appetites mirror Miller's own. The book thus forms a kind of opposite companion volume to *The Air-Conditioned Nightmare*: there was no air-conditioning in Greece, but it was not a sterile, anti-life country like America: 'In Greece one has the desire to bathe in the sky. You want to rid yourself of your clothes, take a running leap and vault into the blue. You want to float in the air like an angel or lie in the grass rigid and enjoy the cataleptic trance. Stone and sky, they marry here. It is the perpetual dawn of man's awakening . . . in his heart man is angelic; in his heart man is united with the whole world.'[15]

Miller returned to New York on 9 October 1941, where he stayed again at Caresse Crosby's apartment. He met both Fernand Léger and André Breton: Breton wittily declared in *La Clé des Champs* (1953) that it was understandable that Miller's work was prohibited in the United States; like the atomic bomb, he was destined for external consumption.[16] *Hamlet, Volume II* was published by Carrefour in April and in December *Wisdom of the Heart* by New Directions, containing seventeen essays and stories. The title essay concerns the work of the English psychologist E. Graham Howe, who had a strong interest in Buddhism, and in his review of *I and Me, Time and the Child* and *War Dance*, Miller advocated Howe's doctrine of 'full surrender', which is the 'religious view of life: the positive acceptance of pain, suffering, defeat, misfortune, and so on'. And in his essay on *The Absolute Collective* by the philosopher Erich Gutkind, Miller declared that 'we stand at the threshold of a new way of life, one in which MAN is about to be realized.'[17] The book also contains an excerpt from Miller's abandoned book on D. H. Lawrence, 'Creative Death', as well as tributes to Blaise Cendrars, Brassaï and Keyserling, 'The Philosopher Who Philosophizes'.

Miller became enthralled by *Cosmic Consciousness: A Study in the Evolution of the Human Mind* (1901) by the Canadian physician Richard M. Bucke, which he also recommended to Durrell. Bucke believed certain great figures, such as Plotinus, William Blake, Whitman, Boehme, Ramakrishna and Balzac (he singles out in particular Balzac's *Louis Lambert* and *Seraphita*), achieved a profound insight into the secret, eternal meaning of existence, which he termed 'cosmic consciousness' and which prefigured the next stage of human spiritual evolution. It is understandable that Miller would find *Cosmic Consciousness* so appealing since Bucke had become a kind of disciple of Walt Whitman and wrote a biography of the poet in 1883. In one of his finest essays, his 'Letter to Pierre Lesdain', which forms Chapter 12 of *The Books in My Life*, Miller argued for Whitman's superiority over Dostoevsky, because Whitman had achieved 'the cosmic sweep' and did not struggle to find God as did the great Russian, but rather had attained complete affirmative acceptance of life in all its contradictions.[18]

He also began reading the British metaphysical writer Claude Houghton, author of *I am Jonathan Scrivener* (1930), and in a letter of 31 January 1942 he shared with Houghton his enthusiasm for Romain Rolland's book on Ramakrishna as well as his meeting with 'a disciple of Ramakrishna's, Swami Nikhilananda, who allowed me the privilege of reading the manuscript of one who sat at Ramakrishna's feet and took down his words verbatim.' Nikhilananda also inspired the comparative mythologist Joseph Campbell, and would play a major role in J. D. Salinger's spiritual quest as Vedanta increasingly influenced his fiction.[19]

He hammered out a draft of *Sexus* at the beginning of 1942, which he would later revise four times while living in Big Sur, and also published an essay on Max Ernst, 'Another Bright Messenger' in *View*, an important magazine (1940–47) edited by Charles Henri Ford and Parker Tyler which introduced Surrealism to American readers.[20] The title is most likely an allusion to Algernon Blackwood's metaphysical novel *Bright Messenger* (1921), in which a *deva* – the Sanskrit term for a benevolent deity – takes human form, about which Miller had become very keen. Miller declared that Ernst's paintings 'are the product of an inventive mind endeavoring to translate in worldly language experiences which belong to another dimension'.[21] Ernst had appeared at the end of *Tropic of Capricorn*, where Miller noted that, while in America in the Twenties, 'I was ignorant of the fact that there were men then living who went by the outlandish names of Blaise Cendrars, Jacques Vaché, Louis Aragon, Tristan Tzara, René Crevel, Henry de Montherlant, André Breton, Max Ernst'.[22] The influence apparently went in the other direction as well, for according to Branko Aleksic, Miller's novel inspired Ernst's spectacular palaeolithic masterpiece, the sculpture *Capricorn*, which depicts a massive enthroned bull whose tremendous right arm holds a huge staff, flanked on the left by a tall, thin, violin-shaped female figure with a giraffe-like, elongated neck.[23]

While in New York, Miller's relationship with Nin began to founder and she refused to leave her husband for him. He had met a woman named Laura Lourie probably first in the late 1930s and again at the end of 1941: he wrote the 'divine' Lourie imploring love letters from early 1942 through May. When she broke with him and went to California, Miller followed but the love affair was over.[24] Now in Los Angeles, Gilbert Neiman – the translator of Lorca – offered Miller accommodation with him and his wife, Margaret, at 1212 Beverly Glen Boulevard, where Miller stayed in their 'Green Room'. Neiman wrote beautifully of his friend during this period:

> Here is a person who grasped, who kept the infant in himself alive, and refused to strangle it. Like holding a red hot iron, he was seared time and again, until he plunged with the iron straight into the pool of the sky. When he lost his suffering he lost his callouses, so now he can touch fire with hands as soft as a baby's. That is one way of losing suffering, yet only a handful of men throughout printed history have been able to do it.[25]

Through Neiman he met Man Ray, who took a famous photo of an attractively bare-breasted, tattoo-faced Margaret standing over a seemingly unaware Miller. He was now in a whirlwind of activity: he met Igor Stravinsky, the actress Geraldine Fitzgerald (to whom he wrote a series of love letters), read Céline's *Death on the Installment Plan*, telling Durrell 'he's got more dynamite in him than Hitler ever had. It's permanent hatred – for the whole human species. But what merry-making'; and wrote as one possessed, wearing out, then breaking, his typewriter and pen.[26] He found life in southern California disconcerting: he noted that when he took his accustomed long walks in the automobile-dominated metropolis, he was the lone stroller. One recalls Ray Bradbury's eerie story 'The Pedestrian' (1951), in which a man walking the streets of a futuristic Los Angeles notes the deserted streets and the people behind dark windows watching flickering television screens, and who is then arrested for the crime of walking: it is now against the law.[27]

On 17 November 1942, Nin wrote him an angry letter describing both his 'helplessness' in dealing with money and her decision to break with him. He made perfunctory efforts to find work as a scriptwriter in Hollywood but was nauseated by the whole movie industry scene.[28] He had been told by his agent that all the studios expected of their writers was 'just plain shit wrapped in cellophane'. In the fall his continued poverty led him to compose begging letters, and he also painted scores of watercolours (this had always given him intense pleasure) full of his customary repertory of clowns, the Star of David, moons and astrological signs. He wrote to the actor Vincent Price, who bought several of his paintings and became a close friend and patron.[29] Miller received a visit from Bern Porter, a Manhattan Project physicist from Berkeley, who would commence publishing his work. An appeal for funds, watercolour supplies, old clothes ('I am 5 feet 8 inches tall, weigh 150 pounds, 15 neck, 38 chest, 32 waist, hat and shoes both sizes 7 to 7. Love corduroys') entitled 'Open Letter to All and Sundry' of 14 March 1943 was mimeographed by Ben Abramson and sent to Miller's supporters and partially reprinted on 8 November in *The New Republic*. By the end of the year he had received $700 in cash and direct book sales, much more than he had earned previously from his writings.[30]

He was introduced by Lawrence Clark Powell early in 1943 to Sevasty Kousaftis, a 23-year-old Greek woman as a possible translator of *The Colossus of Maroussi*. Perhaps partially due to the lingering effects of his passion for Greece, by July Miller was quickly in love with Sevasty and wrote one of the two poems he composed in her honour, 'O Lake of Light', published in *Harper's Bazaar* in 1944. But Miller's *coup de foudre* was not reciprocated

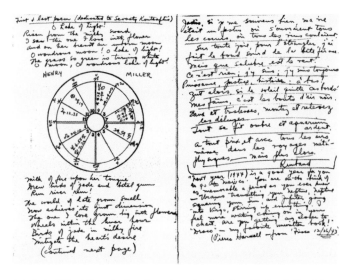

Astrological Chart, Poem for Sevasty, and opening lines from Rimbaud's *Une Saison en Enfer, The Red Notebook* (1943).

and he was devastated.[31] He had fortunately landed in a haven of spiritual aid, with Krishnamurti presiding in Ojai (a small town in a lovely bucolic setting about an hour-and-a-half northwest of Hollywood) and Christopher Isherwood, Gerald Heard, Aldous Huxley and Swami Prabhavananda, founder of the Vedanta Society of Southern California, all living in Los Angeles. In despair and nearly suicidal, he made an appointment to see Prabhavananda, but soon felt that he had recovered his balance. When he arrived and told the Swami that he now had no need of him, the Swami replied: 'Come in anyway. Perhaps it is I who need you. I too have problems. Perhaps you can help me'.[32] Miller

always managed to continue working in the midst of his various upheavals, and he now submitted his first paid book review – Walter Lowrie's *A Short Life of Kierkegaard* – to *The New Republic*. Miller thought the book as fine as Milton O. Percival's *William Blake's Circle of Destiny*, one of his favourite critical studies, declaring that Kierkegaard's 'passion for being honest made his life a crucifixion' and that 'institutions, whether Church or Party have always betrayed the spirit they represent. When has the Church ever represented Christ – or the Democracies democracy – or . . . one can continue *ad infinitum*'.[33]

He met the Greek painter Janko Varda, whom he visited in February 1944 in Monterey, staying in his Red Barn. After a few weeks Varda took him to Big Sur to meet Lynda Sargent: he remained as a guest in her cabin for two months.[34] Sargent told her friend Kathryn Winslow: 'Yanko had a rare bird that flew the coop. I have taken him in. You must come and meet Henry Miller.'[35] The former mayor of Carmel, Keith Evans, offered him his cabin on Partington Ridge, where he moved in May. Just as Martin Heidegger had retreated from Freiburg to the Black Forest mountain village of Todtnauberg to think and write, so Miller's own increasing alienation from American life and his inability to earn a living led to what amounted to almost a complete symbolic break from 'secular life' to the spiritual mountain-top: the influence of his hero, the nature worshipping Jean Giono, perhaps may also have influenced this move.

Big Sur was certainly different from New York City or Paris: 150 miles south of San Francisco, the rugged Santa Lucia mountains extend down to the Pacific Ocean. The Missionary Fathers arrived in Monterey around 1798 and the Spaniards named the area El Sur Grande, the Big South.[36] In 1937 the construction of Highway 1 opened up the area to newcomers: only about 300 inhabitants then lived along a 60-mile stretch of the Pacific coast. Ponderosa pine, oak, bay laurel, madrone, tall redwoods, wild lilac, prickly chamise, black sage as well as poison oak were abundant.[37] The closest town for obtaining food was Monterey, 35 miles away. Miller's cabin was perched about 1,000 feet above sea level and there was no electricity or telephone until the mid-1950s: residents in the area used lamps and candles, while refrigerators operated on butane gas. His closest neighbours were mountain lions, foxes, squirrels, deer, coyotes, hummingbirds, quail, falcons, eagles and scorpions.[38] He learned to kill threatening rattlesnakes with a pickaxe: 'Above all, you mustn't panic', he informed Brassaï. 'You just have to be quick and aim accurately. Cut the snake in half with a single blow.'[39] Clad only in a jockstrap, Miller soon became accustomed to making daily trips hauling groceries in a wooden cart; it was an hour-long climb up the steep, mile-long trail to his cabin.[40]

He acquired a badly mauled young stray dog which he named Pascal and went for walks in the steep hills in pitch dark: 'There are things engraved on the rocks which you notice only at night. And the plants open and give out marvelous scents. But what blackness when the moon is hidden!' The rigours and solitude of the lovely yet forbidding landscape were balanced by a small circle of artists and seekers: he would meet the poet Robinson Jeffers, the Jungian Maud Oakes, the Christian Scientist and spiritual adept Jean Wharton, and Jamie de Angulo, the wild scholar of the Native Americans.[41] Yet Miller now felt isolated and wrote to Emil White, a Viennese fan whom he had met in Chicago two years before, asking him to join him. White would prove an invaluable helper with the practical and mechanical tasks of running a household, which so challenged him: it was Emil who constructed the wooden cart Miller used to transport provisions. He also conducted a romance-by-mail with a young lady in New York named June Lancaster, whom one of Miller's young admirers, Harry Herschkowitz, finally convinced to visit Big Sur at the end of May: the affair quickly fizzled and by mid-August June was gone.[42]

In May Bern Porter brought out Miller's humorous essay to garner support for Alfred Perlès, *What Are You Going to Do About Alf?*, blacking out the 'obscene' words in the text to avoid confiscation by the Post Office. Miller also completed an essay on his painter friend 'Varda: The Master Builder', which appeared in Porter's and George Leite's anti-war *Circle* magazine (volume 1, issue 4), which would also publish William Everson (Brother Antoninus, the pacifist religious poet who would correspond with Miller), Kenneth Rexroth, Robert Duncan, Anaïs Nin, Kenneth Patchen and William Carlos Williams.[43] Miller's anti-war tract *Murder the Murderer* spoke to the 5,500 conscientious objectors who had been 'settled' in camps on the West Coast.[44] *Sunday After the War* published in August 1944, contained three 'fragments' from *The Rosy Crucifixion*, essays on Lawrence, Nin, Anghelos Sikelianos, as well as the moving account of his return to his parents' home in 1940, 'Reunion in Brooklyn'. Herbert Read, who would become a strong supporter of Miller, declared in the *New English Weekly*: 'What makes Miller distinctive among modern writers is his ability to combine without confusion, the aesthetic and prophetic functions.'[45]

Miller's mother fell ill with cancer and he left for New York in early September. Her condition improved and Hershkowitz introduced him to Janina Martha Lepska, a Yale philosophy student who had studied previously with Paul Weiss at Bryn Mawr.[46] Miller had by this time collected a quartet of Ivy League academic advocates, including Weiss, Wallace Fowlie and Henri Peyre, both French scholars at Yale, and Herbert Faulkner West at Dartmouth. Fowlie and Peyre had organized a showing of Miller's watercolours, and on 7 November Miller went to New Haven to meet Fowlie at Yale's Trumbull College.[47] Fowlie had first read Miller in 1940, and the pair exchanged mutually admiring letters. Miller brought him the gift of a watercolour titled *The Clown's Mask* in honour of Fowlie's book *Clowns and Angels*. The President of Yale offered him $1,000 to give a public lecture but he refused.[48] Miller believed all universities should be destroyed because they were 'penal institutions of the mind'.[49] He met with groups of students; Fowlie was impressed by his attentiveness, kindness and patience in their conversations.[50] Miller and Lepska met again, further erotic sparks were kindled and he went on to Dartmouth in Hanover, New Hampshire, to visit Herbert West, where he received love letters from Lepska and spoke to West's comparative literature class. His remarks were construed as anti-American during wartime and he was put under surveillance by the FBI.[51]

He returned to New Haven to meet Lepska and together they went to Washington, DC, where he visited Huntington Cairns (who was, although advisor to the government censors, a great fan of Miller's) and Caresse Crosby and then they continued to Boulder, Colorado, staying there with the Neimans: on 18 December he and Lepska were married on a lovely evening in Denver during a near conjunction of the moon with Venus.[52] The couple then first stayed a week with Kenneth Rexroth at his house on Portrero Hill (Rexroth there assessing Miller as highly egotistical). Next he took his new bride to Varda's place in Monterey, Varda then driving them back to Big Sur.[53] In Miller's absence Bern Porter had published *Semblance of A Devoted Past* in November 1944, a selection of rich letters to Emil Schnellock about his paintings (written in Paris from March 1930 to a final letter from Corfu of 20 September 1939) with nine black-and-white reproductions of Miller's art work, as well as *The Plight of the Creative Artist in the United States of Americ,* which contained his 'Open Letters' criticizing the marginalization of the country's composers, painters and writers.

Indeed, although Miller had now established himself in a beautiful location and had the company of a lovely and intelligent young woman, he was not at ease in his homeland. He wrote to Fowlie on 11 April 1945 that he missed Europe and felt keenly the lack of 'spiritual, moral, cultural, sensual values' in America.[54] His work was now appreciated by major figures in Europe: Fowlie replied a few weeks later that he 'had dinner two nights ago with Jean-Paul Sartre. He came up to my place and was greatly intrigued with your water colors. He spoke with admiration of *Capricorn*.'[55] Miller corresponded with his beloved Jean Giono and became an advocate for the work of the Egyptian novelist Albert Cossery.[56] He worked now in a small studio next to his house built from a horse-shed out of corrugated iron and driftwood, 'like one of Van Gogh's habitations'. He read the life of Milarepa, *The Perennial Philosophy*, which Aldous Huxley had sent him, Krishnamurti's *Ten Talks* and Pierre Loti's *Jerusalem*.[57] As usual, Miller fed his always hungry mind with a constant supply of the most various, and sometimes recherché, provender.

Bern Porter published *The Happy Rock*, printed on coloured paper and graced with a portrait of Miller by Léger, the title of which is from *Tropic of Capricorn*: 'the true rock of the self, the happy rock', and contains tributes to Miller from several writers, while 'Obscenity and the Law of Reflection' was printed by Alicat Bookshop of Yonkers. Judson Crews, a young writer and publisher, came to visit and was impressed by Miller's wife: 'Lepska was never embarrassed to talk to me about Hegel and Marx and Heidegger, and Sidney Hook, the Webbs, or Bertrand Russell, or Meister Eckhart.'[58] Lepska gave birth to a daughter, Valentine Lepska, on 19 November 1945 in Berkeley, and the proud parents named Wallace Fowlie as godfather. *The Air-Conditioned Nightmare* was published in December and begins with Swami Vivekananda: 'The greatest men in the world have passed away unknown. The Buddhas and the Christs that we know are but second-rate heroes in comparison with the greatest men of whom the world knows nothing.' Ramakrishna threads through the book from the epigraph to the 'Preface' to 'Good News! God is Love!' to 'With Edgard Varèse in the Gobi Desert.'[59] John Wain praised Miller's

hurrying, turbulent prose that gives the impression of complete spontaneity, but only the most naïve reader will imagine that such prose can be produced without a great deal of hard work. The rhythms never get out of hand, the pauses are varied with considerable skill, and the words are chosen with great effectiveness.[60]

Miller met the painter Bezalel Schatz as well as D. H. Lawrence's wife, Frieda, who was spending the winter in Big Sur.[61] Perhaps Miller now had Lawrence's novella *The Man Who Died* in mind when he wrote to Fowlie in February:

> I said I would write you about the life of Jesus *after* the resurrection – the period of forty days, was it, between the resurrection and the ascension. But the more I think about it the more I feel that it is important not to communicate what I think I have learned – a most tremendous truth – but to live my life in the light of it. I didn't come by this truth alone, I must tell you. Though for some time now I have been

Swami Vivekananda, 1893.

preparing myself to receive it, so to speak . . . I am almost frightened now by what I know.[62]

Miller led the most intense of spiritual lives, of which few of his admirers and friends were aware. The gap displayed in this quotation between Miller's public reputation as the bad boy of American literature, disrupter of national morality and rectitude, and the actual reverence of his mind and heart cannot be more striking.

He wrote to Gore Vidal, thanking him for sending a copy of his novel *Williwaw*, and attempted unsuccessfully to translate Rimbaud. He instead began work on a biographical and critical study: the first part appeared in *New Directions Year Book* number 9 and the second in the 1949 yearbook, both under the title 'When Do Angels Cease to Resemble Themselves' (the title is from Lautréamont's *Les Chants de Maldoror*), and then in book form as *The Time of the Assassins*, published by New Directions in 1956. His fascination with Jakob Wasserman's *The Maurizius Case*, a novel which dramatized the theme of law versus justice in the struggle between the young Etzel Andergast and his Attorney General father, Wolf, who had unjustly imprisoned a man, resulted in 'Maurizius Forever', while 'Patchen: Man of Anger and Light', his essay on the Ohio-born pacifist poet, was also published. Miller again prefigured the countercultural turn in his 'Preface' to *Life Without Principle: Three Essays by Thoreau*, reprinted as 'Henry David Thoreau' in *Stand Still Like the Hummingbird*. Young American poets and artists now seemed 'helpless' and unable to fulfil the Thoreauvian injunction to simplify their lives by 'wresting a living from the soil, of doing odd jobs, of living on as little as possible. They remain in the cities, flitting from one thing to another, restless, miserable, frustrated, searching in vain for a way out.'[63] And like the American youth of the Sixties, Miller declared his brotherhood with the Native Americans in his 'Introduction' to Haniel Long's *The Marvelous Adventure of Cabeza de Vaca*: 'as a man, and as an American particularly, the shameful record of our relations with the Indians saddened me to a degree beyond anything I had ever felt in connection with man's inhumanity to man.'[64]

Meanwhile, American GIs had bought Miller's books in large quantities, and Maurice Girodias informed Miller that he intended to publish new editions and pay him royalties of 410,000 francs.[65] On both sides of the Atlantic, his work began to stir up controversy. In November *The New York Times* reported that 'the French League for Social and Moral Action brought suit today against two Paris publishing firms to prevent the continued printing and circulation of the novels *The Tropic of Cancer* and *The Tropic of Capricorn* by Henry Miller, United States author. The league declared the books were pornographic and an offence against public morals.'[66] Thus Daniel Parker, the head of the French League, initiated *l'affaire Miller*: Breton, Gide, Bataille, Eluard, Queneau and Sartre all ultimately became involved in defending Miller from charges of pornography. Maurice Nadeau, co-editor with Albert Camus of *Combat*, asked Camus to join the cause, which he did.[67] Bataille had become editor of the journal *Critique* funded by Girodias, and the first issue of July 1946 contained 'La Morale de Miller', a review of *Tropic of Cancer*, *Tropic of Capricorn* and *Black Spring*, and he also composed 'L'Inculpation d'Henry Miller'.[68] In America, Mildred Edie Brady's 'The New Cult of Sex and Anarchy', an acerbic critique of the nascent counterculture in which Miller is pilloried as the centre of a new Dionysian cult, was published in the April 1946 issue of *Harper's*.[69]

There is irony in the fact that while Miller was being prosecuted for his emphasis on sex, the body, 'obscenity' and, in the minds of some, a 'reduction' of life to its most basic appetites, he was simultaneously exploring a complex of related 'anti-materialist', 'paranormal' ideas. In the mid-Forties, Miller joined the Fortean society. Theodore Dreiser, Ben Hecht, H. L. Mencken were also members. Charles Fort (1874–1932) had collected examples of bizarre and unexplained occurrences, and Miller alludes to him in *Big Sur*: 'People are constantly supplying me with startling facts, amazing events, incredible experiences – as if I were another Charles Fort.'[70] In *Circle 7–8* Miller reviewed *Life after Death* by Gustav Theodor Fechner, the German physicist and experimental psychologist, and emphasized the limitations of 'our superior, patronizing scientific viewpoint', which had relegated ancient wisdom to the category of myth. Miller declared that 'to read Fechner is to understand that the whole universe is not only alive in a way that surpasses all comprehension, but that everything in the universe – man, beast, flower, star – is connected and inter-related.' He refers to Algernon Blackwood's *The Centaur* as well as *The Bright Messenger*, 'one of the strangest and most exciting books I have ever read', which takes up the Fechnerian theme of 'the aliveness of the earth', prefiguring the contemporary 'Gaia hypothesis' of planetary consciousness.[71] Miller's critique of 'progress' and the dominance of scientific modes of cognition as well as the increasing dehumanization and mechanization of human life is in the tradition of the German Romantic *Naturphilosophen* as well as the great philosopher of science Paul Feyerabend, who argued in *Against Method* that 'Science' with a capital 'S' had become our modern ideology, a myth of unassailable certainty which both misunderstood and demeaned alternative ways of knowledge. As Miller declared in 1962:

> We are at last beginning to have a worldwide view, instead of the insular one we so long nourished. We are no longer exploring outer space alone but that inner space in which man has his being and through which he will attain in the not too distant future to new levels of consciousness.[72]

In February 1947 Miller and Lepska moved to new quarters they had purchased from Jean Wharton on Partington Ridge. It was an old garage on two and a half acres of hillside which had been rebuilt into a single large space to function as living room, bed-room and kitchen along with a small addition for their baby. It was 'almost Japanese in its austerity', but the south wall was glass, which offered a spectacular view of the Pacific coast.[73] Here he would remain for the next fifteen years. Miller promised to repay Wharton the $7,000 once he received the royalties due him from France: Miller was conscientious about paying back his debts, keeping a large chart above his desk on the wall scrupulously indicating persons and sums owed. He bought an unreliable 1941 Cadillac for $100.[74] Robert Fink, a biochemist from Chicago, came to visit during the summer: he had read Miller in Europe as a GI and he noted that the simple shack which served as Miller's studio was lined with bookshelves made of pine boards and bricks. Both the studio and desk were noteworthy for their orderly appearance: manuscripts, letters and writing implements were all in their proper place.[75] Cyril Connolly, editor of *Horizon*, arrived from England on a visit. Connolly had spoken highly of *Tropic of Cancer* and believed Miller was 'one writer who has solved the problem of how to live happily in America'. Miller reported to Durrell that he thought Connolly had really come to see the otters frolicking off the coast, but left disappointed for none were to be seen.[76]

Of, By and About Henry Miller was published in 1947 by Oscar Bardinsky, and Miller also met Kathryn Winslow in Big Sur. In 1948 she would open 'M, The Studio for Henry Miller' in Chicago's Jackson Park art colony, which would sell his books and water-colours until 1958.[77] Miller now collaborated with Bezalel Schatz to produce *Into the Night Life*, which took sixteen months to create: it included Miller's handwritten text of the dream sequence from *Black Spring* and Schatz's colour illustrations, and was printed in serigraph and silkscreen in Berkeley. He continued his water-colours craze: Lepska remembered his excitement creating *Pink*

Beauford Delaney, 1953.

Nude (1947): he danced about euphorically chanting the names of his favorite colours, squeezing them from their tubes: 'More Rose Madder, more Crimson Alizarin, more Scarlet Lakes!'[78] *Remember to Remember* appeared, which contained his wonderful essay on French bread, 'The Staff of Life'; 'Obscenity and the Law of Reflection', an important attempt to define obscenity; his masterwork essay on France, 'Remember to Remember'; as well as portraits of artists he encountered during his trip, including the tender homage to 'The Amazing and Invariable Beauford Delaney', the painter Harry Herschkowitz had introduced him to in 1943. The following year Delaney painted a striking seated portrait of Miller with a haloed head, and the two friends corresponded regularly over the years. He also now returned to writing *The Rosy Crucifixion*, which he had begun in 1942 in New York, and which he now realized would require three volumes: *Sexus, Plexus and Nexus.*[79]

Sales of Miller's books in Europe had increased and he had $37,000 in his account to be claimed, but it was difficult to get the money out of France. He owed $800 in taxes in August 1947 and yet others needed *his* help. In the fall he received a letter from June begging for aid and Miller contacted Irving Stettner, a friend who lived in New York, who sent her $30.[80] Stettner would later edit *Stroker*, which published many of Miller's final writings. Conrad Moricand, Miller's astrologer friend from Paris, also needed assistance, and Miller invited him to stay in Big Sur. Anaïs Nin came in the summer of 1947, and noticed palpable domestic tension between Lepska and her husband.[81] Nin's observant eye, as so often, would prove to be prescient.

His connections to French writers and culture sustained him as he continued to correspond with his beloved Blaise Cendrars, informing him in a letter of 1 October 1947 that he had met in Hollywood during the early Forties the train robber, lawyer and actor Al Jennings: 'such a sweet, gentle, kind soul – who would believe that he had been the famous outlaw?' Jennings's book *Through the Shadows with O. Henry* had been translated by Cendrars as *Hors-la-Loi* in 1936. In the next paragraph Miller revealed that René Allendy's *Paracelse, le Médecin Maudit* (1937) was always by his side: only Miller could shift from Jennings to Paracelsus without skipping a beat. In France, André Breton, with whom Miller had exchanged some 20 postcards and letters, sought to organize an exhibition of his watercolours in Paris, and Breton included Miller's essay 'Paysages' (actually an excerpt from his essay on France 'Remember to Remember') in the lengthy *Surrealism in 1947* catalogue which also contained articles by Breton, Bataille and many others. The cover of the book was designed by Marcel

Duchamp: a three-dimensional, soft rubber female's breast with the words 'Please Touch'.[82] Miller was also intrigued by *Le Miroir du merveilleux* by Pierre Mabille, editorial director of *Minotaur*, an anthology of writings by Plato, Apuleius, Blake and René Char as well as material on Egyptian and Mayan mythology, which drew connections between Surrealism and the occult tradition.[83]

By March 1948 Moricand was ready to leave and the fiasco of his time in Big Sur with the Millers became the subject of *Devil in Paradise*. Nothing seemed to satisfy the neurasthenic astrologer, no matter what Miller tried to make him feel at home. The relationship ended bitterly, with recriminations from both sides. Léger asked Miller to write a brief work about circus clowns and he created *Smile at the Foot of the Ladder* (1948).[84] Designed by Merle Armitage, the book contained lavish illustrations of clowns by Klee, Picasso, André de Segonzac, Rouault and Toulouse-Lautrec. Miller had been corresponding with Wallace Fowlie, read and reviewed his *Clowns and Angels*, and declared: 'You are the only man I know of, writing today, who understands the singular mystical relationship between the clown, the voyou, and the angel in man. When you touch this theme you make me delirious.'[85] *Star of the Unborn*, a novel by Franz Werfel, also perhaps initiated the germination of Miller's tale:

I finished a marvelous chapter of Werfel's last book last night and went to bed dancing. It was about angels . . . The angels appeared during the trip to Jupiter. However cheap the style, something seeps through . . . the man over-reached himself. And at least we get God, creation, angels, spirit, etc. It's a rum book. I can't drop it, though he irritates me continually.

Thus Werfel, Fowlie's essays, Rouault's clowns, Míro's painting of a ladder, a dog and the moon as well as Rainer Maria Rilke all came together in Miller's touching tale of Auguste, the clown who sought to realize his angelic essence.[86]

One of the most significant intellectual encounters during this period for Miller was with a German author who was then little-known in America. He had reported to Laughlin in 1944 that he was rereading Hermann Hesse's *Steppenwolf.* He also surprised himself by his ability to read *Siddhartha* in the original German (a 'masterpiece'), and praised *Narcissus and Goldmund, Journey to the East*, and the autobiographical sketch Hesse published in *Horizon* in September 1946.[87] Miller's enthusiasm would lead to the publication of *Siddhartha* in English in 1951 and the book sold well, but when the Sixties arrived it became New Directions' bestseller – 1,300,000 copies were sold of the 1957 paperback edition – as well as one of the sacred texts carried in the backpacks of the new generation of flower children.[88]

On 28 August 1948 at 8:35 a.m. in Carmel, Lepska gave birth to Henry Tony Miller, and father Miller reported to Durrell, in an apparent unconscious imitation of the *couvade* of the Native Americans, that he became increasingly thinner, ending at 129 lbs.[89] The Dominican priest and writer Père Bruckberger came to visit and F. J. Temple remarked that 'Father Bruckberger was not far . . . from considering Miller as one of the rare "Saints" of the United States'.[90] By summer 1948 Girodias was able to pay Miller $500 every month, but at the beginning of 1949 Miller was still bartering for provisions. A neighbour, Mary Rose Lopez, recalled Miller borrowing kerosene from her father and being struck by his red corduroy pants, which her father thought he must have obtained at the circus.[91] Miller now made the sixth and final revision of *Sexus*.[92] To relax he began to patronize Nepenthe, a new restaurant and bar on Highway 1.[93]

In August 1949 *Sexus* was published: Miller had wanted the book to appear with the rest of *The Rosy Crucifixion* so that his trilogy would be read in its entirety, but Girodias convinced him

Miller and Tony, 1950.

to release it separately.[94] Like his earlier 'autobiographical fictions', the novel is based on people he knew: 'Ulric' is Emil Schnellock, 'Stanley' is Stanley Borowski, 'Dr Kronski' is Emil Conason, 'MacGregor' is both Alec Considine and William Dewar. 'Miller' is 33 years old as the novel begins, 'the age of Christ crucified', and June is at first 'Mara', but in Chapter 8 changes to 'Mona', which she will remain for the remainder of the trilogy. The constant, varied, athletic and usually humorous sexual scenes, which were probably influenced by Miller's reading of the Indian *Kamasutra* and *Ananga Ranga* (as well as his admiration for Elie Faure's descriptions of erotic Indian sculpture), led the French to suppress the book. Miller wrote a brief text, 'Signs of Love', in 1972 to accompany Cliff Karhu's 'Shunga' paintings of Japanese erotic art, and his remarks there precisely describe his intentions in *Sexus*:

> What we see in the early stages of Shunga is an insatiable appetite for life, something akin in the Western world to the spirit of Chaucer and Brueghel. There is no sentimentality, no romanticism. Things are what they are, and sex is sex, something pleasurable, healthy and to be enjoyed to the full.[95]

Durrell, however, was appalled: he thought the novel full of 'twaddle'; 'the moral vulgarity of so much of it is artistically painful'; it was replete with 'childish explosions of obscenity'.[96] Miller did not take offence: the friendship continued to flourish. Just two years before his death, he declared: 'I've written about 60 books, and only part of them have dealt with obscenity. It was because of my obsession for telling the truth that I fell into this. It was never with the idea of shocking.' He had never seen himself as a 'realist' writer: he used surrealism, fantasy, humour and dream sequences to 'deepen and heighten this thing called reality, because what people call reality is not reality in my mind'.[97]

In a way, Durrell answered his own criticism in his essay in *Horizon*, 'Studies in Genius: Henry Miller':

> There seem to be two distinct types of creative mind. The first controls his material and shapes it. The second delivers himself over, bound hand and foot to his gifts. The first belongs to the family of Pope, the second to the family of Lawrence, of Blake. With this second type of artist it is useless to agitate for measure, form, circumspection. They are entirely mantic, delivered over to their pneuma.[98]

Lepska with Val and Tony in 1950.

Miller 'delivered himself over' and 'stuttered' (as he once said of Dostoevsky) like the great ones, created formless volcanic massive texts, fabricated, went off the deep end, rather than creating a finely shaped aesthetic object. Miller became aware, like Anaïs Nin, that in writing 'autobiography' it was impossible to tell the 'truth' about one's life. In *The Books in My Life* he declared that 'Autobiography is the purest romance. Fiction is always closer to reality than fact.'[99]

At the end of September Miller finished the exactly 700-page manuscript of *Plexus* and then Lawrence Clark Powell, who had suggested Miller make UCLA the repository of his archives, asked him to compile a list of books he considered significant which could be printed as a brochure and sent to friends of the UCLA Library. He began work in January 1950 by exploring the books he read as a child and completed the manuscript a year later.[100] John Kidis (born Mestakidis), published *The Waters Reglitterized*, a letter on painting to Emil Schnellock from 22 February 1939, one of the handwritten books for friends he created in the late Thirties in Paris, and it contains a striking description of Uccello's *The Battle of San Romano*, which Miller had seen in the National Gallery in London.[101] He also began to correspond with one of the heroes of his youth, John Cowper Powys, and he enthusiastically confided in the great Anglo-Welsh author his appreciation for the works of the astrologer Dane Rudhyar and his hope that they would live to see the lost islands of Atlantis, Mu and Lemuria found again.[102] Miller would become a staunch champion of Powys's work, praising in particular his *Autobiography* and *A Glastonbury Romance*. Miller now kept a photograph of an anonymous Chinese sage over the door of his house: he revealed to J. Rives Childs that 'this "unknown" is closer to me than all the known ones – and he radiates light!'[103] The Western literary figure who also exemplified this sense of wholeness was a writer Miller considered 'probably the most "rounded" figure in all literature – human to the core', Rabelais.[104]

Jean-Michel Hornus, a French Christian admirer came to visit, as did the comedian Red Skelton, who performed one of his hilarious skits, which entranced Tony and Valentine. Dylan Thomas wrote to his wife Caitlin to tell her that he had spent a happy evening with a mellow, gentle and gay Miller.[105] But his finances were still difficult in early 1951, when he wrote to Kathryn Winslow for help. He was broke and was struggling to maintain credit with his mailman, the family's source for postage stamps, cheese, eggs, milk, bread and butter, but to whom he owed $40. His voluminous letter-writing, however, continued apace: in February he began corresponding with the celebrated

Nostradamus scholar Dr Max de Fontbrune, recommending that he read Immanuel Velikovsky's catastrophic version of planetary history, *Worlds in Collision* (1950).[106]

In addition to his financial woes, the marriage with Lepska had become increasingly acrimonious and the couple completely disagreed about childrearing. Miller favoured complete freedom while Lepska was more traditional. Furthermore, life in the wilds far from the city and cooped up with an ageing, impractical literary genius could hardly have been easy for the still youthful Lepska. Miller told Edmond Buchet that Lepska had become violent and that several times he struck her back, about which he felt deeply ashamed.[107] Lepska fell in love with a biophysicist and in July 1951 left with the children for New York to stay with her parents: by October she had sued for divorce and moved to southern California, again taking the children.[108] Miller was devastated when Valentine and Tony departed. Late in November 1951 the 27-year-old Eve McClure, who was Bezalel Schatz's sister-in-law (Bezalel was married to her sister Louise), began writing Miller

Miller and the unknown Chinese sage, Big Sur, 1950.

letters from her house in Beverly Hills. She was an admirer of the author of *Tropic of Capricorn*, a book she had recently finished reading.[109] Miller received a rectangular silver Yemeni talisman from Schatz, which he believed to be 400 years old and inscribed with a Hebrew text: 'God bless you and protect you. May the radiance of His vision illumine your countenance. And may He instruct you in his ways.' Miller would wear the pendant night and day for many years and rarely remove it: he had absolute faith that it brought him protection and good fortune.[110] He had increasingly begun to resemble his beloved Balzac, who Stefan Zweig tells us 'believed in amulets, always wore a lucky ring with mysterious oriental symbols, and before taking any important decision he would creep up five flights of steps to consult a fortuneteller, just as any Parisian seamstress would'.[111]

6

Magus on the Mountain, Tropics Triumphant, 1952–62

At the end of March 1952 Miller drove down to Long Beach in southern California to see his children and visited Eve McClure in Beverly Hills: her charm and loveliness overwhelmed him, and they returned to Big Sur together in April.[1] He told Maurice Nadeau that he was now 'like a new being' in a 'dream state', and informed Durrell that to be with Eve was 'like living on velour'.[2] Miller now quickly regained his footing after his marriage crisis: he began work on *Nexus*; in April *Plexus* was published in French; both *Tropic* books appeared in German and Danish, *Black Spring* in Swedish: ten of his books had been translated into foreign languages.[3] *The Books in My Life* was published in November 1952, and Miller included an appendix which lists 'The One Hundred Books Which Influenced Me Most': the French edition, *Les Livres Dans Ma Vie*, contains an even more extensive list.[4] His principle of selection was simple: like Jorge Luis Borges, he was not swayed by whether a book was considered 'good l iterature', classic or canonical: his enthusiasm was reserved for authors who moved *him*, who gave him pleasure, who induced in him a state of *exaltation*. Hence a list that may seem to many a wild heterodoxy: his admired writers include Giono, Cendrars, Hesse, Haggard, Whitman, Algernon Blackwood, Arthur Machen and Maurice Maeterlinck.[5] His method is associative, one recollection of a book leading him to another and hence to autobiographical reflections.

He reveals in Chapter 2, 'Early Reading', that he planned to write a treatise entitled *Draco and the Ecliptic* inspired by the work of Frederick Carter: 'This, the seal or capstone to my 'autobiographical novels', as they are called, I trust will prove to be condensed, transparent, alchemical work, thin as a wafer and absolutely air-tight.'[6] He later told Brassaï: '*Draco* would have been the voice of the medium who, coming out of her trance, begins to reflect lucidly on what has just happened to her, almost unbeknownst to her.'[7] We again sense the Gnostic return to an archaic, secret primal identity, to the hidden, occluded real self. He had been fascinated by the concept of *apocatastasis* in Chapter 10 of Unamuno's *The Tragic Sense of Life*, which he read in the early Thirties, and refers here to the exploration of the concept by Eduardo Sanchez (the occultist cousin of Anaïs Nin) in his book *The Round*. In Chapter Four on Rider Haggard he speaks of

> the return to the source, the only revolution which has meaning for man, is the whole goal of man. It is a revolution which can only occur in man's being. This is the true significance of the plunge into life's stream, of becoming fully alive, awakening, recovering one's complete identity.

Draco and the Ecliptic – had it ever been written – would likely have explored the astrological and occult dimensions of his work, bearing the same relationship to his 'autobiographical romances' as D. H. Lawrence's *Psychoanalysis of the Unconscious, Fantasia of the Unconscious* or *Apocalypse* did to his novels and poetry.

Miller now received enough money from Girodias to enable his partial entry into respectable society: at the age of 60 he opened his first bank account. Until then he had been so poor that he kept what little money he ever had in his pocket.[8] At the end of December he and Eve were married, and his new financial solvency meant that he could now fund a trip to Europe. They

Miller and Eve, Spain, 1953.

arrived in Paris in a snowstorm on 31 December, the start of a honeymoon in Europe which would last for seven months.[9] They stayed with Maurice Nadeau (who had founded the committee to defend Miller in 1946) and his wife in Paris, where he was lionized, and travelled with his publisher Edmond Buchet to his house outside the capital, Le Vesinet.[10] Buchet was impressed by the sexagenarian's vigour, observing that prior to Miller being struck by influenza (Miller thought he became ill because he had not been wearing his lucky Yemeni talisman), he and Eve would disappear once or twice a day to the bedroom.[11] They met Man

Ray, Belmont, Reichel, Brassaï, Eugene Pachoutinsky and Cendrars, and at the end of January travelled to Monte Carlo before spending a month at La Ciotat, the country home of the actor Michel Simon. In Die they met the teacher and writer Albert Maillet, in whom Miller had found 'a kindred spirit. A sort of Christ – the real one, not of the Church'.[12]

They returned to Le Vesinet, met Bezalel and Louise Schatz, and in April Buchet took the Millers and Schatzes to see the painter Maurice de Vlaminck in Rueil-la-Gadelière.[13] In mid-May the couples journeyed to Montpellier, where they met the poet Frédéric Jacques Temple at Tuilerie de Massane, the home of Miller's beloved Joseph Delteil and his Chicago-born wife, Caroline. Temple recalled a deeply tanned Miller, blue eyes flashing, pants fastened by a Navajo belt, declaring that one day the Indians would again be masters of America.[14] The Delteils, Schatzes and Millers left a few days later for Spain with the photographer Denise Bellon, where they spent ten days.[15] Miller composed a vivid and lively account of the trip which originally appeared in *Syntheses* in September 1954, and the recently published *Mejores no hay* (2012) contains both this text as well as the splendid photographs taken by Bellon documenting their journey.

In Barcelona they had a happy reunion with Alfred Perlès and his wife, Anne. In late June he was overwhelmed by Van Eyck's *The Mystic Lamb* in the Cathedral at Ghent, which he felt brought him 'the closest I would ever get to the divine light of Nature', and on his return to France Miller went in July to visit the celebrated Nostradamus scholar Dr De Fontbrune in Perigord: his letters are full of ominous predictions of World War Three over the next year or so.[16] They then travelled to Corwen in Wales, where they visited John Cowper Powys, and then on for a second visit with Perlès to Wells in Somerset, where their main activity seems to have been laughing.[17] They returned to America in late July 1953 and his children stayed with them for the year.[18] Nancy Hopkins, one of

Miller's neighbours, who wrote a memoir of her life in Big Sur, *These Are My Flowers*, described him as being 'full of talk about Val and Tony . . . nothing so delights my heart as a person who really loves his children as Henry does'. And for her part, Eve was by all accounts not only a superb companion to Henry but an excellent mother, adoring the children as if they were her own, and a tireless helpmate.[19] Katsimbalis came for two days and Miller found him as stupendous as ever: following his visit Miller was inspired to read Xenophon's *Anabasis*, which he found 'very exciting'.[20] Van Wyck Brooks, an eminent figure in the East Coast literary establishment, and his wife, Gladys, also paid a visit, and Miller was glad to find that Brooks was not a stuffed shirt.[21] Brooks would later propose

Miller and Joseph Delteil, 1953, at Tuilerie de Massane.

Miller for membership of the National Institute of Arts and Letters and would contribute the 'Introduction' to *Writers at Work: The Paris Review Interviews, Second Series*, which included Miller.

While Miller was in Europe, *Plexus*, the second volume of *The Rosy Crucifixion* trilogy was published by Olympia Press (which printed Beckett's *Watt* the same year). *Plexus* recounts his marriage to June (Mona) and his struggle to be a writer after leaving the Cosmodemonic Telegraph Company, the opening of the speakeasy with Mona, their trip South, June's affair with Jean Kronski.[22] Many of the intellectual passions which drove Miller during the years of its composition made their way into the novel: a quotation from *Louis Lambert*: 'I feel within me a life so luminous that it could animate a world, and I feel myself locked up in some kind of mineral'; a long section of Chapter 8 is devoted to Nostradamus; another passage celebrates his love of the Chinese sage of whom he had a photograph: 'He is not simply 'a man of spirit' – he is all spirit. He is Spirit itself, I might say. All this is concentrated in his expression. The look which he gives forth is completely joyous and luminous. It says without equivocation: "Life is bliss!"'[23] The novel concludes with a panegyric to Spengler: 'There are phrases, sentences, sometimes whole paragraphs from The *Decline of the West* which seem to be engraved in my brainpan . . . for me Oswald Spengler is still alive and kicking. He enriched and uplifted me. As did Nietzsche, Dostoevski, Elie Faure.'[24]

In February 1954, Miller's daughter Barbara, who had found her father mentioned in an issue of *Family Circle* magazine, wrote and visited in June. In November Perlès arrived with the manuscript of *My Friend, Henry Miller*, which would be published in 1956.[25] Members of the counterculture and the emerging Beat movement began to see Miller as a literary force. Allen Ginsberg told his father that *Tropic of Cancer* was 'a great classic' and wrote (15 February 1952) to Neal Cassady and Jack Kerouac: 'Send *me* some peyote. Who else you know? How about digging Henry

Miller?'[26] Miller had prefigured the 'Confessional' writers through his naked revelation of his own sufferings: he had howled long before *Howl*. Kerouac (who would write a novel entitled *Big Sur*) perspicaciously remarked: 'The success of Allen is due to the fact that no one since Henry Miller has had the guts to say cock and cunt in public.'[27] Wallace and Shirley Berman, publishers of the underground Los Angeles journal *Semina*, and the poet Michael McClure came to visit; Richard Brautigan later wrote a novel entitled *A Confederate General from Big Sur* (1964).[28] Ginsberg and Kerouac also both attempted pilgrimages, but never managed to see *cher maître*, and Miller in turn wrote an admiring preface to Kerouac's *The Subterraneans* (1959). Miller's emerging status as a kind of countercultural guru was symbolized by his occasionally magus-like appearance: in addition to the Yemeni talisman, he sometimes donned a Mandarin skull cap, and during his daily walks carried an impressive *shillelagh*, the Irish blackthorn walking-stick John Cowper Powys had given him.[29] Miller's *numen*, however, attracted too many visitors, sometimes as many as 20 in a day. They were often sent away, then returned. One contingent asked to be allowed to handle something Miller had himself touched, so Eve proffered some old handkerchiefs and they left content.[30]

In September, Valentine and Tony joined Lepska for the school year and their proud father returned to his favourite angelic theme: 'They are so wonderful. If only she gets to realize what a privilege it is to live with angels. Not that they are well-behaved! But what shines through them!'[31] Miller then went to Pasadena in southern California to celebrate the 35th birthday of his daughter Barbara. He complained to Nadeau that he found the Los Angeles freeways 'hallucinating' (he let Eve do the driving) and was happy to return to Big Sur after the sterile way of living he found there.[32] He also began corresponding with Georges Simenon, whose novels he admired and whom he would later meet at Cannes.[33] In Autumn 1955 *La Tour de Feu: Henry Miller; ou, Les Mauvaises Frequentations* also appeared, which contained the first serious effort to conceptualize Miller's life and work within a philosophical and spiritual framework. As usual, the French understood him far better than his countrymen.

Miller was now absorbed with *Big Sur and The Oranges of Hieronymus Bosch*: he would typically rise at five in the morning before Eve was up and work hard through the end of the afternoon, unless he needed to chop wood, do chores in the garden or deal with visitors. Eve and he would play several lively games of ping-pong, have an aperitif while dinner cooked and be in bed by nine o'clock in the evening.[34] The artist Bob Nash (about whom Miller would write the essay 'Journey to an Antique Land') remembered spirited dinners with the Millers, furnished with fine wines supplied by their neighbour Giles Healy: Nash's contribution was to wash the pots and pans, usually past midnight. Robert Fink recalled that although he was decades younger than Miller, he found it difficult to keep up with the sexagenarian during mountain hikes: 'his gait was still springy, jaunty and alive'.[35]

In early January 1956 Miller learned his mother was ill: he and Eve travelled to New York at the end of the month.[36] His sister Lauretta was now an emaciated 67, and both mother and daughter were living in poverty. On 21 March at 6:30 a.m. his mother died, and later he told a ghoulish tale that her dead body opened its eyes and shot him a final evil glance: she was buried during a snowstorm. Eve wrote to Anaïs Nin: 'I met his mother on her deathbed. At 86, dying. She frightened the hell out of me. A real tyrant, cold as ice, and she died without "recognizing" Henry. This hurt him deeply.'[37] Miller brought Lauretta back with him to live at Partington Ridge and then placed her in the Del Monte Rest Home in Pacific Grove.[38] While in New York he visited June, and was shocked by her physical infirmities and unkempt appearance; he wept at the sight of his old love and hurried away, but saw to it that the scholar Annette Baxter, who would write *Henry Miller, Expatriate* (1961), and her psychiatrist husband would look after her.[39]

Miller in his Big Sur study, 1958.

When he returned to Big Sur, on the site of the shack he had used previously he built a new studio and a room for the children, while the Carmel artist Ephraim Doner, a close friend, constructed a tile mosaic bearing a blessing in Hebrew to decorate the outside wall. Roger Bloom, a convict in Missouri Penitentiary who had been condemned to life imprisonment for robbing a bank with a toy pistol, wrote to Miller and they began a long relationship which would ultimately involve Nin, Perles, Emil White, Durrell, Elmer Gertz and Robert Fink. Miller succeeded in having Bloom released from prison on parole after eight years.[40] Miller corresponded with other inmates and made efforts to free them, including Tommy Trantino: Miller was in that tradition of literary luminaries – Sartre (Jean Genet), Mailer (Jack Abbott) – who became involved in the cases of inmates they believed were unjustly incarcerated.

Devil in Paradise, the story of Miller's bizarre relationship with his friend from the Paris years, astrologer Conrad Moricand, and his ultimate expulsion from Big Sur, appeared in July, as did his masterful recollection of his days in Paris, *Quiet Days in Clichy*. In October his study of Rimbaud, *The Time of the Assassins*, was published. Miller drew parallels between Rimbaud's life and his own: they both suffered terrible mothers, their common desire for flight and revolt, the mystical angelic quest; and both were fascinated by the occult tradition. Miller had come late to Rimbaud: he had previously avoided him because he was the favourite of his rival for June's affections, Jean Kronski, but he now celebrated him as one of the supreme world spirits, as one of the great crucified figures of the nineteenth century who were tortured in their quest for the ultimate meaning of existence: Dostoevsky, Nietzsche, Van Gogh, Kierkegaard.

Miller was ecstatic over his friend Lawrence Durrell's just-published *Justine*, the first volume of *The Alexandria Quartet*, and declared that Durrell was the greatest contemporary master of English prose.[41] Meanwhile, Miller's own increasing celebrity was now recognized by his election as a member of the National Institute of Arts and Letters. On 22 May 1957 Louise Bogan announced at the induction ceremony:

> Henry Miller, born in New York City in 1891, is the veteran author of many books whose originality and richness of technique are matched by the variety and daring of their subject matter. His boldness of approach and intense curiosity concerning man and nature are unequalled in the prose literature of our time.[42]

Miller now began to gravitate towards 'everything Japanese' and he read with fascination Jiro Osaragi's *Homecoming* and *Five Women Who Loved Love* by Ihara Saikaku (both translations appeared in 1955). He also loved the Japanese films *The Magnificent Seven* and *Ugetsu*. This affinity for Japanese culture would continue to the end of his life.[43]

Big Sur and the Oranges of Hieronymus Bosch (1957) demonstrates the influence of *The Millennium of Hieronymus Bosch* by the art historian Wilhelm Fraenger, from which Miller quotes at the opening: 'The Brothers and Sisters of the Free Spirit called their devotional community-life 'Paradise' and interpreted the word as signifying the quintessence of love.'[44] Bosch's depiction of the preternaturally bright oranges hanging from the trees in his magical masterwork *The Millenium* triptych inspired Miller: 'Seeing the world through his eyes it appears to us once again as a world of indestructible order, beauty, harmony, which it is our privilege to accept as a paradise or convert into a purgatory.'[45] In celebrating the simple and interdependent life of Big Sur as a paradise in which the quest for self-realization might be undertaken, Miller was prefiguring the hippie communes of the Sixties. His attitudes about sharing, borrowing, exchanging his writing and watercolours with others for clothing, food or money recall Lewis Hyde's idea in *The Gift* that 'a work of art is a gift, not a commodity'.[46] The Esselen Indians had once lived in the Big Sur area, after which the Esalen Institute would be named. Founded in 1962 by Richard Price and Michael Murphy with the support of Frederic Spiegelberg (the scholar of Indian religions), Aldous Huxley, Abraham Maslow and Alan Watts, Esalen would become one of the centres of the human potential/transpersonal psychology movement.[47]

Miller's 'otherworldly' interests also appeared in *Big Sur*. In July 1947 an alien spacecraft was said to have crashlanded on a ranch in Roswell, New Mexico, and Miller revealed that off the coast of Big Sur he and his friend Walker Winslow had observed two gyrating lights in the sky which were reported the next day 'as a saucer phenomenon'.[48] Miller had mentioned Donald Keyhoe's book *The Flying Saucers are Real* (1950) in the preface to *The Books in My Life*, and he wrote to Joseph Delteil on 8 June 1954 recommending *Flying Saucers Have Landed* (1953) by Desmond Leslie and George Adamski: 'I have begun to believe that we will be in contact soon

with other worlds here (on earth) and in space . . . Am I mad?
I tremble with anticipation.'[49] His openness to the possibility of
extraterrestrial life during this period coincides with C. G. Jung's
interpretation in *Flying Saucers: A Modern Myth of Things Seen in the
Skies* (1958): 'Now we are approaching the great change to be
expected with the entering of the vernal equinox into Aquarius.'[50]

On 10 May 1957 *Sexus* was ordered confiscated by the Attorney
General of Norway on the grounds that it was 'obscene writing'.[51]
Miller composed three texts during this period explaining his ideas
concerning obscenity, censorship and freedom of speech. He sent
two letters to the defence attorney Trygve Hirsch in Norway
(19 September 1957 and 27 February 1959). But the ban on *Sexus*
was upheld, although the defendants were found not guilty.[52]
Miller also drafted an essay for his Paris lawyer to be used as court
testimony during the trial of *Sexus* in France, and this was published as 'Obscenity in Literature' in *New Directions in Poetry and
Prose 16* in 1957:

> I am a man of peace whose sole aim is to enjoy life to the
> utmost . . . That certain words, certain expressions, usually
> though not always connected with sex, have come to be
> thought of as 'forbidden' is, at bottom, mystifying.[53]

His increasing celebrity was confirmed in June 1957, when Eddie
Schwartz and Tom Moore founded the Henry Miller Literary
Society in Minneapolis, which would publish between 1959 and
1963 a *Newsletter* devoted to his life and work.[54] Even Flannery
O'Connor became a fan after reading *The Colossus of Maroussi* as
she confided to a friend: 'Never read Henry Miller before but this
book is very fine.'[55]

In the summer of 1958 Miller began seeking a good school (the
concept itself was for him an oxymoron) for his children and read
Summerhill by the Scottish educational reformer A. S. Neill, whom

he would meet in London in 1961. He wanted Valentine and Tony to experience as joyous and liberating an 'education' as possible.[56] Meanwhile, Miller's neighbour Nancy Hopkins observed:

> Big Sur is beginning to get rather respectable, for as it has gotten more 'chic' the prices have risen accordingly and fewer and fewer of the Bohemian element can afford to buy or rent homes here . . . And Henry Miller has two cars (one a Cadillac) and plays ping-pong and has become positively bourgeois – his son reads nothing but comic books and his daughter pin-curls her hair at a pink-satin-and-tulle vanity table. Quel malheur! Whither the Left Bank?[57]

Now aged 67, Miller remained healthy: his only ailment was a case of haemorrhoids, for which he was treated in Berkeley in November.[58]

His most significant literary discovery of this period was John Cowper Powys's *A Glastonbury Romance* (1932). He told Durrell: 'My head began bursting as I read. No, I said to myself, it is impossible that any man can put all this – so much! – down on paper. It is super-human.'[59] He also became riveted by Charles Williams's *Arthurian Torso*, which he consistently placed among his favourite critical studies (the other two most frequently cited were Milton O. Percival's *William Blake's Circle of Destiny* and Pandelis Prevelakis's *Nikos Kazantzakis and his Odyssey*). Williams explores the same mythological terrain as Powys – the legend that it was in Glastonbury, identified with Avalon, that Joseph of Arimathea had set the Grail.[60] Miller's high estimation of Powys was shared by George Steiner, who asserted that 'Powys is, with Milton and with Blake, one of the foremost imaginers and narrators of the transcendent, of the "other," in the language.'[61] It is this quality that Miller loved in *A Glastonbury Romance*, just as Powys himself had said of Miller: 'his critical appreciation of certain mystical elements and what might be called prophetic elements in other writers . . . have encouraged in him a certain *seismic mediumship* and psychic clairvoyance'.[62] *Arthurian Torso* and *A Glastonbury Romance* confirmed and continued his childhood fascination with King Arthur, 'light of the Western world', as Miller called Arthur in his essay devoted to Powys, 'The Immortal Bard'.[63]

The idea for the book *Art and Outrage* (1959) began with Durrell and Perlès exchanging letters about Miller, but the third musketeer later joined in, giving an engaging overview of his artistic influences and development. Miller returns to the photograph of the unknown, inscrutably smiling Chinese sage from the close of *Plexus* and compares him to Hesse's *Siddhartha* and the *Tao te Ching*: 'The smile of "above the battle". Overcoming the world. And thus finding it. For we must not only be in it and above it, but of it too. To love it for what it is – how difficult! And yet it's the first, the only task. Evade it, and you are lost. Lose yourself in it and you are free.'[64] Miller now set to work on *Nexus,* the third volume of *The Rosy Crucifixion* trilogy and had completed the manuscript by April 1959.[65]

In mid-April of that year Miller went to Paris with Eve and the children for a five-month stay in Europe. Edmond Buchet, Nadeau and Belmont met them at Orly and Miller was happy at Le Vesinet, playing ping-pong and games with the children. In June he met Barney Rosset, the publisher of Grove Press, and Maurice Girodias for lunch in Paris. Rosset, who had first read Miller while a student at Swarthmore, wanted to publish *Tropic of Cancer* and *Tropic of Capricorn* in America: however, Miller was not yet ready.[66] Miller went to Copenhagen to meet his Danish publisher and Holland with the children, and then with Tony and Valentine, but without Eve, by train to Die in the Drôme to visit Albert Maillet and his family. There were now obvious problems in the marriage: Eve complained to Buchet that she had married an 'old man', and when Brassaï gave a dinner for the couple, Eve went into a long, and understandable, harangue about the other side of the paradise at Big Sur: leaking roofs, their now decrepit 1941

automobile, constant money worries.[67] They went on to visit
Durrell in Sommières in mid-July – Durrell was enjoying a great
success with his *Alexandria Quartet* – and Miller also met Richard
Aldington, whom he would later remember fondly. With his
German publisher, Heinrich M. Ledig-Rowohlt, Miller visited the
grave of Paul Valéry in Sète, where they discussed the transmigration
of souls and rode horses in the Camargue with the children.[68]

When the Millers returned to the United States in August, their
marriage was unimproved: Miller suspected Eve of having an affair
with a neighbour and he became involved with Caryl Hill, a waitress
at Nepenthe Restaurant. Miller was now in a crisis. His state of mind
can be gauged from the fact that he consulted one of his astrologers,
who advised him that he should put off until the following year a trip
he had suddenly contemplated making to Japan, Siam and Burma.[69]
When he rose early in the morning, he put his gramophone on at top
volume and listened to Monteverdi's *Madrigals*, Ravel's *Gaspard de la
nuit* and Scriabin's *Fifth Piano Sonata*.[70] And his rapture about
Joseph Delteil's *François d'Assise* (1960) – whose *Jesus II* (1947) he had
also adored – also sustained him through his dark night of the soul:
'He was the arch enemy of the established order, the most radical of
radicals. His Order was humanity entire. In his dream of universal
love and justice he was prepared to embrace *all* mankind in one
inclusive open order.'[71] Increasing praise from the international
literary world perhaps also salved an ego wounded by yet another
disintegrating marriage. Karl Shapiro called him 'The Greatest
Living American Author', a 'wisdom-writer . . . a holy man . . .
Gandhi with a penis . . . the only American of our time who has
given us a full-scale interpretation of modern America', while
Durrell edited the anthology *The Henry Miller Reader*. By the late
Fifties, Miller had begun to emerge as a major influence on writers
such as Italo Calvino, who declared: 'This was a time when a figure
like Henry Miller was much more important than Hemingway,
whom nobody bothered about any more.'[72]

In April 1960 Miller went to Cannes for the film festival, to which he had been invited to serve as a judge. He stopped first in Paris and ten days later went to Rome, where he found cold rain, scores of stray cats and was appalled by 'the hideous vulgarity' of St Peter's.[73] He went on to Hamburg to meet Ledig-Rowohlt of Rowohlt Verlag in Reinbek, and encountered his publisher's young and attractive assistant Renate Gerhardt, by whom he was instantly smitten. Ledig-Rowohlt set up a ping-pong table in Hamburg and encouraged his staff to play with the visiting genius during office hours. Miller also enjoyed Bremen and Lübeck, where he found great pleasure eating and drinking in the famous *ratskellers*. Miller had last been in Germany in 1928 and was now struck by the contemporary Germans' 'prosperity, ease and contentment'. In Cannes, where the festival began on 4 May, he saw about 32 films, which he found poor except for the Japanese *Kagi*, based on Junichiro Tanizaki's erotic masterpiece *The Key*. Miller was intrigued by the combination of violence, love and tenderness in Japanese cinema as well as by the Samurai tradition: 'the older films that refer to historical Japanese times, that have lots of action, sort of like cowboy movies, are my favorite'.[74] He met Caryl Hill in Cannes – they had arranged earlier to meet up there – but Miller was already becoming emotionally involved with Renate Gerhardt, to whom he wrote love letters, and he surprised Caryl by telling her they would sleep in separate rooms. While in Cannes, Miller received a letter from Eve seeking a divorce, which he conceded was the right course of action.[75]

Miller told Brassaï he wanted to meet Picasso, who in turn told the photographer 'I have great admiration for Henry Miller. Perhaps you could come back with him after the festival?' The encounter was duly arranged, and at the last minute, Miller backed out – again displaying his fear and shyness regarding his heroes.[76] At the end of May he visited Michel Simon again in La Ciotat, then on to Juan-les-Pins for a week and to Èze-sur-Mer for a visit with Brassaï and his wife, Gilberte. He saw Durrell in Nîmes, and in Milan met his Italian publisher, Feltrinelli, staying at his sumptuous villa on Lake Garda for a week. He also visited Pisa, Florence, Volterra, Lucca and San Gimignano, and was struck by 'the vital, progressive spirit of the Italians'. He returned to Paris for a few days, where he visited his old friend the painter Beauford Delaney at his studio in Clamart on the edge of Paris, and then headed back to America.[77]

Nexus was published by Obelisk in June 1960, and details the relationship between Mona and Jean Kronski and their abandonment of Miller to travel in Europe, Mona's return alone, and Miller and his wife leaving for Europe together. Miller had told Elmer Gertz about his admiration for Cantor Sirota, and wrote him on 2 October 1963 that he wanted to find the passage in *Nexus* regarding him:

> I read *Nexus* all through to find it. I was almost overcome by my own writing. This is a marvelous book, I find, about the Jew in my life, music, art, literature, and the struggle (for a Goy) to become an artist. Now I think it superior to most of the other books I wrote; it's from the center of my being. Mad, a good part of it. Sublime even, sometimes.[78]

His intellectual enthusiasms found their way into his 'autobiographical romances', erasing the line between 'life' and 'art', between autobiography and fiction. Allusions to sources as diverse as Dante, Strindberg, Swedenborg and the *Dhammapada* abound. He told Durrell: 'I love Berdyaev. It's like my "alter ego" writing.'[79] Nikolai Berdyaev's ideas on creativity and his statement on apocatastasis – the doctrine of universal salvation and resurrection – clearly appealed to Miller and they permeate the opening pages of *Nexus*, as well as references to Dostoevsky and *Oblomov* by Ivan Goncharov.[80] Miller thus sets the scene for the Dostoevskyan struggle about to take place between himself, June and Jean: he is writing a kind of American

Notes from the Underground in which he, like Dostoevsky's tortured anti-hero, struggles for his soul. We remember that Miller would take long walks in New York, stopping in front of the portrait of Dostoevsky in a bookshop window and staring at it for hours. In addition to *Nexus*, the year 1960 included the appearance of *To Paint is to Love Again*, which contained his text on his 'watercolor mania' as well as fourteen colour reproductions of his paintings.

His restlessness now led him to decide to go to Europe for nearly a year, and in late September 1960 he flew from California to Paris with Vincent Birge, a pilot for TWA. They spent a few days in Paris and then went south to Die (Drôme), where Miller had left his 1953 Fiat (which constantly broke down) with Albert Maillet. In mid October they left Die and went to Reinbek for two weeks, where Miller continued to woo Renata while the Fiat was being repaired. In early November they left for Georges Simenon's château in Épalinges near Lausanne, where Miller spent four days.[81] One night Charlie Chaplin was also a guest and there was much laughter and revelry. Chaplin elaborated his theory of artistic creativity: 'We're all of us psychos. But a few, like the three of us, are unbelievably lucky. When they feel a crisis coming on, they don't have to spend a lot of money on psychoanalysis. You two start writing, I make a film, and we're temporarily cured. And we get paid for it to boot.'[82] Simenon noted that his children bonded immediately with Miller, responding to his childlike enthusiasm.[83] Miller was now on a mission to find a place to live with Renate and her boys, which would take almost a year. In early November Emil White joined them and they went on to Vienna, Emil's home town, and after a week, Henry flew back to see Renate in Hamburg.[84]

Renata introduced him to Dr Wilhelm Wulff, who had been Himmler's astrologer, and Miller was impressed to find on his wall a photograph of one of the two 'Masters' from *Letters from the Mahatmas*.[85] Miller reconnected with his German heritage: he signed his name on Rowohlt's autograph wall in Gothic

German letters as 'Heinrich Muller' with the message 'God is Love'. He admired the lovely landscape of Schleswig-Holstein, and Dortmund, the city of his maternal grandfather, Valentin Nieting, wondering why his relatives abandoned Germany for the nightmare of New York. However, he also bemoaned the fact that it was due to his German genes that 'I have toiled my whole life like a horse, although I do not believe in work.'[86] Miller wanted to be a Zen Master – able to recline and enjoy the view without concern – but he felt his Germanic heritage had made it nearly impossible for him to stand still like the hummingbird.

As if to prove his point, he started work on Christmas Eve on a play that took him back to his time with June, *Just Wild About Harry*, influenced by Saroyan and Ionesco and the burlesk of his youth, which he would dedicate to Renate.[87] He also composed one of his best essays, published as a preface to Faure's *History of Art* in his *Oeuvres complètes* in 1964, celebrating his beloved art historian's conception of art as the true religion. Faure had written in one of Miller's favourite books, *La Danse sur le feu et l'eau*: 'Religion does not create art. It is art which creates religion, by incarnating into its images our desire to overcome life, to affirm ourselves, to spread ourselves, and impose upon our external universe the form even of our dreams, which torment us up to the moment in which we have formulated them.'[88] He also completed a text in nonsense German along with several drawings on 15 January 1961 which was published in *Rhinozeros*, 'Ein ungebumbelte Fuchselbiss'.[89]

He was still vacillating about publishing the two *Tropic* works and wrote to Rosset:

I would triumph as the King of Smut. I would be given the liberty to thrill, to amuse, to shock, but not to edify or instruct, not to inspire revolt. Certainly you must be aware that throughout my autobiographical works, including *The Colossus of Maroussi*, *The Books in My Life*, *Hamlet* and the *Oranges*, the

overlying thought is to inspire and to awaken, not merely to
titillate and amuse the reader.

But Rosset, learning that possible pirated editions were being
planned, offered Miller a generous deal and flew to Hamburg;
both Girodias and Ledig-Rowohlt urged him to accept, and Miller
finally signed the contract on 18 February 1961.[90] He had been in
daily correspondence with Vincent Birge, and wrote to him in late
February that he was ready to resume his travels in search of a
home for himself, his children, Renate and her two boys. They set
out for Ticino, then to Montpellier in April, where F. J. Temple
arranged for Miller to try on the robes of Rabelais in the university
museum. He was plagued by various ailments, including hip pain,
fatigue and digestion problems, and was suffering over the uncer-
tainty of his affair with Renate, so instead of going to church or
using drugs, alcohol or psychoanalysis, he turned as usual to the
stars: he consulted his astrologer *du jour*, Dr Wulff in Hamburg,
who advised him to go to Lisbon, where he arrived in May.[91]
They even looked for 'Shangri-La', as Miller joked, in Monaco,
Liechtenstein and San Marino: in eight months they had travelled
20,000 kilometres but no suitable place could be found. He did,
however, get some useful work done correcting proofs for Grove
Press of the *Tropic* books, and spent a happy week with the actress
Hildegard Knef in Berlin.[92] Grove Press published *Tropic of Cancer*
on 24 June 1961, after a ban in America for 27 years: 68,000 copies
were sold in the first week and it hit the bestsellers' list.[93]

But his burgeoning riches and fame did little to lift his
spirits and he had given up the quest for a home in Europe: he
was demoralized and returned to Reinbek. In late July he visited
his Danish publisher in Copenhagen, where he met Antonio
Bibalo, who had written an opera based on *The Smile at the Foot
of the Ladder*, saw Hamlet's castle at Elsinore, and went on to
Milan to meet his publisher Mondadori, where Mario Marini

created a bust of him. Then he, Perlès and his wife toured England and Ireland.[94] Miller's romantic dreams about Renate seemed to be crashing to earth. She (revealed in his late *The Book of Friends*) had consulted with Wilhelm Wulff, who advised her that the stars were not in the right alignment and so marriage was not recommended.[95]

Miller returned to America in September to Pacific Palisades, where he rented a furnished room at 661 Las Lomas to be near his children. He met Aldous Huxley, Colin Wilson and Christopher Isherwood and wrote more than 100 pages of the second volume of *Nexus* but then stopped, continued a year later, and then abandoned the project.[96] E. R. Hutchinson remarked that in early 1961 most Americans had never heard of either Henry Miller or *Tropic of Cancer*, but by 1964 one 'would have had to climb the hills to discover a citizen who hadn't heard about the one man and the one book that had ignited the censorship holocaust searing the whole United States'. Ultimately, Miller would become the most controversial and censored writer in American literary history. On 9 October 1961 Bradley Smith, a bookstore owner in Los Angeles, sold a copy to an undercover policeman, and the following February was given a 30-day prison sentence; bookstores, drug-store counters, newsstands and even public libraries were raided by the police.[97] Charles Rembar, chief counsel for Grove Press, suggested Rosset engage Elmer Gertz to deal with the obscenity charges against the book in Illinois. Miller was fortunate to have Gertz as an advocate for he had a deep interest in literature and would become a close friend.

The trial began on 10 January 1962 with Judge Samuel B. Epstein presiding and ended on 21 February. Epstein declared: 'Literature which has some social merit, even if controversial, should be left to individual taste rather than to government edict. Let not the government or the courts dictate the reading matter of a free people.'[98] Many of the major figures of the American literary establishment became advocates for Miller, including Robert Lowell, who wrote in a letter of 14 April 1962: 'This seems to be a censorship year. English faculties and unlikely persons such as Harry Levin and Dick Wilbur are everywhere testifying for Henry Miller. We are all signing testimonials for Miller, between signing other ones against using the bomb.'[99] And while America's justice system was preoccupied with Miller's use of four-letter words, Miller had discovered the Trappist monk Thomas Merton and wrote James Laughlin several enthusiastic letters, finding Merton's dialogue with the great Zen scholar D. T. Suzuki as well as his fragment on the Desert Fathers illuminating: 'I feel closer to him, his way of thinking, than any other American writer I know of.'[100]

In January 1962 Miller published 'I Defy You' in *Playboy* (for which he would write several articles over the next few years) in response to the censorship of *Tropic of Cancer* in Massachusetts, and ultimately the Supreme Judicial Court of Massachusetts lifted the ban on 17 July.[101] He returned to Europe in March 1962 to be a judge at the Prix Formentor in Mallorca. He visited Paris, London and Berlin, where he saw the Marini bronze head of himself at the Galerie Springer, which he thought 'magnificent, if I say so myself'.[102] He met Ionesco at Edmond Buchet's in April and Joan Miró in May in Majorca.[103] He returned to America at the end of May, meeting Eddie Schwartz and Tom Moore of the Henry Miller Literary Society as well as Elmer Gertz for first time in Minneapolis in June, and then went on to visit Roger Bloom in prison in Jefferson City, Missouri.[104]

He returned to Pacific Palisades in July and stayed only a few weeks before returning to Europe again in August: the British publisher John Calder had invited him to the Edinburgh Festival to participate in an International Writers' Conference. He stopped in Reinbek to see Renate, with whom he had been in contact, and he would later send her sizeable sums of money to help finance the publishing house she had begun.[105] In Edinburgh, Norman Mailer, William S. Burroughs, Mary McCarthy, Alexander Trocchi and Lawrence Durrell were in attendance, and Calder remarked that although Miller spoke little, on the fourth day, when the subject of censorship came up, he gave a speech on literary freedom which 'received a standing ovation from nearly three thousand people packed into Edinburgh's McEwan Hall. It was obvious that, at least to a younger generation, he had become a legendary literary figure.'[106] At one big party of sherry-drinking literati, Burroughs recalled that Miller said to him

> 'So you're Burroughs.' I didn't feel quite up to 'Yes, maître', and to say 'So you're Miller' didn't seem quite right, so I said, 'A long-time admirer' and we smiled. The next time I met him he did not remember who I was but finally said, 'So you're Burroughs.'

Anthony Blond in his article 'Unshockable Edinburgh' quipped: 'If Henry Miller was the hero of the week, William Burroughs was certainly the heroin.'[107] Interestingly, there were many points of comparison between the two renegades: both disbelieved in psychoanalysis, inclined towards Gnosticism and Native American shamans, were keen on *The Tibetan Book of the Dead*, Oswald Spengler, Dianetics and UFOs (Burroughs went so far as to become a convert to Whitley Streiber's tales of alien abduction), although Miller never felt the need to utilize a Reichian Orgone Box.

He went on to Paris, Copenhagen and then to Percha-bei-Starnberg in Bavaria to visit Hildegard Knef, who remembered Miller's charismatic *Freundlichkeit*; he even made a friend out of her usually sullen and grumpy Bavarian postman, who had now become cheerful and subsequently always inquired after Miller. While staying with Knef, he found time to contribute to the volume devoted to Céline in the celebrated *L'Herne* series: 'I adore

Miller, Elmer Gertz and son at the Loop Synagogue in front of Abraham Rattner's stained-glass windows, Chicago, 1962.

the works of Céline and owe him a great deal . . . Céline lives in me, he will always live there.'[108] He visited Mad King Ludwig's castle Neuschwanstein, which he found particularly astonishing, went to the Salzkammergut, Mozart's house in Salzburg, and was cheered by a visit from Renate.[109] In Berlin he met Nicholas Nabokov, attended the George Grosz exhibition and stayed with Renate, whose Gerhardt Verlag was planning to publish *Just Wild About Harry* in German.[110]

Miller returned to New York at the end of October and went on to Chicago, where he met Elmer Gertz and saw Abraham Rattner's stained-glass windows at the Loop Synagogue; he returned to Pacific Palisades at the start of November. Rosset published *Tropic of Capricorn*, which also became a bestseller, and New Directions brought out *Stand Still Like the Hummingbird*, a collection of Miller's essays. Things had heated up in the *Tropic of Cancer* brouhaha: the grand jury in Brooklyn decided Miller should be prosecuted under

Section 1141 of the New York Penal Code, while the District Attorney referred to it as 'a certain obscene, lewd, lascivious, filthy, indecent, sadistic, masochistic and disgusting book'. There were threats to have him arrested and extradited from California, but he stayed put. Charles Rembar recalled an amusing dialogue:

> Miller asked, 'Tell me, how is all this going to come out?' The New York Court of Appeals has held the book obscene, the score on the various trials around the country was pretty bad, and Miller's extradition was a hovering possibility. I felt sure, though, that when a case got to the Supreme Court, the decision would be in our favor. 'There'll be a lot of trouble along the way,' I answered, 'but it will end right.' 'Isn't that interesting,' said Miller, quite serious, 'that's just what my astrologer told me.'[111]

Miller had nothing to fear, for the case was dismissed. He now sold the film rights for *Tropic of Cancer* to Joseph E. Levine for $125,000, but his income tax situation was now dire: he had given away much of the several hundred thousand dollars he had earned the past few years and had to pay taxes on his income, so he wrote Elmer Gertz about his plan to paint watercolours he could donate to institutions to lessen his liability. He now painted as many as five watercolours a day.[112] When Gertz expressed astonishment at Miller's 'very sensible attitude', Miller replied: 'Don't understand your surprise. After all, I'm a realist . . . My aim, God willing, is to get clever enough to not pay *any* taxes.'[113]

Miller now became friends with Joe Gray, a former boxer, stuntman and Dean Martin double, who became his liaison into the Hollywood set. He toured the movie studios, meeting Shirley MacLaine, Marlon Brando and Cary Grant, and was invited to a private screening of *Cape Fear*: Robert Mitchum's acting greatly impressed him.[114] Anaïs Nin paid a visit: he gave her the copyright

Miller and Joe Gray, Los Angeles, 1966.

on his letters to her, spoke of his love for his children, his belief in reincarnation, and Nin thought he looked like a 'jolly' Buddhist monk.[115] He began to go house-hunting so that he could live again with his children, but would have preferred to find a place in Mexico than one in southern California.[116] His intellectual life continued to be robust: he became immersed in Maisie Ward's biography of G. K. Chesterton, one of his 'favorites', who was 'much better, bigger, than I had thought – even tho' an ardent Catholic'. But he seemed to contradict Nin's assessment of him as an impervious Buddha. Now, at a time when his worldwide fame was dawning and he was besieged by admirers, he wrote Gertz at Christmas time, usually the time of year he felt lowest, 'despite family, friends and all that, I feel lonelier (almost) than ever before in my life. I would almost say – I have gotten nowhere. I end up as I began – a failure.'[117]

7

Fame and Insomnia in Pacific Palisades, 1963–71

On 6 January 1963 Miller sent several telegrams to friends including Lawrence Durrell, requesting a minimum of $5,000 to purchase a house he had found at 444 Ocampo Drive, Pacific Palisades: a two-storey, white stucco Georgian with a wrought-iron balcony, large stone fireplace, brass door-knocker and finely maintained lawn priced at $77,000.[1] He was convinced by a friend that the swimming pool would be therapeutic for his health. As previously in his life in Paris and Big Sur, he had fallen into a new situation. Bern Porter recalled: 'Henry was allergic to houses, real estate agents, banks, and checks. Someone had to do all this for him. Someone had to go pick it out and buy it and almost bring him in by the hand and say, "Henry, this is a house."'[2] He had landed in the tony neighbourhood where the German writer Lion Feuchtwanger entertained Thomas Mann; the great American composer Roy Harris lived nearby.[3] Lush, exotic southern Californian flora filled his backyard: palm trees, cacti, banana trees. Valentine, now aged seventeen, and Tony, fourteen, moved in along with their mother. The staid exterior was deceptive, however, for the house's lively interior would reflect Miller's original, zany imagination: an open ping-pong table in the living-room (which doubled as the surface on which he drafted his watercolours), a piano, walls covered with his own paintings as well as graffiti and quotations in Chinese, Japanese, Russian and German, to which visitors were encouraged to contribute. Psychedelic posters of

Maxwell Parrish, Gustav Klimt and Jimi Hendrix soon adorned the ceiling courtesy of Tony. Miller's bedroom was downstairs, and on his dresser he kept a framed photograph of Ramakrishna.[4]

Lawrence Durrell and Henry Miller: A Private Correspondence was published in 1963 by Dutton; a much-expanded edition containing letters from 1935 to 1980 appeared in 1988. Ian MacNiven commented on Miller's 'almost pathological' epistolary urge: by the 1970s, he had composed between 100,000 and 200,000 letters.[5] This vital exchange revealed the excitement of the two friends' explosive enthusiasms. Grove also published *Black Spring* in 1963 and New Directions brought out *Just Wild About Harry*. The play's world première took place in July 1963 in Spoleto: in August the play was closed as obscene at the Edinburgh Festival.[6] A disguised version of his life with June, it was influenced by Saroyan, Ionesco and Artaud: 'Here was revolution, genuine revolution. Except for a small circle of admirers, no one seemed to take Artaud's views seriously. Literature, that's all it was. Besides, wasn't he a bit of a madman? (What innovator isn't?).'[7]

Miller had learned copperplate engraving while in Copenhagen and now in March 1963 began learning silkscreening in order to produce serigraphic prints. He studied it under Sister Mary Corita and her colleagues at Immaculate Heart College in Hollywood, and when his stretched sacrosciatic muscle gave him trouble, the Sisters went to his house to continue the lessons.[8] And for his watercolours, he now had a huge table (above which he posted images from India, Africa, China and Japan as inspiration), a double sink for cleaning brushes and pans and storage space for his creations. He continued to enjoy his daily naps, took therapeutic daily swims in the pool, which was kept heated to 84 degrees, rode his bicycle and started a new romance with Ziva Rodann, Miss Israel of 1960.[9] Now aged 72, Miller was described by Lionel Olay as 'slim as a boy, spry and alert as a fox, with nervous, graceful movements.'[10]

In September he began writing a one-act burlesk about a writer on trial for writing an obscene book. He considered depicting a jury in the play wearing large masks with the faces of jackals, foxes and hyenas. His old friend George Seferis won the Nobel Prize for Literature and Miller sent a congratulatory cablegram.[11] Joan Baez brought the 23-year-old Bob Dylan for a visit, but the encounter did not go well. Miller thought the singer-poet 'snooty and arrogant', while Dylan thought the writer dismissive.[12] Dylan devoted two pages to Miller in *Tarantula* (1971) and later apparently had no hard feelings. When asked about his favourite reading, Dylan replied: 'Rilke. Chekhov. Chekhov is my favorite writer. I like Henry Miller. I think he's the greatest American writer . . . I met him. Years ago. Played ping-pong with him.'[13] And when probed by Ron Rosenbaum about his 'purpose and mission', Dylan replied: 'Henry Miller said it: the role of an artist is to inoculate the world with disillusionment', which demonstrates he knew his Miller: this is a paraphrase from *Sexus*:

A man writes to throw off the poison which he has accumulated because of his false way of life. He is trying to recapture his innocence, yet all he succeeds in doing (by writing) is to inoculate the world with the virus of his disillusionment. No man would set a word down on paper if he had the courage to live out what he believed in.

But Miller remained unenchanted: 'Bob Dylan leaves me stone cold, though he's Number One for all the teenagers.'[14]

He had always made friends easily, and he now socialized with a surprising number of classical musicians, going to a violinist's house to hear Jascha Heifetz and Gregor Piatigorsky play chamber music, meeting conductors Zubin Mehta and William Steinberg, the film composer Bronislaw Kaper as well as Hilda Somers, a specialist in the piano music of his favourite composer, the

Theosophy-inspired Alexander Scriabin, whose *La Poème de l'extase* he memorably compared in *Nexus* to 'a bath of ice, cocaine and rainbows'. Perhaps most importantly he became close friends with the pianist Jakob Gimpel, whose masterclasses he attended with great enjoyment and for whose recording of Beethoven's *Emperor Concerto* he contributed the admiring liner notes.[15] And he fed his mind as always with books as well as music. In an unintentionally amusing exchange with a French interviewer, Miller insisted the French people were great readers. He, however, had been immersed in books in his youth but 'now I don't read any more than two or three or four books a week'.[16] He was then absorbed in Laurens Van der Post's *The Lost Bushmen of the Kalahari* and a biography of Alexander the Great while reacquainting himself with one of the favourites of his youth, Marie Corelli's *Life Everlasting* (1911).[17] And if Miller was still heterodox in his iterary taste, he also continued to flout 'American values', such as celebrating Christmas. He always abhorred the holiday season and this year was no exception: he implored his friends not to send cards or gifts: 'This is a sad time of the year for me – worse than Yom Kippur, for some reason. The world seems more than ever crazy to me at X'mas. They've really fucked Jesus up good and proper. I refuse to observe the day any more – or New Year's either. What's "new" about it, eh?'[18]

Although he had always found the holiday season depressing, his creative zest rarely flagged. His stationery had been embossed with his name and address: he now asked Eddie Schwartz of the Henry Miller Literary Society to create letterheads with a Zulu saying, 'The time of the hyena is upon us', stencilled in red ink at the bottom.[19] Over the next two decades a plethora of provocative aphorisms would grace his letters. His friend Florian Steiner provided two: the Portuguese 'When shit has value, the poor will be born without assholes' and 'Henry, now and then I may be obliged to sleep in my car, but when I need to take a shit I go to the Beverly Hills Hotel.' Céline provided 'I piss on it all from a considerable height', while the occultist Eliphas Levi contributed 'When love comes to the fore woman will be the queen of the universe.' 'Every eel in the world is born in the Sargasso Sea' came from Colin Wilson and 'I obtained not the least thing from complete, unexcelled awakening, and for that very reason it is called complete, unexcelled awakening' from Gautama the Buddha.[20]

Miller's literary status was now curious. A flood of translations of his works appeared worldwide but he was (in)famous mainly for a single book – *Tropic of Cancer* – as well as *Tropic of Capricorn* and the erotic passages in *Sexus*. Yet he had achieved a great deal beyond these (chiefly early) works, and the public had a completely distorted sense of his range as an author. The situation had been similar with Vladimir Nabokov, who became world famous due to *Lolita*, but reading only *Lolita* would give an anomalous impression of the style and meaning of Nabokov's massive and varied oeuvre. In a sense, Miller's fear that he would become known as the 'King of Smut' had come to pass: the uproar over censorship issues had overshadowed virtually every other aspect of his artistic vision. Indeed, the legal fireworks continued, with a Florida circuit court forbidding the sale of *Tropic of Cancer*. The Supreme Court of the United States finally delivered its verdict on 22 June 1964, reversing the Florida decision, with Justices Black and Douglas affirming 'that all censorship is unconstitutional'. Miller wondered whether 'the enemies of progress' in America would try – were it possible under the Constitution – to impeach the Supreme Court's members.[21]

His domestic situation by now had become rather byzantine. Lepska had met a man during her trip to Europe during the summer of 1963: she and her lover were now installed with Miller and his children under the same roof (Valentine was about to be married and Tony was about to go to a military academy). The situation became understandably touchy: the couple had decamped by April of 1964. When Lepska left, she took her belongings with her – all the chairs, tables, armoires and rugs – so Miller obtained boxes from the grocery store to use as furniture. He then bought rollerskates and enjoyed himself by skating through the empty rooms: he liked his new house, but he had always exhibited a Buddhist detachment towards being encumbered by objects and possessions.[22] He seemed able to keep his equilibrium through the *sturm und drang* of his emotional life without recourse to the typical means taken to 'escape' during the Sixties. He had always smoked cigarettes, but his alcohol intake was moderate and he never felt the need to use drugs.[23] Miller got high on his watercolour mania, on Blavatsky and esoteric lore. He had the temperament in many ways of a Zen monk, essentially abstemious in his habits and contemplative in his orientation, although perhaps his two rather consistent routes to Nirvana were his addiction to astrologers and the lure of romance.

One of the main oracles he consulted during this period of upheaval was Jacqueline Langmann of Lausanne, Switzerland, 'one of my best astrologers', author of *Henry Miller et son destin* (1974), who warned him of his burgeoning legal problems, increasing public visibility and eventual triumph: 'it's in the stars that *Cancer* won't fail'.[24] As for infatuation or falling in love, perhaps Miller's familiarity with the theatrical in the person of June Mansfield, whom he considered 'an actress – both on and off stage', explains his penchant for the scores of thespians he would encounter, become friends with or be smitten by, beginning with Geraldine Fitzgerald (to whom he had written love letters) in the Forties, through Hildegard Knef to Ziva Rodann, Ava Gardner, Kim Novak, Gia Scala, Diane Baker, Inger Stevens, Elke Sommer, Zofia Staboszowska and Lisa Lu. Now he relentlessly pursued the Canadian actress Gail Gerber, who was simultaneously being courted by Terry Southern, writing her love letters and sending her a book of his paintings. He acknowledged that 'somehow the actress in a woman always gets me', and he thrived on the 'touch of evil' in their 'multiple personalities'. Along with stars (in the sky and on earth), he confessed to Brassaï during this period that 'I have love affairs and passing fancies, yes! with such beautiful young women from every corner of the globe. It's ridiculous at my age.' During this phase he appeared to be taking Goethe as his model, who in 1821 at the age of 72 had fallen for the seventeen-year-old Ulrike von Levetzow in Marienbad.[25]

Miller, however, was not just absorbed in his private universe. Watching a Southerner defend segregation on television in June 1964, he observed that the white man 'left it very clear that "they" would fight any bill or law tooth and nail – to hold "the niggers" down or in their place. He never once said Negro. It was disgraceful, but I hope the whole country listened in, just to see what mentalities these ignorant white bastards have.'[26] His daughter Valentine and her husband came to live with him as well as his son, Tony, who sought to avoid the Vietnam War draft.[27] Miller had his friend Bill Webb, who had been a conscientious objector during World War Two, visit and speak to his son. One day Miller called Webb in a panic. Webb went to the door and Miller collapsed weeping in his arms: Tony had enlisted in the Army. However, Tony later went absent without leave and headed for Montreal, then turned himself in at Fort Ord near Carmel and succeeded in absenting himself from military service, thus continuing the pacifism of his father and grandfathers.[28]

In 1964, *Greece*, a short text with illustrations by Anne Poor, appeared as well as *Henry Miller on Writing*, an anthology edited by Thomas H. Moore of the Henry Miller Literary Society, containing passages from his major works that dealt with his struggles as a writer as well as selections on obscenity and manuscript notes for *Plexus* from 1947. He now spent a great deal of time making watercolours and even spoke of giving up writing books so he could spend all his time painting.[29] But Miller demonstrated that he had not lost his creative spark when in January 1965 'Revolt in the Desert', a superb uncollected essay on education, appeared in

Cavalier: 'A child must indeed be strong and healthy to survive our crazy educational system . . . Real education is a process that never ends; it can begin anywhere, anytime, and its goal is not "to receive an education," but to nourish the spirit.' Miller salutes his great exemplars, Alexander the Great, Milarepa and Swami Vivekananda, the last 'an awakener, if ever there was one. Pure dynamite. A realist to the core, but with a spiritual flavor unpalatable to our American taste.'[30]

In 1965, another breakthrough year, more titles reached the market. A pirated edition of *The Rosy Crucifixion* created by the publisher H. L. Hamling and his 'Greenleaf Classics' was now threatened, which forced Grove Press into issuing *Sexus*, *Plexus* and *Nexus*. Grove also brought out *Quiet Days in Clichy* and *The World of Sex*, the latter in a new edition which included reproductions of manuscript pages and Miller's copious revisions of the book (dated February–April, 1957, Big Sur) made prior to the book's republication in France by Olympia Press in 1957. G. P. Putnam published *Letters to Anais Nin* (Nin's own *Diaries* began to appear in 1966), a rich collection of their correspondence spanning several decades, while MacGibbon & Kee in London brought out *Selected Prose: Volumes I and II*.

Miller met the 27-year old Hoki Tokuda in February 1966 at the home of Dr Lee Siegel.[31] She was a pianist and jazz singer who entertained patrons at the Imperial Gardens, a Japanese restaurant on Sunset Strip. The victim of yet another *coup de foudre*, he immediately began bombarding Hoki with a barrage of letters (published in 1986 as *Letters from Henry Miller to Hoki Tokuda Miller*), which he frequently signed 'Henry-San' and punctuated with the Japanese he was trying to learn: 'Maybe in my next incarnation I will become a real *Sensei*. And then I will play the samisen or the koto. Or write beautiful poems like Basho, or paint beautiful women like Utamaro.'[32] His new passion however was interrupted by a ghost from the past: Eve died in September, possibly by suicide for she had been drinking alcohol all day followed by a dose of barbiturates.[33] He was wracked with grief, for a while. He engaged in some brief self-analysis, regretting that he had left Eve for his short-lived idyll with Caryl Hill. He wept copiously, then went to play ping-pong at Dr Siegel's and his spirits began to revive, ending the day in a restaurant with four girls from Canada – three sitting at the table and one on his lap – and arranged a date with his French waitress, another of his fans. It was F. Scott Fitzgerald who declared in *The Crack-Up*: 'The test of a first rate intelligence is the ability to hold two opposed ideas in the mind at the same time, and still retain the ability to function.' Indeed, during this phase Miller's soul seemed scattered. Every day his mind shifted: he planned various trips to Japan, Haiti, Europe, Hong Kong and Hawaii. He requested Hoki's horoscope from Jacqueline Langmann and sent handprints of his right and left palms, which he had made in 1957, to the graphologist Dorothy Sara for analysis. In short, he appeared to be in the same state of psychological disarray as when he had courted Renate Gebhardt.[34] He also began to need practical help, hiring Connie Perry to assist with housekeeping and with his increasingly burdensome paperwork.

Miller corresponded with the German-American Los Angeles writer Charles Bukowski, who had been published by Jon and Gypsy Lou Webb's Loujon Press in New Orleans. Miller's letters to Walter Lowenfels had appeared in the Fall 1961, Summer 1962 and Spring 1963 issues of the Webbs' magazine, *The Outsider*. The couple had published Bukowski's first two volumes of poetry in lavish editions – *It Catches My Heart In Its Hands* (1963) and *Crucifix in a Deathhand* (1965) – and now began the creation of *Order and Chaos Chez Hans Reichel*, which appeared in December 1966.[35] Originally written in Paris in 1937–8 as one of his handwritten books to friends, *Order and Chaos* contains Miller's letters to the German painter. Lawrence Durrell provided the Introduction.

And *Ecce Homo* by George Grosz was published by Grove Press
with an Introduction by Miller, which George Steiner found
'exceptionally thoughtful and well considered'.[36]

Miller continued vigorously to court Hoki, frequently going to
hear her play the piano and sing while maintaining his unremitting
campaign by letter. At last, the stars were in alignment: in the
summer of 1967, Hoki's visa was about expire and in order to be
able to remain in America she agreed to tie the knot. On 10
September 1967 they married (Miller's fifth time) at Dr Lee Siegel's
with Judge Edward R. Brand presiding. It was stipulated that the
marriage would not be consummated and that Puko, one of Hoki's
female friends, would live with them.[37] Miller needed to be in
Paris on 20 September for a watercolour show sponsored by the
Westwood Art Association, and the *vernissage* took place on 22
September. The exhibition contained 60 paintings and ten etch-
ings: the following month it travelled to Uppsala, Sweden, and then
to Stockholm's Museum of Modern Art and to London. Miller was
a huge success in Paris and was mobbed by fans.[38] Robert Snyder,
the director who had made films about Casals, De Kooning,
Michelangelo and Buckminster Fuller, was along for the trip to get
footage for his upcoming documentary on Miller. The couple took
an apartment near the Luxembourg Gardens, where Gerald
Robitaille, a fan of Miller's who now began work as his secretary
and factotum, and his wife also stayed. Miller and Hoki went to the
south of France to see Durrell in Sommières, who then went with
them to Paris. Durrell's presence meant lots of partying (he was
exceedingly fond of alcohol: Hoki claimed that the liquor bill was
higher than their rent). Miller made a special visit to the studio of
his dear painter friend Beauford Delaney at 53 rue Vercingetorix,
returning to America on 14 October.[39]

But there were now some knots to unravel in Miller's marital
history: because the validity of his divorce from June by proxy in
Mexico in 1934 was questioned by the Immigration Department,

his marriage to Hoki could possibly be nullified. The newlyweds made a trip to the Sands Hotel in Las Vegas to be remarried and Hoki's friend Puko, the judge and the bell captain served as witnesses.[40] Miller continued to suffer from his hip – he was now keeping his pool overheated to 86–88 degrees – and visited the doctor, who gave him an injection and prescribed medication. His children were also having issues: Tony with the draft board; and Val, who had been divorced in 1966 and arrested on marijuana charges, seemingly directionless.[41] In addition to Puko, another friend, Michiyo Watanabe, was also now a member of the Miller ménage.[42]

On 14 March 1968 Durrell arrived to spend two weeks at Pacific Palisades. Connie Perry, Hoki and Puko took him to Disneyland, which thrilled him except for his extreme disappointment upon learning that no alcohol was sold on the premises. Durrell spent fifteen hours enjoying the 'marvelously inventive toys', but throughout the day kept asking 'Where is the booze?'[43] In April Hoki travelled to Japan for the second time in 1968 to promote an exhibition of Miller's paintings in Tokyo (she had been there in February to be with her ill father). Miller began complaining of insomnia and took sleeping pills to assuage the pain in his little toe. In November he conducted amusing conversations in Japanese with Michiyo (who had been his Japanese teacher) and Puko while waiting for Hoki to return from her third trip to Japan, which she had made in September to pursue her career in film, television, radio and recordings.[44] Things went from bad to worse in their 'marriage': Miller bought Hoki a white Jaguar, in which she fled at night to play mahjong and returned at daybreak.[45]

To assuage the torments of love Miller had begun to make what he named his 'Insomnia' watercolours. The first of the twelve paintings date from seven months after he first met Hoki (August 1966), and the series continued until 27 September 1969. He had been reading Allen Edwardes and R.E.L. Masters's *The Cradle of*

Erotica, which describes the sexual customs of Africans, Arabs, Hindus, Chinese and Japanese, from which several of the Japanese expressions he used in the text of the paintings derived. In the fifth painting with 'Je Suis Pas plus con qu'un autre' inscribed at the top, Miller employed the following words: Dokyo, or 'guy with strongest penis in the world'; Harigata, 'artificial penis'; Hara-Hiri, 'cock, cunt'; Ai-name, 'Mutual love licking, reciprocal sucking'.[46] If Miller was chaste in his relationship with the actual Hoki, he let his imagination run wild in his art. By February 1968, Jon and Louise Webb had negotiated with Miller to publish his water-colours, which would lead eventually to *Insomnia* (1970), and he began writing the text to accompany them at the beginning of May.[47]

While Miller couldn't sleep, the crazy Sixties veered towards an apocalypse: the Vietnam War escalated, on 4 April Martin Luther King, Jr was assassinated, Robert F. Kennedy was shot dead two months later on 6 June, major American cities erupted in racial violence, and in August the Chicago Police rioted at the Democratic National Convention. Miller believed the country was on the verge of a revolution and that the United States was 'bankrupt, physically as well as morally'. He signed, along with 528 others, the Writers and Editors War Tax Protest, thus refusing to 'pay the proposed 10% income tax surcharge or any war-designated tax increase'.[48] The mindless violence of the times was symbolized by the film *Bonnie and Clyde* (1967), and he swiftly composed a diatribe, '*Bonnie and Clyde*: A Toccata for Half-Wits', condemning the American valorization of the basest criminality.[49] When writing to Durrell about this essay, he expressed his horror of violence but went on to reveal he had taken a walk at one a.m. the previous night: some (probably drugged) teenagers in a car began to threaten and curse him. Miller was so enraged that he imagined a scenario in which he would allow the two boys to follow him to his house, let them enter, then retrieve his razor-sharp machete and hack them to pieces. The just-arrived Age of Aquarius celebrated making love, not war, but he confessed to Durrell: 'Beware of the peace lovers, I always say. Beware of the just man! Do you know what it is to dance with rage? That's what I do inwardly again and again. Fortunately I always wear my Buddha-like mask.'[50] Underneath his joyous and usually serene exterior there pulsated a chaotic and sometimes raging soul.

In 1968, *Collector's Quest: The Correspondence of Henry Miller and J. Rives Childs, 1947–1965*, an exchange of letters between Miller and the former ambassador to Saudi Arabia and Ethiopia, was published. William. A. Gordon's *Writer and Critic: A Correspondence with Henry Miller* included letters written while Gordon was working on *The Mind and Art of Henry Miller* (1967). Miller had sharp objections to many of Gordon's interpretations, setting the stage for his frequent disagreements with other biographers, including Brassaï, George Wickes and Jay Martin. Robert Snyder continued work on *The Henry Miller Odyssey*, which would be released in 1969. At first Miller refused to be filmed at his home, but relented after persuading Snyder to agree to specific rules: no light-meters or lights, no direction or retakes or noisy clapsticks used to synchronize film to soundtrack.[51]

Miller now fell into the habit of banging on a large, red-lacquered drum and chanting the mantra central to Nichiren Buddhism, 'Nam Myo Ho Renge Kyo' (There is nothing so exquisite as the law of the lotus sutra). He was overjoyed to find that he had a string of unremitting luck once he began chanting, sometimes several times a day. He confided to his sceptical, practical and hard-nosed wife: 'As you know, I do lots of things other people regard as ridiculous or superstitious. I am a born believer, and a "fool" in the best sense of the word, a fool like Parsifal, for example.' But no mantra seemed able to bridge the differences between two people separated by such wide gulfs of age, culture and intelligence. By the beginning of January 1969, Miller announced: 'I've finally come to the conclusion that there is no sense in our living together any longer as man and wife.' In May 1970 they separated: Hoki moved to an apartment in Marina del Rey, but the formal divorce did not take place until 1978.[52]

Miller flew to Paris at the end of June 1969 to be consultant for Joseph Strick's adaptation of *Tropic of Cancer* (1970); he made a cameo appearance toward the end of the film. Pauline Kael wrote in the *New Yorker*, that

> the movie is so much less than the book that it almost seems deliberately intended to reduce Henry Miller – probably the funniest writer since Mark Twain – to pipsqueak size . . .
> I enjoyed the movie and I think others will, too, although there's something rather tacky and second-hand about it that prevents us from laughing very deeply. One could hardly guess from this thin trickle of jokes that Henry Miller is the closest an American has come to Rabelais.[53]

In June 1970 *Playboy* also published an essay by Miller about the film's production. The book, like James Joyce's *Ulysses*, which the director also adapted, proved challenging to translate into cinematic language. But Miller continued to love films: as much as he abhorred *Bonnie and Clyde*, he thought Fellini's *Satyricon* (1969) marvellous. He adored Fellini's poetic, surrealistic, oneiric, vivid flow of entracing tableaux: he saw no need to worry about the 'meaning' of *Satyricon* because here 'form and image obey the ceaseless logic of dream', as he remarked in his essay of 1947 on experimental cinema. He believed the potential of film had barely begun to be realized and that one day it might replace literature.[54]

Miller's sister, Lauretta, died in December 1969, and the following month he confessed to Durrell: 'I am going thru inner upheavals, partly because of age, partly as a result of foolish behavior. I think this year will see me doing new, strange things. Don't be surprised at anything.'[55] By May, as we have seen, he and Hoki had separated, and as if perfectly timed to celebrate and mourn the whole mad passion, Jon and Gypsy Lou Webb's Loujon Press published *Insomnia*. Their most elaborate production, it was fraught with difficulties, and Miller loaned them $6,000 to get the project off the ground. The production included twelve 17 x 22 inch, signed large watercolour reproductions in a specially made 19 x 24 inch wooden box weighing over seven pounds.[56] Together with the paintings, the book contains a 33-page handwritten text which documents the rollercoaster ride of Miller's doomed passion – 'First it was a broken toe, then a broken brow, and finally a broken heart' – and ends with a marvellous 'Cadenza', a comic virtuoso nonsense performance in which Miller cites Kurt Schwitters and Dada (he was reading Kate Steinitz's *Kurt Schwitters: Portrait from Life* of 1968 during this period). He wrote an essay for the *New York Times* in 1972 in which he declared that 'the one strong, true desire I have is to write absolute nonsense, but for this I need lots of vacant, lazy days, freedom from chores of any kind'.[57] Doubleday issued *Insomnia* in a trade edition in 1974.

The pace of Miller's life in 1970 continued hectic. He met Isaac Bashevis Singer, with whom he discussed Knut Hamsun's *Mysteries*, and Singer would become one of his favourite writers.[58] The 91-minute, black-and-white movie of *Quiet Days in Clichy* was filmed on the streets of Paris by Danish director Jens Jorgen Thorsen and screened in Cannes on 8 May; the U.S. Government seized the only English-language prints of the film on charges of obscenity.[59] Bradley Smith came to interview and photograph Miller, which evolved into the autobiographical coffee-table book *My Life and Times* (1971).

As the new decade began, the appearance of Kate Millett's *Sexual Politics* (1970) occasioned major controversy. Arguing that D. H. Lawrence, Norman Mailer and Miller were chauvinistic,

Alison Bechdel's contribution to 'Let's Read About Sex', *New York Times Book Review*, 3 October 2013.

misogynistic, phallocratic and sexist, Millett chose passages from Miller's work which she argued portrayed women in a subservient, 'objectified' manner. Mailer leapt to Miller's defence in *The Prisoner of Sex* (1971). Nin accused Millett of taking Miller's sexual hijinks seriously: 'All he was trying to do really was to revolt against Puritanism and be a picaresque writer, such as we had in France in Rabelais.'[60] Gore Vidal joined the fray and published his essay 'In Another Country' in *The New York Review of Books*: 'The Patriarchalists have been conditioned to think of women as, at best, breeders of sons, at worst, objects to be poked, humiliated, killed . . . There has been from Henry Miller to Norman Mailer to Charles Manson a logical progression.'[61] In the revised version of the essay included in *United States: Essays, 1952–1992*, Vidal altered the sentence to: 'There has been from Henry Miller to Norman Mailer to Phyllis Schafly a logical progression', thus placing Mailer and Miller in the same company as the arch-conservative Schlafly rather than with the serial murderer of women Manson:

SOON KATE MILLETT INTERRUPTS HER QUOTATION OF HENRY MILLER TO EXPLAIN HOW HE'S DEHUMANIZING THE WOMAN IN HIS STORY.

THE BOOK GOES ON LIKE THIS. ANALYSIS INTERSPERSED WITH QUOTATIONS.

TV 20

IT WAS TEMPTING TO SKIP AHEAD TO THE PARTS BY MILLER, BUT I DIDN'T WANT TO MISS ANYTHING.

MILLETT'S COMMENTARY HELPFULLY ELUCIDATED SOME OF THE MORE MYSTIFYING ACTIVITIES.

AND SOMEHOW, IN THE FRICTION BETWEEN THEIR TWO VOICES, THERE WAS SOMETHING IN ITSELF STRANGELY EROTIC.

it is unclear whether for Vidal this represented a demotion or elevation in ethical status. Camille Paglia argued that Millett's wrong-headed feminism had contributed to rendering great writers like Hemingway, Lawrence and Miller taboo in university humanities curricula.[62]

Miller's interest in the ancient Gnostics revived due to his thrilling discovery of *La Cendre et les étoiles* (1970) by Jacques Lacarrière, translated as *The Gnostics* (1977). Durrell, who had explored Gnostic themes in his *Alexandria Quartet* as well as the *Avignon Quincunx*, the quintet of novels including *Monsieur*, in which Akkad explains Gnostic rituals (1974), *Livia* (1978), *Constance* (1982), *Sebastian* (1983) and *Quinx* (1985), had copies sent to both Miller and Denis de Rougemont. Miller was unable to sleep after reading the book: it immediately made him feel 'as one does on hearing opening bars of a favorite symphony'. He too had always felt that everything in the world was 'utterly crazy' and that the Gnostics were correct: Planet Earth could only be understood as a 'cosmic mistake'.[63] In Miller's beloved *William Blake's Circle of Destiny*, Milton O. Percival had observed:

> A circular movement of the soul in its absence from God
> is all but incumbent upon mystical religions. A wheel of
> birth, a cycle of destiny, a ring of return – these conceptions
> . . . came in through the Mysteries, and were basic in the
> Gnostic systems. In this type of thinking, the soul has its
> origin in a supersensible world, incurs a fall, undergoes
> expiation and purification, and returns at last to its primal
> source . . . the cosmos follows the cycle along with man. It,
> too, falls from its primal purity and oneness into materiality
> and multiplicity, only to undergo renovation and return to
> the One from which it fell.[64]

Percival noted that Blake 'would have been more at home in the Alexandria of the third century than he was in the London of his own time', and the same might be said of Miller, with his belief in the divine spark and angelic light occluded within. This fall and restoration is *apocatastasis*, the Greek word for restoring things to their primordial condition, a notion which had intrigued Miller for decades. As with his fascination for astrology, apocatastasis implies a harmony between macrocosm and microcosm, the motions of the human *psyche*, or soul, mirror the planetary cycles.[65] As Hermes Trisgmegistus said: 'As above, so below'.

Indeed, during the Sixties and Seventies Miller's thought seemed in perfect accord with the emerging 'New Age/Perennial Philosophy', which posited a tradition of spiritual belief across the ages which had a core set of shared ideas. The list of names he repeatedly invokes – Pythagoras, Buddha, Hermes Trismegistus, Heraclitus, Lao-Tzu, Jakob Boehme, Paracelsus, Meister Eckhart, Milarepa, Ramakrishna, Vivekananda, Blavatsky and many others – fits perfectly within the conception. The notion of *prisca theologia*

– that there is an originary truth which has been in existence
since ancient times (which in Theosophy is ascribed, for example,
to Tibetan Masters living in the Himalayas) but is now lost –
recalls Miller's belief that the earliest thinkers, as well as 'primitive'
peoples, such as the Native Americans, the Bushmen of the
Kalihari and the Pygmies, possessed a wisdom modern humanity
has forgotten and also explains his allegiance to the 'lost continent'
theory: that Atlantis, Lemuria and Mu were inhabited by god-like
beings from which *homo sapiens* has 'devolved'. His attraction to
exotic and faraway places – he often spoke of desiring to visit
Tahiti, Timbuktu, Lhasa or Patagonia – is also a reflection of this
essentially romantic yearning for the place where the hidden
secrets of existence may be revealed, a place which may lie just
over the horizon.

My Life and Times was published by *Playboy* in 1971, a large-
format autobiography lavishly illustrated with photographs
and reproductions of manuscript pages from Miller's Paris notebooks, unpublished work on D. H. Lawrence as well as color
reproductions of his paintings, and a photograph of Miller playing
ping-pong with a nude blonde lady. Throughout the text he
dispenses his Gnostic philosophy of self-salvation: 'You have to
get to the point of no return before you come up again. There's no
God protecting you. In the end you have to come back to yourself.
It has got to be *you* doing something, whatever you decide upon.'[66]
In June Miller had surgery: an artificial artery was put in to aid the
circulation in his right leg, and he quit smoking after half a century.
He also finished a 33-page essay on the death of Yukio Mishima for
a Japanese newspaper, *Shukan Post*, which appeared in five weekly
instalments beginning 26 October 1971 and for which he was paid
$10,000.[67] He returned to his old love Knut Hamsun, composing
an essay on *Mysteries* for the *New York Times*, a work he felt was
'closer to me than any other book I have read', as well as 'Picasso at
90' for *Life* magazine.[68] Hamsun's magnificent novel concerning

Johann Nagel's seeming lack of a stable identity, his inventive lying and lyrical praise of mystery, dreams and poetry, along with the lovely visionary scene in Chapter Eight of the myriad white angels, seemed to sum up Miller's own lifelong spiritual struggles. He believed Hamsun ready for a revival: 'I notice that Hermann Hesse's work has made a strong appeal to the young; perhaps Hamsun will too. He should be right up their street, since he too was a dropout, a wanderer, an outcast, an everlasting rebel and an eternal foe of the establishment.' And Durrell came to visit again at the end of 1971 for Henry's 80th birthday celebration at the UCLA Research Library. Connie Perry met Durrell and Margaret McCall at the airport and took them to Pacific Palisades. Henry recalled: 'All of a glorious drunken (or semi-drunken) evening he was at the top of his form, never more subtle, boisterous, elusive and diabolically Irish.'[69]

8

On the Way to Devachan, 1972–80

In his final decade Miller continued to be prolific, but his large books were behind him: *Big Sur and the Oranges of Hieronymus Bosch* (1957) was his last ambitious effort, and he had by now definitively abandoned the composition of *Nexus II*, although an excerpt from the manuscript appeared in *El Corno Emplumado* in 1964. He kept Meng-Tse's plea to ward away visitors posted on his door:

> When a man has reached old age and has fulfilled his mission, he has a right to confront the idea of death in peace. He has no need of other men; he knows them already and has seen enough of them. What he needs is peace. It is not seemly to seek out such a man, plague him with chatter, and make him suffer banalities. One should pass by the door of his house as if no one lived there.

He had discovered this quotation in his readings of Hermann Hesse, who had placed a German translation of the Chinese text on his door.[1] Miller now began creating a series of ten small books – taking to heart Callimachus' counsel concerning the 'badness' of big books, *mega biblion, mega kakon* – with his friend Noel Young for Young's Capra Press in Santa Barbara. The first appeared in July: *Reflections on the Death of Mishima*, a wide-ranging provocative meditation on Yukio Mishima's *hara-kiri* as well as discussions of Zen, Japanese samurais and militarism, and the notion that 'only the genius seems to understand and appreciate the joy of sheer nonsense'. Miller had met Mishima briefly in Germany, and here he imagines encountering him in Devachan, where they would conduct a scintillating conversation on everything from 'angels Buddhist and otherwise' to 'Freud, Hegel, Marx, Blavatsky, Ouspensky, Proust, Rimbaud, Nietzsche . . . We might even take up the riddle of the universe, both from Haeckel's standpoint and our own.' The essay demonstrates Miller's gift, even at this late stage in his career, for composing joyful, effortless, fluent and effervescent prose.[2]

Anais Nin, who had been divorced from Hugh Guiler and was now living with Rupert Pole in California, came to visit. She had appeared with Miller in Robert Snyder's *The Henry Miller Odyssey*, and the scene in which they are conversing is noteworthy for her stiffness and reserve: it is difficult to imagine that the two had once been passionate lovers. After the Hoki debacle, Miller declared that he had no desire to get married again, but continually falling in love suited him perfectly: 'I am dead unless I am in love.' Miller proceeded to replace Hoki with the Chinese actress Lisa Lu, whom he had actually first met in the mid-1960s.[3] He was up at three or four a.m. writing to Lisa: over one nine-month period in 1974–5 he composed 224 love letters, often long ones in which he laid his soul bare and which he believed were among his best.[4] Indeed, Miller was perhaps most like D. H. Lawrence in the liveliness, spontaneity and excitement of his wonderful letters to Durrell, Nin, Schnellock and the thousands to non-literary acquaintances, friends and lovers: they give the impression of coming straight from the fiery source of his creativity, a confirmation of his belief that life and art were inseparable. Their energy and integrity is apparent in one letter or postcard after another, typed or written on front and back, along the sides, replete with exclamation marks and full of the fervour to communicate, sometimes with the envoi 'in haste': all striking evidence of his passionate desire to have an *exchange* with the other person.

Miller was still vital, quick, energetic, and over the last few years felt he had achieved a new 'level of serenity'. When he went to bed at two or three a.m. he enjoyed 'a peace of mind which I suppose is the fruit of much struggle, frustration and despair'. The second of the chapbooks for Capra Press, *On Turning Eighty*, was published in October and opens with his still affirmative vision:

If at eighty you're not a cripple or an invalid, if you have your health, if you still enjoy a good walk, a good meal (with all the trimmings), if you can sleep without first taking a pill . . . if you can whistle up your ass, if you can be turned on by a fetching bottom or a lovely pair of teats, if you can fall in love again and again . . . man, you've got it half licked.

Miller admired the two Pablos – Picasso and Casals – because they, although over 90 at the time, remained creative and youthful, while he remains true to his Emersonian vision: 'There is nothing wrong with life itself. It is the ocean in which we swim and we either adapt to it or sink to the bottom. But it is in our power as human beings not to pollute the waters of life, not to destroy the spirit which animates us.'[5]

At the beginning of 1973 Marcel Marceau wrote concerning obtaining the rights to make a movie of *The Smile at the Foot of the Ladder*, and the 20-year-old filmmaker Tom Schiller, who had created short films for *Saturday Night Live*, began to make a documentary on Miller to be called *Henry Miller Asleep and Awake*. The pair became good friends, sharing gin and tonics, and Miller actively made various editing suggestions as the film progressed.[6] He also began a larger writing project, *The Book of Friends*: the earliest chapter he drafted memorialized his first friend, Stanley Borowski ('Stasiu'), whom he had met at age five. He contributed an Introduction entitled 'The Astrologer Seen through the Eyes of a Friend' to Sydney Omarr's *Astrological Guide to 1973*.[7] Miller believed that 'the purpose of astrology is not to teach how to thwart destiny but how to live up to it, in accordance with it.'[8] Omarr, who had written *Henry Miller: His World of Urania*, thus joined the long list of astrologers that included Moricand, Rudhyar, Wilhelm Wulff and Langmann as well as Jessica Hensley of Paris, Pierce Harwell and Blanca Holmes in Los Angeles, Constanza Camargo in Colombia, and a practitioner in Denmark.[9] Miller wanted to paint his horoscope on his bedroom ceiling so he could see it while lying in bed.[10]

His interest in the Armenian-Greek thinker G. I. Gurdjieff was ignited during this period, as can be seen in one sequence of Tom Schiller's film, in which Miller describes his love of Fritz Peters's *Boyhood with Gurdjieff*: it had become one of his favourite books, for which he wrote an admiring Preface. Schiller brought over a bottle of Armagnac one evening – Gurdjieff's favourite liquor – and they drank to his memory: Miller enjoyed a sound fourteen hours of sleep that night. He praised Maggi Lidchi's *Man of Earth* (1968), which depicts a man's journey to India in search of enlightenment and features a character reminiscent of Gurdjieff. He also wrote a series of letters to the Vietnamese poet, philosopher and Zen Buddhist monk Pham Cong Thien, in which he frequently alluded to Gurdjieff.[11] He met Thien in 1965, a gifted, multi-lingual scholar who wrote a monograph about Miller in Vietnamese as well as works on poetry, metaphysics, Nietzsche, Hölderlin and Heidegger. Miller asked his friend Maurice Nadeau to try to help Thien find employment while he was living in Paris.[12] In addition to Gurdjieff, he found pleasure in everything, from 'a big beautiful book about Strindberg' to Gabriele D'Annunzio's *The Flame of Life*.[13] He became particularly enamoured by Nadeau's *Gustave Flaubert, écrivain* (1969), which appeared in English translation as *The Greatness of Flaubert* (1972): 'I don't know when a book has seized me by the throat like this one. I suppose I see a great deal of my own struggles in Flaubert's struggle with the art of writing.'

Miller was no lazy scanner of lines on the page: as he had done in Paris when he first studied Proust, he was an attentive reader and thoroughly annotated Nadeau's text with copious appreciative comments.[14]

Capra Press published *First Impressions of Greece* in April: Miller had retrieved the manuscript from George Seferis's wife after the poet's death. He had begun the handwritten text on the island of Hydra at the home of the painter Ghika in November 1939, which he then gave as a gift to Seferis. This act astounded the great poet, who told Edmund Keeley: 'Can you imagine somebody doing a thing as generous as that . . . The only manuscript of his notes for the book he will write given as a gift to a friend before he has written the book?'[15] This was a glorious phase in Miller's voyage to Greece: 'the whiskey excellent, especially favorable for discussions about Blavatsky and Tibet'.[16] Miller eulogized the island of Zakythnos (Zante), which 'obsessed' him: 'Perhaps because I had discovered it in a dream which fused with reality. I wanted to come to the frontier of a new world, a very tiny world which would

Miller and Twinka Thiebaud, 1978.

answer to every demand. Zante seems like such a world. For me it is the threshold of Greece.'[17] The Greek word *kosmos* encapsulates the meaning of his spiritual quest in Greece:

> To make a world again, a cosmos, we must have men with new eyes. Man must be re-endowed with a soul. This world, *our* world of today, belongs not to man, nor even to the beast, but to the machine. *Alors*, down with the world! Up with the Cosmos.[18]

One wonders what Miller would make of today's cellphone, internet, tablet, video game, automatic checkout lane, computer-screen saturated cosmos. Two other chapbooks (which had been previously published), *The Waters Reglitterized* and *Reflections on the Maurizius Case*, appeared in August and December, respectively.

In August, as the Watergate scandal intensified, Miller had some choice words about the American President: 'I think Nixon is pushing himself over the edge of the precipice. Amazing, though, what a man without charisma, can accomplish. I can understand Hitler's and Mussolini's rise to power but not Nixon's. What a quiet little monster he is!'[19] At the beginning of September 1973 he underwent his third surgery to improve a circulatory problem. The operation for a heart bypass took fourteen hours: he had a stroke, which left him blind in the right eye and with only partial use of his left arm and leg. A positive result of the ordeal was a euphoric post-operative vision in which he was back on the island of Crete, able to speak Greek, and ecstatic that he had returned to Greece. Tony and Valentine cared for their father, and Valentine asked her friend Twinka Thiebaud, the daughter of artist Wayne Thiebaud, to move in as a more permanent caretaker.[20] Miller managed to keep his spirits and energy high despite his increasingly limited mobility, exemplifying the credo contained in *The Waters Reglitterized*:

Who is the man who triumphs? The one who *believes*. Let the 'intelligent' ones doubt, criticize, categorize and define. The man of heart believes. And the world belongs to him who believes most. Nothing is too silly, too trivial, too far-fetched or too stupendous for man to believe. Learning crushes the spirit; belief opens one up, delivers one.[21]

Miller became the enthusiastic advocate for several women authors during this period, including the Greek scholar and translator of Kazantzakis, Amy Mims, whose memoir *The Book of Amy* (1972) he praised extravagantly, the Danish feminist Suzanne Brogger, and Erica Jong, author of *Fear of Flying* (1973): he contributed an essay to the *New York Times* declaring *Fear of Flying* the 'feminine counterpart to my own *Tropic of Cancer*'.[22] He and Jong would begin corresponding in April 1974 and they met the following October.[23]

Simply by virtue of outliving all of the major twentieth-century writers (Hemingway was dead at 62, Steinbeck at 66, Faulkner at 65), Miller by the Seventies had the field to himself as elder states-man of American letters. He indeed became the oldest major American writer, ultimately outliving even the wizened T. S. Eliot (died age 76) and Ezra Pound (died age 87). Because he had come to fame in his early seventies, he was old enough to appear as a kind of guru to the youth revelling in the 'Sexual Revolution' of the Sixties – a role he did not relish. Norman Mailer and Kenzaburo Oe were committed fans, and Phillip Roth's *Portnoy's Complaint* (1969) was possible because, as Roth admitted, it was 'Henry Miller, I think, who educated me about letting the repellent in, let the repellent into the fiction. Let the repellent into literature.'[24] Hunter S. Thompson had written of Miller in Big Sur and frequently alluded to him in his letters. Charles Bukowski enjoyed his sexual writing, but was less than thrilled when he began to hold forth about Pisces, Leo and Taurus. Jim

Harrison believed Miller 'was like a continuous transfusion, food to avoid melancholy'.[25] John Updike followed Miller's example in the sexual frankness of *Couples* (1968), in which Piet Hanema admires Freddy's collection of Grove Press titles. Even Vladimir Nabokov paid a typically supercilious nod to his cultural omnipresence during this period in Chapter 21 of *Ada or Ardor: A Family Chronicle* (1969): 'They liked Rabelais and Casanova; they loathed *le sieur* Sade and Herr Masoch and Heinrich Müller.' This sentence is glossed in the 'Notes' to *Ada* (by Nabokov's anagrammatized *doppelgänger* 'Vivian Darkbloom'): 'Heinrich Müller: author of *Poxus*, etc.'[26]

This is Henry, Henry Miller from Brooklyn appeared in 1974, the book version of Robert Snyder's documentary *The Henry Miller Odyssey*. Like *My Life and Times*, it was a large-format work with text and images taken from the film. Lawrence Durrell's *Monsieur* was published in the same year. Miller found it confusing (although as ever he was ravished by his friend's style) but later found *Livia* (1978) easier going.[27] He continued to play ping-pong with guests: one reason was that he became weary of people having intellectual discussions about art and literature in his house.[28] But ping-pong was also the perfect symbolic expression of the Zen philosophy of detachment he had embraced: 'chop wood, carry water'. He wrote to the French author Gaston Criel about his book *La Grande Foutaise*:

As the Zen masters say: 'Think only and entirely and completely of what you are doing at the moment and you are free as a bird.' No Westerner wants to accept such a statement, naturally – it seems too simple to be true. We prefer to complicate things, with our prejudices, our principles, our beliefs, our judgments. And so we continue to feed the machine which grinds us to nothingness.[29]

The easiest and yet most difficult thing for most people is to do just what is before their nose to do: thus the Zen of ping-pong.

The Nightmare Notebook was published in 1975, some 30 years after *The Air-Conditioned Nightmare*. The *Notebook* is a facsimile reproduction of the bound printer's dummy of an edition of Walt Whitman's *Leaves of Grass* published by Doubleday in which Miller made notes of his American trip. It is a lavish book – 700 signed copies were printed selling at $150 –with colour reproductions of the paintings Miller drew during his travels, lists of places visited and notes recording a visit to John Steinbeck in Pacific Grove, California: 'Impression of an over-sensitive man. Acting tough but very tender underneath.'[30] Miller's and Wallace Fowlie's *Letters* were also published in 1975. As we have seen, Miller and the eminent French literature scholar developed a close friendship: Fowlie dedicated his study *Rimbaud* (1966) to Miller. Fowlie also wrote *Rimbaud and Jim Morrison: The Rebel as Poet, A Memoir* in which he suggested: 'A phrase complementary to "living on the edge", this time from Rimbaud, was known to Jim: "Voici le temps des Assassins." Jim had probably read Henry Miller's book on Rimbaud of which this sentence serves as title.'[31]

In 1975 Tom Schiller released *Henry Miller Asleep and Awake*, in which Miller gave him a tour of his famous bathroom, where every square inch of the walls were covered with illustrations which included Hermann Hesse, Gurdjieff, Junichiro Tanizaki, serene statues of Buddha, naked ladies, Mad King Ludwig's castle at Neuschwanstein, erotic scenes and Sri Aurobindo, Blaise Cendrars, Bosch, Gauguin and 'an absence of all Christian iconography'.[32] Miller is, as always, irresistably enthusiastic, a marvelous raconteur and a character. He looks straight into the camera and tells us without a hint of dissimulation that when he travels on a jet he hears playing in his head not only the most indescribable symphonic music but also *the music of the spheres*. All his life he had been, and was still so at 83, a wild man, a misfit, an anarchist, a creative, innocent, zany, humorous and engaging free spirit. We are as fascinated – if not more so – with the man as with the work, with his acceptance of the chaos of the subconscious and the unresolvable contradictions of the human condition, of madness. As he told William A. Gordon:

> In Tibet, for example, they do not have the same fear of insanity as the Western world has. When a man becomes insane they look upon it as though he were revealing another side of himself. His soul is a fasces – multifold. And did not Whitman say: 'Do I contradict myself? Very well, I contradict myself.'[33]

Miller took an active interest in the making of the film, giving many suggestions as Schiller proceeded. As we have seen, he was interested in the new possibilities of film and television, and although he enjoyed watching championship wrestling, he also admired Rod Serling's innovative and imaginative *The Twilight Zone* (1959–64): 'All weirdee stuff, via science-fiction pseudo-knowledge . . . Marvelous stuff in this area for TV or films. Much better than the mystery dope we've been fed up with over the years.'[34]

Miller became a fan of Germaine Greer and entertained a variety of guests, including the actor Jack Nicholson (he wrote a brief appreciative essay on the film *Five Easy Pieces* entitled 'On Seeing Jack Nicholson for the First Time'), the musician Robbie Robertson, the director Terence Malick and Norman Mailer. He also met the Korean pianist Hak Soon Hahn through Jacob Gimpel's Master Class and began corresponding with her in November: she visited his home, adding her Korean words to his wall of international graffiti.[35] Miller liked to eat well and invited many people to cook for him, including his friend Susan Kidder Herr, who recalled that 'food prepared unimaginatively was a crime to him'. Frawley Becker came with quart jars with puréed vegetables like the soups Miller had in Paris as well as *osso buco*, one of his favourite dishes.[36]

In December 1975 Miller completed a 32-page typed text in French which Gallimard had asked him to compose, later to be published as *J'suis pas plus con qu'un autre*, and in 1976 the French government awarded him the Légion d'Honneur.[37] *Henry Miller's Book of Friends: A Tribute to Friends of Long Age*, the first of a trilogy which would later include *My Bike and Other Friends* (1978) and *Joey* (1979), was published by Capra Press in 1976. Here Miller continues his obsessive return to the past, his Proustian effort to bring back memory. He drew lively portraits of his early boyhood pals, Stasiu, Joey and Tony Imhof, Cousin Henry, Jimmy Pasta, as well as his adult friends, Joe O'Regan, Max Winthrop and Alec Considine. Robert Kirsch in his review remarked: 'But the more you read of Miller the more you realize that this ingenuousness – this freedom from reserve, restraint, dissimulation, this seeming artlessness and innocence – is engaging and the source of his strength.'[38] In *My Bike and Other Friends* he composed a hymn to his bicycle, joining several other famous writers, including William Saroyan and Samuel Beckett, who were fond of their bikes. His memoirs of people he knew were fictionalized: Miller acknowledged that he exaggerated a bit to make the characters more interesting. For example, in the section entitled 'Other Women in My Life' in *Joey*, Miller claimed his love affair with Sevasty Koutsaftis had become physically rather intimate, a suggestion Koutsaftis herself later vehemently denied: 'His imaginings overrode actuality, I'm afraid.'[39]

Yet his approach to biography in *The Book of Friends* followed precisely the advice he had given during this period to Jay Martin, who was then writing a biography of Miller. He told Martin that he did not want a biography full of details, but rather 'purely poetical evocations, in which the facts don't matter in the slightest. Why, you could even invent the facts. I'd prefer that. So long as you were interesting, I wouldn't care.'[40] Miller ended up dissatisfied with virtually all the biographical/critical studies which appeared during his lifetime: by Brassaï, George Wickes, Jane A. Nelson's Jungian study, *Form and Image in the Fiction of Henry Miller*, William A. Gordon's *The Mind and Art of Henry Miller* and Martin's own *Always Merry and Bright: The Life of Henry Miller* (1978).

On 9 June 1976, he sent the first of some 1,500 letters to Brenda Venus, an aspiring actress from Mississippi who had written asking to meet him. Since losing sight in his right eye during the bypass operation for his artery, his reading, painting and writing were severely handicapped, so he composed his letters to her by hand, sometimes two or three daily.[41] Miller acted as a kind of philosopher/ teacher to Brenda and recommended Pierre Loti's *Disenchanted*, Huysmans' *À Rebours* and Mohammed Mrabet's *Look and Move On*, emphasizing that she should read for enjoyment rather than instruction, and shared his enthusiasm for new films such as Lina Wertmuller's *Swept Away* (1974), which he said reminded him of *Tropic of Cancer* and *Sexus*.[42] He wrote to her often about his sexual fantasies over the next four years: apparently Miller in his mid to late eighties had not yet arrived at that *ataraxia* which the aged Sophocles had achieved. According to Plato, the great playwright reputedly exclaimed about sexual desire: 'I am glad to have left it behind me and escaped from a fierce and frenzied master'.[43] Miller even desired to swear a *Blutbrüderschaft* with Brenda: they took a penknife and made incisions, but the cut to Miller's aged wrist caused an unexpectedly copious, but swiftly staunched, flow of blood.[44] He also met the Danish writer Suzanne Brogger, whom he would christen his 'Danish Sheherazade', and would promote her book *Deliver Us From Love*. They conducted a fascinating correspondence published posthumously (like the Brenda Venus letters) in 1998. He conceded to her that although he was constantly in love with women, he was more in love with his writing: 'I give myself over completely and utterly to my work.'[45]

J'suis pas plus con qu'un autre was published by Buchet/Chastel in 1976 and a facsimile holograph edition (1980) by Stanke in Montreal; the title may be translated as *I'm no more of a dope than the next guy.* It is the only text Miller composed in French, and he forbade it to be translated into English. It was a playful exercise in which he challenged himself to see if he could write in the French language, and although he never mastered the intricacies of its syntax and grammar, the text is a pleasurable sequence of random associations. He tells us he dislikes Mozart's perfection, he prefers 'monsters' like Rabelais, Cendrars (he recalls his early days reading *Moravagine* with a dictionary) and Rimbaud over Hemingway, he names Ramakrishna as his Master and Alexander the Great merits a two-page fanfare, again demonstrating Alexander was on his mind in the early to mid-Seventies. He returns to angels: '*La seule chose qui nous manque ce sont des anges. Dans ce vaste monde il n'y a pas de place pour eux. D'ailleurs, est-ce que nous avons ces yeux pour les reconnaître? Peut-être nous sommes entoures par les anges sans le savoir.*'[46] The book improvises effortlessly over a huge array of subjects with a deft and humorous touch, rather like a late Beethoven bagatelle.

Norman Mailer had been approached by Barney Rosset to compile an anthology of Miller's writings, advancing him $50,000, half of which was to be shared with Miller. *Genius and Lust* appeared in October. Mailer had some odd notions, one of which was that Miller wrote *Colossus* to 'grease' (with a pun on 'Greece') the wheels of the literary establishment, which had looked askance at Miller's 'obscene' writings. He would also write a screenplay based on *The Rosy Crucifixion* series which has never been produced. Miller liked Mailer personally but found his writing too intellectualized and baroque.

Miller had always been fond of making lists: of favourite wines, of characters and events to include in his novels, of women he loved, so he was only too happy to contribute his own most recent list of his '10 Greatest Writers' to *The Book of Lists* (1977): 1 Lao-Tzu; 2 François Rabelais; 3 Friedrich Nietzsche; 4 Rabindranath Tagore; 5 Walt Whitman; 6 Marcel Proust; 7 Elie Faure; 8 Marie Corelli; 9 Fyodor Dostoevsky; 10 Isaac Bashevis Singer.[47] The appearance of Tagore is a bit surprising, but the other nine names were fairly constant members of his pantheon.

The new year brought a farewell and a reconciliation: Anaïs Nin died on 14 January and Capra published *Mother, China, and the World Beyond*, in which Miller narrates a rapprochement with his mother. He meets her in Devachan, which, according to chapter Five of A. P. Sinnett's *Esoteric Buddhism*, is the temporary, intermediate place where souls go after death before being reborn, and there is a tearful forgiveness scene. Miller combines here his life-long interest in theosophy – it is in Devachan and not the Christian afterlife that he encounters his mother – with the effort to heal the psychological wounds which had afflicted him. His constant searching for affirmation from a long series of women seems to be an obvious reflection of his need to find solace for his early trauma in childhood. Perhaps the closest real mother he would find was the character Aunt Roussaki in Pandelis Prevelakis's novel *The Sun of Death* (1964). In his Preface to the book, Miller declared:

> If on this earth we could all find such mothers, such teachers of life as Aunt Roussaki, what more could we ask, what greater blessing. Through this simple soul the author reveals to us the true nature of wisdom, the true method of education, the true means of implanting faith and love of life.[48]

Another essay, 'A Nation of Lunatics' – the title is taken from Walt Whitman's description of what he feared the United States would one day become – appeared in *Four Visions of America*, and Miller demonstrates that he had lost none of his anger: 'In the brief span of our history we managed to poison the world. We poisoned it with our ideas of progress, efficiency, mechanization.'[49] In an interview with Thomas Ayck, he again railed against the American way of life and values: 'In my opinion it is all absurd, all of it, these questions of earning money, how much someone earns, is absurd. The banks are absurd, the stock market. For me that is all a sickness, a collective sickness. We should get rid of it all, destroy it all, live completely differently! Yes!'[50] Miller was very close to his hero John Cowper Powys, who wrote in his *Autobiography*, one of Miller's favourite books, that he wanted to 'commune with angels and demons . . . worship the elements . . . to return to the imaginative and poetic life that Science has for so long been destroying'.[51] Like Powys, Jean Giono and D. H. Lawrence, Miller lamented the direction modern life had taken, and as we have seen would not have grieved were an apocalypse to arrive and cause that apocatastasis, the return to primal purity, for which he had in a quintessentially Romantic way always yearned.

In 1978 Miller began to contribute to *Stroker*, the magazine his friend Irving Stettner had started in 1974, and he also lobbied for the Nobel Prize. He sent cards to people asking them to send 'a few succinct lines' recommending him to the Nobel Committee of the Swedish Academy.[52] Isaac Bashevis Singer wrote a strong recommendation for his friend, but Miller did not receive the Prize that year (Singer received the prize in 1978 and Odysseus Elytis in 1979), and he heard from Lawrence Durrell that someone on the committee had said: 'I'm afraid Mr Durrell that we're waiting for Mr Miller to become respectable.' Miller believed he had shared the fate of Theodore Dreiser: the committee had also looked askance at *Jennie Gerhardt* and *Sister Carrie* and shunned Dreiser 'for breaking rules'.[53] In addition to Singer, Miller had another advocate in Italo Calvino, who wrote in a letter to Pirkko-Liisa Stahl in Helsinki: 'Amongst the writers who are already recognized as being first rate and who have not yet received the Prize are Borges and Henry Miller.'[54]

Miller's dear friend Joseph Delteil died in April 1978: he wrote to his wife, 'Caroline, I do not cry over the disappearance of Joseph. His spirit is living in me and always will . . . He was the man of the past and of the future, like King Arthur.'[55] California's Governor, Jerry Brown, came to visit in August 1978, and Miller greeted him with 'If you'll excuse my honesty, I've always held the opinion that politicians are rather on the bottom rung, at the bottom of the barrel of humanity, so to speak.' (In an alternate version of the encounter, Miller said: 'You know, I think politicians are the scum of the earth, next to evangelists. I can't stand Billy Graham.')[56] In December, Elmer and Mamie Gertz came to visit and were impressed by his *joie de vivre* despite his multiplying infirmities. He typically wore a plaid or blue terrycloth bathrobe, was deaf in one ear and wore a hearing aid in the other, and no longer swam because he lost his balance and could see only with his left eye; but he was still his disciplined self, carefully rolling his napkin and placing it in its monogrammed silver holder and keeping his writing materials and paintbrushes where they belonged. He was now being looked after by his secretary, Sandra Stahl, and Brenda Venus picked him up twice a week to go to a restaurant; on those occasions he would discard his walker, hold Brenda by the arm and hold his cane in his other hand.[57]

Miller was enthusiastic about the Moroccan storyteller and artist Mohammed Mrabet, whom Stettner would publish in *Stroker*. This led to an exchange of letters with Paul Bowles, who wrote to Miller on 21 January 1979 that Mrabet 'was pleased, particularly with the concept of writing with the guts, which made him reiterate: He's right, that man! He understands!'[58] Miller wrote to Mrabet on 7 June of the same year: 'Your writing is quite unique and an inspiration not only to young writers but to veterans too.'[59] As usual, Miller was besieged by admirers. Pascal Vrebos visited in February 1979 and reported that as he entered the house Miller was sitting by the window in an

Miller with watercolours, 1978.

armchair reading a book by Madame Blavatsky.[60] The Vietnamese writer Nguyen Huu Hieu, who had been a political prisoner, visited and wrote a fine essay on Miller's spirituality entitled 'Hail to the Cosmological Writer'.[61] Irving Stettner came for three days and they discussed Tommy Trantino, who had been charged with killing two policemen and was incarcerated in New Jersey. Miller had been impressed by Trantino's book *Lock the Lock* (1974), and wrote an impassioned review entitled 'An Open Letter to Stroker!', in which he suggested judges be forced to spend time in prison to prevent them from giving harsh sentences.[62] His son Tony visited, and revealed to Stettner in a private moment that he had a rather sceptical view of his father's continual romantic entanglements: 'The trouble with my father . . . is that he's in love with love.'[63]

Warren Beatty asked Miller to participate in his movie *Reds* (1981) about the American communist John Reed: he began filming in August and Miller spoke in several cameos about the mood in America during the Russian Revolution. He continued to paint watercolours, and in August 1979 told Durrell that he had just created three of his very best: his new favourite painter was Shiko Munakata, the Japanese woodblock printmaker. In Japan the art critic Sadojiro Kubo continued to be an enthusiastic advocate of Miller's paintings, and at his death in 1996 had the largest collection of Miller's work outside America. Miller had had several recent exhibitions of his paintings and would have more over the next few years: at Galerie Espace in Los Angeles (1975), the Tel Aviv International Art Fair (1978) and the Coast Gallery in Big Sur (1978–80).[64] His astrologer Jacqueline Langmann was a guest for a few weeks in October – they spent hours talking in French about the planet Uranus – and Miller continued to read and reread favourite books: Edmondo de Amicis's *The Heart of a Boy*, Pierre Loti's *The Disenchanted*, a biography of Marie Corelli.[65]

In early 1980 Miller wrote to Stettner complaining of a new ailment, hypoglycaemia, and went on a special diet to try to control it. He was visited by Einar Moos, his 23-year-old 'genius' friend from Chile, whom Miller considered the 'most interesting person in my entourage'.[66] Moos recalled his final dinners with Miller, when he would drink a glass of Châteauneuf-du-Pape, take a handful of pills, some so tiny they would slip through his fingers, and make a toast: 'Fuck the doctors!' Miller wondered if perhaps the best way to die would be to walk out peacefully on the ice like the Eskimos.[67]

Devachan must have been on Miller's mind in his last years since, as we have seen, he mentioned it in his Mishima essay as well as in 'Mother, China and the World Beyond'. Miller's health had severely weakened and in a letter dated 8 May to Alfred Perlès he ended with the words: 'See you in Devachan, Joey'.[68] Barbara Kraft had been interviewing Eugene Ionesco and tried to arrange a meeting between Miller and the Romanian playwright, but Miller said: 'Oh, I don't want him to see me like this, how I am now.' Adding a few minutes later, 'If Ionesco could see me now, that's something he could write a play about.'[69] He began to have increasingly bizarre dreams, rolled out of bed at night, fell down repeatedly and was badly cut and bruised. His carotid arteries had become compromised and he was too frail for an operation. Kraft prevailed on Miller to allow his friend and housekeeper Bill Pickerill to move in permanently as a caretaker, and on 27 May he finished his last painting.[70] Miller died on Saturday 7 June 1980 at about 3:30 p.m. in Pickerill's arms.[71] As he had stipulated, on what would have been his 92nd birthday Valentine scattered some of his ashes in the sea beneath Partington Ridge and divided the remainder between herself and Tony.[72]

In 1981 Emil White, assisted by the Big Sur Land Trust, converted his own home into the Henry Miller Memorial Library, and upon White's death in 1989 the Library became a non-profit organization.

In 1983 *Opus Pistorum* was marketed as a pornographic text by Miller, but was in fact not written by him. Several biographies followed, including Kathryn Winslow's *Henry Miller: Full of Life* (1986), Mary V. Dearborn's *The Happiest Man Alive* (1991), Robert Ferguson's *Henry Miller: A Life* (1991), Beatrice Commenge's *Henry Miller: Ange, Clown, Voyou* (1991) and Erica Jong's *The Devil at Large* (1993). Philip Kaufman directed *Henry & June* (1990), an effort to depict the Miller/June/Nin triangle. The French continued their devotion to their adopted son by publishing a superb volume entitled *Cahiers Henry Miller* in 1994, and volumes of letters have appeared regularly, such as the Cendrars–Miller correspondence (1994) and *Lettres à Maurice Nadeau, 1947–1978* (2012). *Nexus: The International Henry Miller Journal* began publishing in 2004, and to date ten issues have appeared. The unfinished *Nexus II* was published as *Paris 1928* in 2012, as was *Mejores no hay!* with spectacular photographs by Denise Bellon.

The 26 January 2012 issue of the *New York Times Book Review* contained Jeanette Winterson's review of Frederick W. Turner's *Renegade: Henry Miller and the Making of Tropic of Cancer* (2011), which reignited the controversy over Miller's supposed 'sexism', while the graphic novelist Alison Bechdel contributed an imaginative cartoon to a series in the 3 October 2013 issue called 'Let's Read About Sex', depicting a contrapuntal dialogue between Miller and Kate Millett (see pp. 150–51). In May 2013 the Henry Miller Memorial Library sponsored a week-long Big Sur Brooklyn Bridge Festival, which hosted readings and performances as well as a panel discussion, 'Henry Miller: Libertine, Communard'. More than 30 years after his departure for Devachan, Miller's genius continues to engage readers throughout the world who find in his ultimately affirmative message a way through the darkness to light.

References

1 Paradise in the 14th Ward, 1891–1908

1 Robert Snyder, *This is Henry, Henry Miller from Brooklyn* (Los Angeles, 1974), p. 9; Jay Martin, *Always Merry and Bright: The Life of Henry Miller* (Santa Barbara, CA, 1978), p. 3.
2 Henry Miller, *Tropic of Capricorn* (New York, 1961), pp. 61, 62.
3 Henry Miller, *The Nightmare Notebook* (New York, 1975), n.p.
4 Twinka Thiebaud, *What Doncha Know about Henry Miller?* (Belvedere, CA, 2011), p. 18.
5 Evan Hughes, *Literary Brooklyn: The Writers of Brooklyn and the Story of American City Life* (New York, 2011), pp. 26, 27; Henry Miller, *My Life and Times* (New York, 1971), p. 182.
6 Snyder, *This is Henry*, p. 9.
7 Kathleen Conzen, 'The Germans', in *The Harvard Encyclopedia of American Ethnic Groups*, ed. Stephan Thernstrom (Cambridge, MA, 1981), pp. 409, 413.
8 Edwin G. Burrows and Mike Wallace, *Gotham: A History of New York City to 1898* (New York, 1999), pp. 745, 1111–12. See also Stanley Nadel, *Little Germany: Ethnicity, Religion, and Class in New York City, 1845–80* (Urbana and Chicago, 1990).
9 Richard Panchyk, *German New York City* (Charleston, SC, 2008), pp. 50, 31.
10 Henry Miller, 'Autobiographical Note', *The Cosmological Eye* (Norfolk, CT, 1939), p. 365.
11 *Dear, Dear Brenda: The Love Letters of Henry Miller to Brenda Venus*, ed. Gerald Seth Sindell (New York, 1986), p. 136; Mary Dearborn, *The Happiest Man Alive: A Biography of Henry Miller* (New York, 1991), p. 21.

12 Dearborn, *The Happiest Man Alive*, p. 20; Brassaï, *Henry Miller: Happy Rock* (Chicago, 2002), pp. 102–3.

13 Dearborn, *The Happiest Man Alive*, p. 20; Robert Ferguson, *Henry Miller: A Life* (New York, 1991), p. 2.

14 Dearborn, *The Happiest Man Alive*, p. 20.

15 Ibid., p. 22; Henry Miller, *Flashback: Entretiens de Pacific Palisades avec Christian de Bartillat* (Paris, 1976), p. 22.

16 Miller, *Flashback*, p. 22; Henry Miller, *Stand Still Like the Hummingbird* (Norfolk, CT, 1962), p. 79; Frank L. Kersnowski and Alice Hughes, eds, *Conversations with Henry Miller* (Jackson, MS, 1994), p. 186.

17 Ian S. MacNiven, ed., *The Durrell–Miller Letters, 1935–80* (New York, 1988), p. 85.

18 Henry Miller, 'A Boyhood View of the Nineties', *New York Times*, CXX (17 October 1971), p. 1; Henry Miller, 'Childhood in Brooklyn', *From Your Capricorn Friend* (New York, 1984), p. 79; Henry Miller, 'The Old Neighborhood', *Playboy*, XII /12 (December 1965), p. 148.

19 Snyder, *This is Henry*, p. 25.

20 *Conversations with Henry Miller*, p. 197; Clifford Terry, 'Dirty Old Henry Miller at 86', *Chicago Tribune Magazine* (12 February 1978), p. 34.

21 William A. Gordon, *Writer and Critic: A Correspondence with Henry Miller* (Baton Rouge, LA, 1968), p. 6.

22 *Dear, Dear Brenda*, p. 147; also see Kathleen Neils Conzen, 'Ethnicity as Festive Culture: Nineteenth-century German America on Parade', in *The Invention of Ethnicity*, ed. Werner Sollors (New York, 1989). Conzen points out that 'the increasing visibility of German–American public celebration in the 1840s was linked to the intensifying pace of German immigration and to the consequent growth of the German-language press and elaboration of the German *Vereinswesen* – associational life – in America', p. 49.

23 Gordon, *Writer and Critic*, p. 43.

24 Snyder, *This is Henry*, p. 28; Patricia Burstein, 'A Feisty 86, Henry Miller writes his own epitaph: "I beat those bastards!"', *People Magazine*, X/8 (21 August 1978), p. 62.

25 Miller, *Flashback*, p. 19.

26 Miller, *Tropic of Capricorn*, p. 10; Anaïs Nin, *The Diary of Anaïs Nin*, vol. III: *1939–1944* (New York, 1969), pp. 199, 200.

27 *Henry Miller in Conversation with Georges Belmont* (Chicago, 1972), pp. 29, 101.

28 Miller, 'The Old Neighborhood', p. 148.

29 Miller, 'Autobiographical Note', p. 366.

30 *Miller in Conversation with Georges Belmont*, p. 29.

31 Miller, *Flashback*, p. 25.

32 Brassaï, *Henry Miller: Happy Rock*, p. 81; Miller, *Flashback*, p. 20.

33 Miller, *Tropic of Capricorn*, p. 14.

34 Thiebaud, *What Doncha Know About Henry Miller?*, p. 112.

35 Henry Miller, 'The Tailor Shop', *Black Spring* (New York, 1963), pp. 91–3; Miller, *Flashback*, pp. 21–2.

36 Miller, *Black Spring*, pp. 95, 96.

37 Miller, *My Life and Times*, p. 34; Miller, *Flashback*, p. 31.

38 'It was a wonderful tender neighborhood. Tender with violence. Again, American. You know, such warmth, and then this ferocity for no reason – I can't understand', Snyder, *This is Henry*, p. 28.

39 Pete Hamill, 'Introduction' to *The Brooklyn Reader*, ed. Andrea Wyatt Sexton and Alice Leccese Powers (New York, 1994), p. xiii; Miller, 'The Old Neighborhood', p. 120.

40 Brassaï, *Henry Miller: Happy Rock*, p. 16.

41 Miller, 'The Old Neighborhood', p. 148.

42 Alfred Perlès, *My Friend Henry Miller* (London, 1973), p. 16; Miller, *From Your Capricorn Friend*, p. 77.

43 On elementary school, see Henry Miller, *Book of Friends* (Santa Barbara, CA, 1976), p. 95; on his pals, see *Black Spring*, p. 4; Pascal Vrebos, *444 Ocampo Drive*, ed. Karl Orend (Ann Arbor, MI, 2003), p. 35; Nordine Haddad, ed., *Henry Miller–John Cowper Powys, Correspondence privée* (Paris, 1994), p. 77.

44 Miller, *Flashback*, p. 47.

45 Miller, *Book of Friends*, p. 19.

46 Henry Miller, *To Paint is to Love Again* (New York, 1968), p. 3.

47 Miller, 'The Old Neighborhood', p. 234; Henry Miller, 'A Nation of Lunatics', in *Four Visions of America* (Santa Barbara, CA, 1977), p. 121; Branko Aleksic, 'The Unpublished Correspondence of Henry Miller and André Breton, the "Steady Rock", 1947–50', *Nexus*, 5 (2008), p. 165.

48 Henry Miller, *The World of Sex* (New York, 1965), pp. 29, 30.

49 Miller, *My Life and Times*, p. 182.

50 Ibid., p. 182.

51 Kathryn Winslow, *Henry Miller: Full of Life* (Los Angeles, 1986), p. 4.

52 Miller *Black Spring*, p. 3; Snyder, *This is Henry*, p. 30.

53 Miller, *Flashback*, p. 43.

54 Dearborn, *The Happiest Man Alive*, p. 27; Ferguson, *Henry Miller: A Life*, p. 11.

55 Miller, *Flashback*, pp. 43–4.

56 Snyder, *This is Henry*, p. 30.

57 Emil Schnellock, 'Just a Brooklyn Boy', in *The Happy Rock: A Book About Henry Miller*, ed. Bern Porter (Berkeley, CA, 1945), p. 7.

58 Henry Miller, *Joey: A Loving Portrait of Alfred Perlès Together with Some Bizarre Episodes Relating to the Other Sex* – vol. III: *A Book of Friends* (Santa Barbara, CA, 1979), p. 70; Walter Schmiele, *Henry Miller* (Paris, 1969), p. 27.

59 Miller, *Flashback*, p. 42.

60 Snyder, *This is Henry*, p. 27; Miller, *My Life and Times*, p. 185; 'A Boyhood View of the Nineties', *New York Times*, p. 12.

61 At age 77 Miller puzzled: 'But coupled with my image of her is a question equally untouched upon, a problem I have never been able to solve: what this kind of conflict within me over this girl is all about', *Henry Miller in Conversation with Georges Belmont*, p. 8.

62 Henry Miller, *The Time of the Assassins* (Norfolk, CT, 1956), p.18; Miller, *Flashback*, p. 48.

63 Joyce Howard, ed., *Letters by Henry Miller to Hoki Tokuda Miller* (New York, 1986), p. 152; Henry Miller, *From Your Capricorn Friend*, p. 34.

64 Gordon, *Writer and Critic*, p. 15.

65 Henry Miller, 'Preface' to Jacqueline Langmann, *Henry Miller et son destin* (Paris, 1974), p. 9; George A. Henty, *The Lion of the North* (New York, n.d.), p. 290; also see *Letters of Henry Miller and Wallace Fowlie, 1943–1972* (New York, 1975), pp. 119–20.

66 Snyder, *This is Henry*, p. 102; Lise Bloch-Morhange and David Alper, *Artiste et métèque à Paris* (Paris, 1980), p. 258; Sydney Omarr, *Henry Miller: His World of Urania* (London, 1960), p. 73, quoted from *Hamlet*.

67 Henry Miller, *Remember to Remember* (Norfolk, CT, 1947), p. 339.

68 'The Theatre', in Miller, *From Your Capricorn Friend*, p. 70.

69 Miller, *My Life and Times*, p. 182; Henry Miller, *Frère Jacques: Lettres à*

Frédéric Jacques Temple (Fontenay-le-Comte, 2012), p. 84.

70 Vrebos, *444 Ocampo Drive*, p. 111 (translation mine).

71 *Letters of Henry Miller and Wallace Fowlie*, p. 126.

72 Robert Snyder, 'Henry Miller: A Reminiscence', in *Critical Essays on Henry Miller*, ed. Ronald Gottesman (New York, 1992), p. 393.

73 *Henry Miller in Conversation with Georges Belmont*, p. 3.

2 Go West, Young Man, 1909–19

1 Henry Miller, 'Revolt in the Desert', *Cavalier*, xv (January 1965), p. 30.

2 Robert Snyder, *This is Henry, Henry Miller from Brooklyn* (Los Angeles, 1974), p. 9; Henry Miller, *My Life and Times* (New York, 1971), p. 185; Mary Dearborn, *The Happiest Man Alive: A Biography of Henry Miller* (New York, 1991), pp. 43, 44; Henry Miller, *Farewell from France: A Letter to Huntington Cairns, April 30, 1939* (Ann Arbor, MI, 1995), n.p.

3 Ian S. MacNiven, ed., *The Durrell–Miller Letters, 1935–80* (New York, 1988), pp. 364–5; A. Norman Jeffares, *W. B. Yeats: A New Biography* (New York, 1988), p. 20. On Miller's interest in Indian thought, see R. K. Gupta, *The Great Encounter: A Study of Indo-American Literary and Cultural Relations* (Riverdale, MD, 1987), pp. 188–91.

4 *Collector's Quest: The Correspondence of Henry Miller and J. Rives Childs, 1947–1965*, ed. Richard Clement Wood (Charlottesville, VA, 1968), p. 60; on Maeterlinck, see 'Henry Miller ou Les Mauvaises Fréquentations', *La Tour de Feu*, 47 (Autumn 1955), pp. 12–13; on Corelli, see Joyce Howard, ed., *Letters by Henry Miller to Hoki Tokuda Miller* (New York, 1986), p. 153.

5 Frank L. Kersnowski and Alice Hughes, eds, *Conversations with Henry Miller* (Jackson, MS, 1994), p. 186; *Henry Miller in Conversation with Georges Belmont* (Chicago, 1972), p. 41.

6 Henry Miller, *The Air Conditioned Nightmare* (Norfolk, CT, 1945), p. 244.

7 Henry Miller, *My Life and Times* (New York, 1971), p. 185; Dearborn, *The Happiest Man Alive*, p. 44.

8 *Henry Miller in Conversation with Georges Belmont*, p. 27.

9 Jay Martin, *Always Merry and Bright: The Life of Henry Miller* (Santa Barbara, CA, 1978), p. 47.

10 Henry Miller, 'Love and How it Gets that Way', *Mademoiselle*, LVIII (January 1964), p. 49.

11 Dearborn, *The Happiest Man Alive*, p. 45.

12 Henry Miller, *Flashback: Entretiens de Pacific Palisades avec Christian de Bartillat* (Paris, 1976), p. 51.

13 Henry Miller, *The Nightmare Notebook* (New York, 1975), n.p.

14 Erica Jong, *The Devil at Large* (New York, 1993), p. 68.

15 Miller, *My Life and Times*, p. 185; Henry Miller, *My Bike and Other Friends* (Santa Barbara, CA, 1978), p. 105; Henry Miller, *Frère Jacques: Lettres à Frédéric Jacques Temple* (Fontenay-le-Comte, 2012), pp. 84, 87.

16 Henry Miller, *Plexus* (New York, 1965), p. 160; Miller, *My Life and Times*, p. 187; Miller, *Frère Jacques*, p. 84.

17 Miller, *Frère Jacques*, p. 84.

18 Miller, *My Life and Times*, p. 187; Miller, *Flashback*, p. 58.

19 Miller, *My Life and Times*, p. 188.

20 F. J. Temple, *Henry Miller, Qui suis je?* (Lyon, 1986), pp. 154, 158; Miller, *Flashback*, p. 72.

21 Miller, *My Life and Times*, p. 188.

22 MacNiven, ed., *The Durrell–Miller Letters*, p. 47.

23 Thomas Nesbit, *Henry Miller and Religion* (New York, 2007), p. 3; John R. Hinnells, ed., *The Penguin Dictionary of Religions* (London, 1984), pp. 328, 329.

24 Henry Miller, *Stand Still Like the Hummingbird* (Norfolk, CT, 1962), p. 157.

25 Henry Miller, *Tropic of Capricorn* (New York, 1961), p. 147.

26 Martin, *Always Merry and Bright*, p. 35; Dearborn, *The Happiest Man Alive*, p. 51.

27 Miller, *Frère Jacques*, p. 77.

28 Ibid., p. 85. Miller refers here to Roosevelt's famous speech in Chicago on 10 April 1899: 'I wish to preach, not the doctrine of ignoble ease, but the doctrine of the strenuous life, the life of toil and effort, of labor and strife'.

29 Harry Kiakis, 'Henry Steps Out', *Nexus*, 3 (2006), pp. 102–3; Dearborn, *The Happiest Man Alive*, p. 49; *Farewell from France*, n.p.

30 Martin, *Always Merry and Bright*, p. 37.

31 Lawrence Clark Powell, 'Remembering Henry Miller', in *Henry Miller: A Book of Tributes, 1931–1994*, ed. Craig Peter Standish (Orlando, FL,

1994), p. 325; Twinka Thiebaud, *What Doncha Know about Henry Miller?* (Belvedere, CA, 2011), p. 65.

32 Miller, 'Where am I? What am I Doing Here?', in *This is My Best in the Third Quarter of the Century*, ed. Whit Burnett (New York, 1970), p. 720; 'The Brooklyn Bridge', in *The Cosmological Eye* (Norfolk, CT, 1939), p. 349.

33 Jack Kerouac, *On the Road* (New York, 2011), p. 14.

34 Miller, *Frère Jacques*, p. 87.

35 Dearborn, *The Happiest Man Alive*, p. 50.

36 Ibid., p. 50; Jerry Bauer, 'Interview: Henry Miller', *Adelina*, XV/10 (January 1981), p. 25.

37 Elsa Dixler, review of Paul Avrich and Karen Avrich, *Sasha and Emma: The Anarchist Odyssey of Alexander Berkman and Emma Goldman*, in *New York Times* (9 December 2012).

38 Miller, *My Life and Times*, p. 190; PBS, *American Experience*, 'American Experience: Emma Goldman, May 20, 1913', at www.pbs.org/wgbh/amex/goldman/index.html.

39 Kersnowski and Hughes, eds, *Conversations with Henry Miller*, p. 182.

40 Sindell, ed., *Dear, Dear Brenda*, p. 129.

41 Miller, *My Life and Times*, p. 190.

42 Dearborn, *The Happiest Man Alive*, p. 51.

43 Miller, *My Life and Times*, pp. 28, 196; 'The Tailor Shop: Between the Cracks', at www.cosmotc.blogspot.co.uk.

44 Miller, *My Life and Times*, p. 193.

45 George Wickes, *Henry Miller* (Minneapolis, MN, 1966), p. 14.

46 *Dear, Dear Brenda*, p. 73; Snyder, *This is Henry*, p. 31.

47 Miller, 'The Tailor Shop', *Black Spring*, p. 82.

48 Miller, *Tropic of Capricorn*, p. 222.

49 Leszek Kolakowski, *Bergson* (Oxford, 1985), p. 53; Nesbit, *Henry Miller and Religion*, pp. 32, 64, 72.

50 Henry Miller, 'A Sense of Wonder', *Vogue*, CXLIV (December 1964), p. 216.

51 Brassaï, *Henry Miller: Happy Rock* (Chicago, 2002), pp. 73, 74; Miller, 'An Autobiographical Note', in *The Cosmological Eye*, p. 367.

52 David Stephen Calonne, *The Colossus of Armenia: G. I. Gurdjieff and Henry Miller, with Five Unpublished Letters to Pham Cong Thien* (Ann Arbor, MI, 1997), p. 38; Henry Miller, 'Man in the Zoo: Georg Grosz,

"Ecce Homo"', *Evergreen Review Reader, 1957–1966* (New York, 1993), p. 341.

53 Miller, *Farewell from France*, n.p.

54 Snyder, *This is Henry*, p. 34; 'On His Sins of Omission', *New York Times Book Review* (2 January 1972), pp. 10–11; Miller, *My Life and Times*, p. 196.

55 Elmer Gertz, *To Life: The Story of a Chicago Lawyer* (Carbondale and Edwardsville, IL, 1990), p. 262.

56 Miller, *My Life and Times*, p. 196; Roger Jackson, *Henry Miller: His Life in Ephemera, 1914–1980* (Ann Arbor, MI, 2012), pp. 33, 34, 46.

57 Robert Ferguson, *Henry Miller: A Life* (New York, 1991), p. 40.

58 Jackson, *Ephemera*, p. 15; Dearborn, *The Happiest Man Alive*, p. 56.

59 Jackson, *Ephemera*, p. 15; Dearborn, *The Happiest Man Alive*, p. 56.

60 Jackson, *Ephemera*, p. 16.

61 Ibid.

62 Robert Ferguson, *Henry Miller: A Life* (New York, 1991), p. 46; Martin, *Always Merry and Bright*, p. 47; Miller, 'Autobiographical Note', in *The Cosmological Eye*, p. 367.

63 Ferguson, *Henry Miller: A Life*, pp. 48, 50; Dearborn, *The Happiest Man Alive*, p. 59; Jackson, *Ephemera*, p. 15.

64 Henry Miller, *The Books in My Life* (Norfolk, CT, 1952), p. 135.

65 George Steiner, 'The Problem of Powys', *Times Literary Supplement*, 3819 (16 May 1975), p. 541.

66 William A. Gordon, *Writer and Critic: A Correspondence with Henry Miller* (Baton Rouge, LA, 1968), p. 16.

67 Barbara Kraft, 'A Conversation with Henry Miller', *Michigan Quarterly Review*, XX/2 (Spring 1981), pp. 53, 54; Miller, *Plexus*, p. 561.

68 Ferguson, *Henry Miller: A Life*, p. 51.

69 Snyder, *This is Henry*, p. 37.

70 Dearborn, *The Happiest Man Alive*, p. 60; personal communication from Roger Jackson concerning Beatrice Wickens's annotations of Miller texts.

71 David Stephen Calonne, Foreword, *Henry Miller: Letters to 'The Black Cat'* (Ann Arbor, MI, 1996), p. 13.

72 Ibid., p. 15.

73 Ibid., p. 18.

74 Ibid., pp. 23–4.

75 Jackson, *Ephemera*, pp. 12–13.
76 Ferguson, *Henry Miller: A Life*, p. 60.
77 Calonne, *Letters to 'The Black Cat'*, p. 22.

3 Cosmodemonia, Mona, the Daimon of Writing, 1920–29

1 Jay Martin, *Always Merry and Bright: The Life of Henry Miller* (Santa Barbara, CA, 1978), pp. 55–6; Mary Dearborn, *The Happiest Man Alive: A Biography of Henry Miller* (New York, 1991), pp. 64–5.
2 Henry Miller, *Flashback: Entretiens de Pacific Palisades avec Christian de Bartillat* (Paris, 1976), pp. 45–6; Henry Miller, *Frère Jacques: Lettres à Frédéric Jacques Temple* (Fontenay-le-Comte, 2012), p. 88; Mike Rivise, 'I Remember Henry Miller', *Fling*, IX (July 1962), p. 52.
3 Mike Rivise, 'Henry Miller: An Impolite Biography', *Jaguar*, I/ 5 (September 1965), p. 14.
4 Roger Jackson, *Henry Miller: His Life in Ephemera, 1914–1980* (Ann Arbor, MI, 2012), p. 15.
5 Robert Ferguson, *Henry Miller: A Life* (New York, 1991), p. 62.
6 Martin, *Always Merry and Bright*, p. 58; Dearborn, *The Happiest Man Alive*, p. 66; Ferguson, *Henry Miller: A Life*, p. 62; Jackson, *Ephemera*, p. 22.
7 Emil Schnellock, 'Just a Brooklyn Boy', in *The Happy Rock: A Book About Henry Miller*, ed. Bern Porter (Berkeley, CA, 1945), p. 9; Rivise, 'Henry Miller: An Impolite Biography', p. 14.
8 Rivise, 'Henry Miller: An Impolite Biography', p. 15.
9 Dearborn, *The Happiest Man Alive*, p. 68.
10 Ferguson, *Henry Miller: A Life*, p. 66.
11 Martin, *Always Merry and Bright*, pp. 62–3.
12 Ibid., p. 67.
13 Henry Miller, *Letters to Emil*, ed. George Wickes (New York, 1989), p. viii; Emil Schnellock. 'Just a Brooklyn Boy', in *The Happy Rock: A Book About Henry Miller*, ed. Bern Porter (Berkeley, CA, 1945), p. 15.
14 Emil Schnellock, 'Just a Brooklyn Boy', in *The Happy Rock*, p. 15; Brassaï, *Henry Miller: Happy Rock* (Chicago, 2002), p. 150; Elmer Gertz and Felice Flanery Lewis, eds, *Henry Miller: Years of Trial and Triumph,*

1962–1964, the Correspondence of Henry Miller and Elmer Gertz (Carbondale and Edwardsville, IL, 1978), p. 43.

15 Schnellock, 'Just a Brooklyn Boy', pp. 21, 10.

16 Ibid., pp. 10, 11, 21, 22.

17 Jackson, *Ephemera*, p. 19.

18 Ibid.

19 Ibid., p. 20.

20 Ibid.

21 Henry Miller, *Tropic of Capricorn* (New York, 1961), p. 31.

22 'I suppose it was the worst book any man has ever written. It was a colossal tome and faulty from start to finish. But it was my first book and I was in love with it': Miller, *Tropic of Capricorn*, p. 34.

23 Dearborn, *The Happiest Man Alive*, p. 69; Jackson, *Ephemera*, p. 22; Henry Miller, *Joey: A Loving Portrait of Alfred Perlès Together with Some Bizarre Episodes Relating to the Other Sex* – vol. III: *A Book of Friends* (Santa Barbara, CA, 1979), pp. 77, 78; Ferguson, *Henry Miller: A Life*, p. 75.

24 Jackson, *Ephemera*, p. 21.

25 Frank L. Kersnowski and Alice Hughes, eds, *Conversations with Henry Miller* (Jackson, MS, 1994), p. 101.

26 Robert Snyder, *This is Henry, Henry Miller from Brooklyn* (Los Angeles, 1974), p. 37; Isaac Bashevis Singer and Richard Burgin, *Conversations with Isaac Bashevis Singer* (New York, 1986), p. 156.

27 Dearborn, *The Happiest Man Alive*, p. 78; Rivise, 'Henry Miller: An Impolite Biography', p. 67. See also David Freeland, *Automats, Taxi Dances and Vaudeville: Excavating Manhattan's Lost Places of Leisure* (New York, 2009), pp. 194, 247, n.10.

28 Dearborn, *The Happiest Man Alive*, p. 78.

29 Ibid., p. 79; Henry Miller, *The Mezzotints* (Ann Arbor, MI, 1993), p. 2.

30 Ferguson, *Henry Miller: A Life*, p. 77.

31 Dearborn, *The Happiest Man Alive*, p. 80; Martin, *Always Merry and Bright*, p. 92; Jackson, *Ephemera*, p. 762.

32 Miller, *Tropic of Capricorn*, p. 340.

33 Dearborn, *The Happiest Man Alive*, p. 80.

34 *Dear, Dear Brenda: The Love Letters of Henry Miller to Brenda Venus*, ed. Gerald Seth Sindell (New York, 1986), p. 112.

35 Miller, *Sexus* (New York, 1965), p. 9.

36 Martin, *Always Merry and Bright*, p. 75.

37 Dearborn, *The Happiest Man Alive*, p. 81.

38 Ibid., pp. 83, 85; Ferguson, *Henry Miller: A Life*, p. 94; Martin, *Always Merry and Bright*, p. 90.

39 Miller, *The Mezzotints*, p. 2.

40 Jackson, *Ephemera*, pp. 27–8.

41 Miller, *My Life and Times*, p. 143.

42 Dearborn, *The Happiest Man Alive*, p. 87; Ferguson, *Henry Miller: A Life*, p. 96.

43 Ibid., p. 87; Martin, *Always Merry and Bright*, p. 94; *Henry Miller and James Laughlin: Selected Letters*, ed. George Wickes (New York, 1996), p. 247.

44 Jackson, *Ephemera*, p. 29.

45 Henry Miller, *Plexus* (New York, 1965), pp. 10–11, 30.

46 Rivise, 'Henry Miller: An Impolite Biography', p. 68.

47 Snyder, *This is Henry*, pp. 39, 41.

48 Mike Rivise, *Inside Western Union* (New York, 1950), p. 133.

49 Roger Jackson, personal communication.

50 Brassaï, *Happy Rock*, p. 56; Dearborn, *The Happiest Man Alive*, p. 90.

51 Jackson, *Ephemera*, pp. 29–31.

52 Henry Miller, *Letters to Emil*, ed. George Wickes (New York, 1989), p. 10.

53 Jackson, *Ephemera*, p. 32.

54 Miller, *The Mezzotints*, p. 6; Martin, *Always Merry and Bright*, pp. 102, 103.

55 Martin, *Always Merry and Bright*, p. 104; Miller, *The Mezzotints*, p. 7.

56 Dearborn, *The Happiest Man Alive*, p. 95.

57 Ibid., pp. 96–7.

58 John Strausbaugh, *The Village: 400 Years of Beats and Bohemians, Radicals and Rogues – A History of Greenwich Village* (New York, 2013), p. 160; Dearborn, *The Happiest Man Alive*, p. 97; Mary Dearborn, 'Introduction' to Henry Miller, *Moloch; or, This Gentile World* (New York, 1992), p. ix.

59 Miller, *Plexus*, p. 197.

60 Dearborn, *The Happiest Man Alive*, p. 97; Martin, *Always Merry and Bright*, p. 105.

61 Martin, *Always Merry and Bright*, p. 106.

62 Henry Miller, *Gliding into the Everglades* (Lake Oswego, OR, 1977), p. 11.

63 Dearborn, *The Happiest Man Alive*, p. 98.

64 Ferguson, *Henry Miller: A Life*, p. 117; Dearborn, *The Happiest Man Alive*, pp. 99–100.

65 Dearborn, *The Happiest Man Alive*, p. 100; Jackson, *Ephemera*, p. 46.

66 Henry Miller, 'Dreiser's Style', *New Republic*, 46 (28 April 1926), p. 306.

67 Martin, *Always Merry and Bright*, p. 111.

68 Dearborn, *The Happiest Man Alive*, p. 101; Martin, *Always Merry and Bright*, pp. 113–15, 118, 121; Ferguson, *Henry Miller: A Life*, p. 120; Strausbaugh, *The Village*, p. 130; Barbara Kraft, 'The Last Days of Henry Miller', *Ping Pong*, 1/1 (1994), p. 14; Harry Kiakis, 'Henry Visits Daughter Barbara', *Nexus*, 5 (2008), p. 246.

69 Walter Lowenfels, 'Extracts from *My Many Lives*', *The Expatriate Review*, 1 (Summer 1971); *Dear, Dear Brenda*, p. 112; Lionel Abel, *Intellectual Follies: A Memoir of the Literary Venture in New York and Paris*, quoted in Jackson, *Ephemera*, p. 45.

70 Jackson, *Ephemera*, p. 38; Dearborn, *The Happiest Man Alive*, p. 103.

71 Dearborn, *The Happiest Man Alive*, p. 106; Henry Miller, *Crazy Cock* (New York, 1991), pp. 77–8.

72 *Henry and June: From the Unexpurgated Diary of Anaïs Nin* (San Diego, CA, 1986), p. 46.

73 Martin, *Always Merry and Bright*, pp. 126–7.

74 Ibid., p. 130; Dearborn, *The Happiest Man Alive*, pp. 107–8.

75 Martin, *Always Merry and Bright*, p. 131.

76 Miller, *Book of Friends*, p. 76; Dearborn, *The Happiest Man Alive*, pp. 108, 109.

77 Martin, *Always Merry and Bright*, p. 132; Dearborn, *The Happiest Man Alive*, p. 110; Harry Kiakis, 'Love, Pain, Big Sur, and Life as a Bedbug', *Nexus*, 8 (2011), p. 107.

78 Martin, *Always Merry and Bright*, pp. 135, 138.

79 Snyder, *This is Henry*, p. 9; Dearborn, *The Happiest Man Alive*, p. 110.

80 Martin, *Always Merry and Bright*, pp. 139, 140–41; Jackson, *Ephemera*, p. 38.

81 Dearborn, *The Happiest Man Alive*, p. 111.

82 Dearborn, 'Introduction' to Miller, *Moloch*, p. ix; Jackson, *Ephemera*, p. 41.

83 Allen Ginsberg, *Howl: Original Draft Facsimile*, ed. Barry Miles (New York, 1986), p. 6.

84 Miller, *Moloch*, p. 3.

85 Martin, *Always Merry and Bright*, p. 145.

86 Jackson, *Ephemera*, p. 41.

87 Henry Miller, *Paris 1928: Nexus II* (Bloomington and Indianapolis, IN, 2012), p. 1.

88 Martin, *Always Merry and Bright*, pp. 156–157; 158; Brassaï, *Happy Rock*, p. 70.

89 Brassaï, *Happy Rock*, p. 70; Miller, 'Where Am I? What Am I Doing Here?', p. 722; *Ephemera*, p. 41; *Dear Brenda*, p. 139.

90 'The Henry Miller to Lowenfels Letters', *The Outsider*, I/3 (Spring 1963), p. 79.

91 Jackson, *Ephemera*, p. 41; Martin, *Always Merry and Bright*, p. 160; Dearborn, *The Happiest Man Alive*, p. 117.

92 Dearborn, *The Happiest Man Alive*, pp. 117, 118; Martin, *Always Merry and Bright*, p. 161.

93 Dearborn, *The Happiest Man Alive*, p. 118; Martin, *Always Merry and Bright*, p. 164.

4 Finding his Genius: Paris, 1930–39

1 Dearborn, *The Happiest Man Alive*, p. 123; Mark Jackson and Mike Scutari, eds, *Where Nothing Happens: The Best of the Henry Miller Memorial Library* (Big Sur, CA, 2012), p. 7.

2 Lise Bloch-Morhange and David Alper, *Artiste et métèque à Paris* (Paris, 1980), p. 255; Jay Martin, *Always Merry and Bright: The Life of Henry Miller* (Santa Barbara, CA, 1978), pp. 180, 183.

3 Martin, *Always Merry and Bright*, p. 185.

4 Henry Miller, *J'suis pas plus con qu'un autre* (Paris, 1976), p. 54; Edmond Buchet, *Les Auteurs dans ma vie* (Paris, 1969), p. 217; Brassaï, *Henry Miller: The Paris Years* (New York, 1995), p. 5.

5 Brassaï, *The Paris Years*, pp. 9, 10, 11.

6 Ibid., pp. 10, 11.

7 Miriam Cendrars, *Blaise Cendrars* (Paris, 1993), p. 486.

8 Brassaï, *The Paris Years*, p. 22.

9 Henry Miller and Michael Fraenkel, *Hamlet, Volume II* (New York, 1941), p. 161.

10 Martin, *Always Merry and Bright*, pp. 200–201.

11 Ibid., pp. 211, 213–15.

12 Henry Miller, 'Preface' to Brassaï, *Conversations with Picasso* (Chicago, 1999), p. ix; Brassaï, *The Paris Years*, p. 1.

13 Brassaï, *The Paris Years*, pp. 30, 4.

14 Martin, *Always Merry and Bright*, p. 217; Brassaï, *The Paris Years*, p. 46.

15 Brassaï, *The Paris Years*, p. 46; Suzanne Brøgger, *To My Danish Sheherezade* (Ann Arbor, MI, 1998), p. 15.

16 Roger Jackson, *Henry Miller: His Life in Ephemera, 1914–1980* (Ann Arbor, MI, 2012), pp. 55–6.

17 Brassaï, *The Paris Years*, pp. 29, 113, 39.

18 Martin, *Always Merry and Bright*, p. 220.

19 *Letters of Henry Miller and Wallace Fowlie* (New York, 1965), p. 126; Martin, *Always Merry and Bright*, p. 220.

20 Martin, *Always Merry and Bright*, pp. 224, 225.

21 Ibid., p. 229.

22 Jackson, *Ephemera*, p. 64; Ralph Jules Frantz, 'Recollections', in *The Left Bank Revisited: Selections from the Paris Tribune, 1917–1934*, ed. Hugh Ford (University Park, PA, 1972), p. 312; Kathryn Winslow, *Henry Miller: Full of Life* (Los Angeles, 1986), p. 20.

23 Jackson, *Ephemera*, p. 64.

24 Martin, *Always Merry and Bright*, p. 232.

25 Ibid., p. 219; Jackson, *Ephemera*, p. 67.

26 Kath Kiernen and Michael M. Moore, eds, *First Fiction: An Anthology of the First Published Stories by Famous Writers* (Boston, MA, 1994), p. 261.

27 Martin, *Always Merry and Bright*, p. 235.

28 Wambly Bald, 'The Sweet Madness of Montparnasse', in Ford, ed., *The Left Bank Revisited*, p. 288; Walter Lowenfels, 'Extracts', *The Expatriate Review* (1971), p. 19.

29 Anaïs Nin, *The Diaries of Anaïs Nin*, vol. I: *1931–1934* (New York, 1966), p. 7; Hugh Ford, *Published in Paris* (Stamford, CT, 1980), p. 159.

30 Erica Jong, *The Devil at Large: Erica Jong on Henry Miller* (New York, 1993), p. 98.

31 *Henry and June: From the Unexpurgated Diary of Anaïs Nin* (San Diego, CA, 1986), p. 6.

32 Wambly Bald in Jackson, *Ephemera*, p. 58; Evelyn J. Hinz, ed., *Anaïs Nin: A Woman Speaks* (Chicago, 1975), p. 66.

33 Anaïs Nin, *The Diaries of Anaïs Nin*, vol. I, pp. 27, 28.

34 See David Stephen Calonne, 'Henry Miller, Anaïs Nin and Psychoanalysis', in *Anaïs Nin: A Book of Mirrors*, ed. Paul Herron (Huntington Woods, MI, 1996), pp. 284–91.

35 Brassaï, *The Paris Years*, p. 57; Lawrence Clark Powell, 'Remembering Henry Miller', in *Henry Miller: A Book of Tributes, 1931–1994*, ed. Craig Peter Standish (Orlando, FL, 1994), p. 320.

36 *Letters of Henry Miller and Wallace Fowlie, 1943–1972* (New York, 1975), p. 168; Brassaï, *The Paris Years*, pp. 59, 95; Martin, *Always Merry and Bright*, p. 245.

37 Brassaï, *Henry Miller: Happy Rock* (Chicago, 2002), p. 152.

38 Henry Miller, *Letters to Anaïs Nin* (London, 1965), p. 43.

39 Martin, *Always Merry and Bright*, pp. 246, 247.

40 Ibid., p. 248; Brassaï, *The Paris Years*, pp. 60, 62.

41 Brassaï, *The Paris Years*, p. 69.

42 Martin, *Always Merry and Bright*, p. 252.

43 Brassaï, *The Paris Years*, p. 120.

44 Martin, *Always Merry and Bright*, p. 265; Dearborn, *The Happiest Man Alive*, p. 151.

45 Dearborn, *The Happiest Man Alive*, p. 158; Jackson, *Ephemera*, p. 68; Winslow, p. 22.

46 Dearborn, *The Happiest Man Alive*, pp. 159, 160.

47 Martin, *Always Merry and Bright*, p. 250; Brassaï, *The Paris Years*, p. 107.

48 Martin, *Always Merry and Bright*, p. 261; Petronius, *Satyricon*, trans. Michael Heseltine (Cambridge, 1969), p. 73.

49 Brassaï, *The Paris Years*, p. 119.

50 Henry Miller, *Letters to Emil*, ed. George Wickes (New York, 1989), p. 15; Brassaï, *Happy Rock*, p. 149.

51 Brassaï, *Happy Rock*, p. 152.

52 John De St Jorre, *Venus Bound: The Erotic Voyage of the Olympia Press and its Writers* (New York, 1994), pp. 23, 3.

53 See David Stephen Calonne, 'Euphoria in Paris: Henry Miller Meets D. H. Lawrence', *The Library Chronicle of the University of Texas at Austin*, n.s. 34 (1986), pp. 88–98; Winslow, *Henry Miller: Full of Life*,

p. 23; Brassaï, *The Paris Years*, p. 122; Martin, *Always Merry and Bright*, pp. 287, 298.

54 Wendy M. DuBow, ed., *Conversations with Anaïs Nin* (Jackson, MS, 1994), p. 222; Stephen Barber, *Antonin Artaud: Blows and Bombs* (London, 1993), pp. 59, 65.

55 Miller, *Just Wild About Harry* (Norfolk, CT, 1963), pp. 8–9, 12–13; *The Waters Reglitterized* (Santa Barbara, CA, 1973), p. 9.

56 Brassaï, *The Paris Years*, p. 108.

57 Miller, 'Utrillo', *Tricolor*, II/8 (November 1944), p. 95; Brassaï, *Happy Rock*, p. 6; *A Literate Passion: Letters of Anaïs Nin and Henry Miller, 1932–1953*, ed. Gunther Stuhlmann (New York, 1987), p. 231.

58 Walter Schmiele, *Henry Miller* (Paris, 1969), p. 126.

59 Herbert Faulkner West, *The Mind on the Wing: A Book for Readers and Collectors* (New York, 1947), p. 129.

60 Winslow, *Henry Miller: Full of Life*, p. 26.

61 Dearborn, *The Happiest Man Alive*, p. 173.

62 Henry Miller, *The World of Sex* (New York, 1965), p. 16.

63 Mario Praz, 'Civiltà in sfacelo', in *Prefazione ai Tropici* (Milan, 1962) (translation mine).

64 Patricia Burstein, 'A Feisty 86, Henry Miller Writes his Own Epitaph: "I Beat Those Bastards!"', *People*, X/8 (21 August 1978), p. 60.

65 Forrest Read, ed., *Pound/Joyce: The Letters of Ezra Pound to James Joyce* (New York, 1967), p. 256.

66 Aldous Huxley, quoted in Winslow, *Henry Miller: Full of Life*, p. 28.

67 Cendrars, 'Un Ecrivain Américain nous est né', *Orbes*, 2nd series, no. 4 (Summer 1935), reprinted in George Wickes, ed., *Henry Miller and the Critics* (Carbondale, IL, 1963), pp. 23–4.

68 Jay Bochner, *Blaise Cendrars: Discovery and Recreation* (Toronto, 1978), p. 75; Brassaï, *Happy Rock*, pp. 20, 21.

69 Ian S. MacNiven, ed., *The Durrell–Miller Letters, 1935–80* (New York, 1988), p. 311.

70 Dearborn, *The Happiest Man Alive*, p. 174.

71 Ibid., p. 175.

72 Miriam Cendrars, ed., *Blaise Cendrars–Henry Miller: Correspondence, 1934–1979* (Paris, 1995), p. 359; Martin, *Always Merry and Bright*, p. 308.

73 Dearborn, *The Happiest Man Alive*, p. 187; Edward De Grazia, *Girls Lean Back Everywhere: The Law of Obscenity and the Assault on Genius*

(New York, 1993), p. 367; see also W. G. Rogers, *Wise Men Fish Here: The Story of Frances Steloff and the Gotham Book Mart* (New York, 1965).

74 Martin, *Always Merry and Bright*, pp. 308, 309; Dearborn, *The Happiest Man Alive*, p. 180.

75 *Henry Miller and James Laughlin: Selected Letters*, ed. George Wickes (New York, 1996), p. x; also see James Laughlin, *Pound as Wuz* (London, 1989), p. 4.

76 Henry Miller, 'Glittering Pie', *Harvard Advocate*, CXXII (September 1935); Ian S. MacNiven, ed., *The Durrell–Miller Letters, 1935–80* (New York, 1988), p. 8; Dearborn, *The Happiest Man Alive*, pp. 186–7.

77 Dearborn, *The Happiest Man Alive*, p. 185.

78 MacNiven, ed., *The Durrell–Miller Letters*, pp. 2, 3.

79 Martin, *Always Merry and Bright*, p. 315.

80 Dearborn, *The Happiest Man Alive*, p. 182.

81 Martin, *Always Merry and Bright*, p. 315; Dearborn, *The Happiest Man Alive*, p. 182.

82 Dearborn, *The Happiest Man Alive*, p. 188.

83 Martin, *Always Merry and Bright*, p. 315; Miller, Preface to Jacqueline Langmann, *Henry Miller et son destin* (Paris, 1974), p. 9; Brassaï, *The Paris Years*, pp. 208, 209; Sydney Omarr, *Henry Miller: His World of Urania* (London, 1960), p. 56.

84 Herbert Faulkner West, *The Mind on the Wing: A Book for Readers and Collectors* (New York, 1947), p. 130.

85 Petronius, *The Satyricon*, trans. J. P. Sullivan (London, 2011); see Helen Morales, 'Introduction', pp. xxiv–xxv.

86 Miller, *Black Spring*, pp. 44, 45.

87 Ibid., p. 91.

88 Ibid., pp. 12–13.

89 Raymond Queneau, 'Tropic of Cancer; Black Spring', *La Nouvelle Revue Française*, XXV (1 December 1936), p. 1084 (translation mine); on Miller and Queneau, see Michel Lecureur, *Raymond Queneau: Biographie* (Paris, 2002), pp. 201–3, 210, 219–20, 224, 294–5, 320, 338–40, 357, 362, 419.

90 James Gifford, ed., *The Henry Miller–Herbert Read Letters, 1935–1958* (Ann Arbor, MI, 2007), p. 85.

91 MacNiven, ed., *The Durrell–Miller Letters*, p. 16.

92 Alfred Perlès, *My Friend, Henry Miller* (London, 1955), pp. 156–9.

93 MacNiven, ed., *The Durrell–Miller Letters*, pp. 33–4.

94 Winslow, *Henry Miller: Full of Life*, p. 30.

95 Martin, *Always Merry and Bright*, p. 320.

96 MacNiven, ed., *The Durrell–Miller Letters*, pp. 16, 87.

97 Ibid., p. 49.

98 Dearborn, *The Happiest Man Alive*, p. 192; Ian S. MacNiven, *Lawrence Durrell: A Biography* (London, 1998), p. 166.

99 Perlès, *My Friend, Lawrence Durrell*, pp. 10, 11; MacNiven, ed., *The Durrell–Miller Letters*, p. x.

100 Ferguson, *Henry Miller: A Life*, p. 252.

101 MacNiven, ed., *The Durrell–Miller Letters*, p. 89.

102 *Henry Miller: A Personal Archive*, sale catalogue compiled by Roger Jackson and William E. Ashley (Ann Arbor, MI, 1994), p. 91: copy of a letter dated 15 December 1937 written by Miller to his father, Heinrich.

103 Martin, *Always Merry and Bright*, p. 316.

104 Dearborn, *The Happiest Man Alive*, p. 200; Jackson, *Ephemera*, p. 118.

105 Anaïs Nin, *The Diaries of Anaïs Nin*, vol. II: *1934–1939* (New York, 1967), pp. 320, 324–5, 333–4. On Esoteric Buddhism, see Henry Miller, *Farewell from France: A Letter to Huntington Cairns, April 30, 1939* (Ann Arbor, MI, 1995), n.p.; on Moricand, see Thomas Nesbit, *Henry Miller and Religion* (New York, 2007), pp. 31, 132.

106 Alfred Perlès, 'Henry Miller – Dead?', *London Magazine*, XXIX/7 (October 1980); Brassaï, *The Paris Years*, p. 23.

107 *The Letters of Samuel Beckett, 1929–1940*, ed. Martha Dow Fehsenfeld and Lois More Overbeck (Cambridge, 2009), p. 707.

108 *Henry Miller on Writing* (Norfolk, CT, 1964), p. 116.

109 Ibid., p. 117.

110 E. R. Curtius, *European Literature and the Latin Middle Ages* (Princeton, NJ, 1973), p. 105.

111 Helena Petrovna Blavatsky, *Isis Unveiled, Volume I: Science* (New York, 1892), p. x; Frank L. Kersnowski and Alice Hughes, eds, *Conversations with Henry Miller* (Jackson, MS, 1994), pp. 196–7.

112 Henry Miller, *The Books in my Life* (New York, 1969), p. 100; 'Positions of the Sun', *View*, VI (May 1946), p. 22.

113 Walter Schmiele, *Henry Miller* (Paris, 1969), p. 133.

114 Dearborn, *The Happiest Man Alive*, p. 201.

115 Gilles Deleuze and Félix Guattari, *Anti-Oedipus*, trans. Robert Hurley,
    Mark Seem and Helen R. Lane (New York, 2009), pp. 298–9; *Hamlet,
    Volume 1* (Santurce, Puerto Rico, 1939), pp. 125–9.

116 Henry Miller, *Frère Jacques: Lettres à Frédéric Jacques Temple* (Fontenay-
    le-Comte, 2012), p. 94; Indrek Manniste, 'Henry Miller's Inhuman
    Philosophy', *Nexus*, 9 (2012), p. 37.

117 *Hamlet, Volume 2* (New York, 1941), p. 449; David Stephen Calonne,
    'Henry Miller: Cosmologist', in *Henry Miller: A Book of Tributes,
    1931–1994*, ed. Craig Peter Standish (Orlando, FL, 1994).

118 David Stephen Calonne, 'Henry Miller and Tibet', *Stroker 68* (2000),
    pp. 8–19; MacNiven, ed., *The Durrell–Miller Letters*, p. 122.

119 West, *The Mind on the Wing*, p. 132.

120 Miller, *Tropic of Capricorn*, p. 343.

121 Ibid., pp. 340, 341.

122 H. Rider Haggard, *She*, ed. Patrick Brantlinger (London, 2001),
    pp. 146, 158, 159.

123 Brassaï, *Happy Rock*, p. 168; Nesbit, *Henry Miller and Religion*; *Tropic of
    Capricorn*, pp. 232, 234.

124 *Henry Miller on Writing*, p. 135; Henry Miller, *Big Sur and the Oranges of
    Hieronymus Bosch* (New York, 1957), pp. 126–9.

125 Gilbert Highet, 'Henry Miller's Stream of Self-Consciousness',
    Horizon, IV/2 (November 1961), pp. 104, 105.

126 Clifford Terry, 'Dirty Old Henry Miller at 86', *Chicago Tribune
    Magazine* (12 February 1978), p. 38; Pascal Vrebos, *444 Ocampo Drive*,
    ed. Karl Orend (Ann Arbor, MI, 2003), p. 152.

127 Winslow, *Henry Miller: Full of Life*, pp. 42–3; Miller, *The Cosmological
    Eye*, p. 3.

128 MacNiven, ed., *The Durrell–Miller Letters*, p. 101.

129 Frances Steloff, 'In Touch with Genius', *Journal of Modern Literature*,
    IV/4 (April 1975); Henry Miller, *Remember to Remember* (Norfolk, CT,
    1947), p. 295.

130 Henry Miller, 'Vive La France!', in *The Air-Conditioned Nightmare*
    (New York, 1970), pp. 70–75; Brassaï, *The Paris Years*, p. 220; *Happy
    Rock*, p. 7; Miller, *Letters to Anaïs Nin*, p. 191.

131 MacNiven, ed., *The Durrell–Miller Letters*, p. 113; Nesbit, *Henry Miller
    and Religion*, p. 30; Brassaï, *The Paris Years*, pp. 206–7.

132 MacNiven, ed., *The Durrell–Miller Letters*, p. 99.

133 Miller, *Letters to Anaïs Nin*, p. 206; Beatrice Commenge, *Henry Miller: Ange, Clown, Voyou* (Paris, 1991), p. 240; Brassaï, *The Paris Years*, p. 221; Brassaï, *Happy Rock*, p. 149; see also Edmund Keeley's superb *Inventing Paradise: The Greek Journey, 1937–47* (New York, 1999).

134 Martin, *Always Merry and Bright*, pp. 359, 360–61; Bertrand Mathieu, 'Henry Miller's *The Colossus of Maroussi*: Forty Years Later', *The Athenian*, vii/78 (April 1980), p. 23.

135 *Writers at Work: Fourth Series: The Paris Review Interviews* (New York, 1977), p. 165.

136 *George Seferis: Collected Poems*, trans. Edmund Keeley (Princeton, nj, 1969), p. 259; MacNiven, ed., *The Durrell–Miller Letters*, p. 118; Martin, *Always Merry and Bright*, p. 361; quoted in Roderick Beaton, *George Seferis: Waiting for the Angel, A Biography* (New Haven, ct, 2003), p. 176.

137 Miller, *Tropic of Capricorn*, p. 233.

138 Steloff, 'In Touch with Genius', p. 810.

5 The Exile Returns: Air-Conditioned Nightmare and Big Sur Paradise, 1940–51

1 'Interview with Henry Miller', *San Francisco Review of Books*, ii/10 (February 1977), p. 10; Miller, *Sunday After the War* (Norfolk, ct, 1944), 'Reunion in Brooklyn', p. 63ff.; Kathryn Winslow, *Henry Miller: Full of Life* (Los Angeles, 1986), p. 45.

2 Winslow, *Henry Miller: Full of Life*, p. 48; W. G. Rogers, *Wise Men Fish Here: The Story of Frances Steloff and the Gotham Book Mart* (New York, 1965), p. 126.

3 Ian S. MacNiven, ed., *The Durrell–Miller Letters, 1935–80* (New York, 1988), p. 456 (31 March 1972); Henry Miller, *Frère Jacques: Lettres à Frédéric Jacques Temple* (Fontenay-le-Comte, 2012), p. 84; Ian Gibson, *The Shameful Life of Salvador Dalí* (New York, 1998), p. 461; Anaïs Nin, *The Diaries of Anaïs Nin*, vol. iii: *1939–1944*, ed. Gunther Stuhlmann (New York, 1969), p. 47.

4 George Orwell, 'Inside the Whale', *A Collection of Essays* (New York, 1954), p. 256; Richard Seaver, *The Tender Hour of Twilight: Paris in the '50s, New York in the '60s: A Memoir of Publishing's Golden Age* (New York, 2012), p. 183.

5 Roger Jackson, *Henry Miller: His Life in Ephemera, 1914–1980* (Ann Arbor, MI, 2012), p. 146.

6 Robert Young, Jr, *From a Different Angle: A Personal Memoir of Henry Miller* (Ann Arbor, MI, 1997), p. 44; Henry Miller, *Farewell from France: A Letter to Huntington Cairns, April 30, 1939* (Ann Arbor, MI, 1995), n.p.

7 Henry Miller, *Letters to Anaïs Nin* (London, 1965), p. 261.

8 MacNiven, ed., *The Durrell–Miller Letters*, p. 146; Miller, 'Murder the Murderer' in *Remember to Remember* (Norfolk, CT, 1947), p. 127; Nin, *The Diaries of Anaïs Nin*, vol. III, p. 97; 'Henry Miller Letters to Swami Nikhilananda', facebook.com/pages/Ramakrishna Vivekananda Center of New York, Treasure #23.

9 Miller, *Letters to Anaïs Nin*, p. 264; *The Nightmare Notebook*, n.p.

10 Brassaï, *Henry Miller: Happy Rock* (Chicago, 2002), p. 98.

11 Miller, *Letters to Anaïs Nin*, pp. 288, 294.

12 Powell, Introduction, *The Intimate Henry Miller* (New York, 1959), p. vii; Frank L. Kersnowski and Alice Hughes, eds, *Conversations with Henry Miller* (Jackson, MS, 1994), p. 8; Powell, 'Remembering Henry Miller', in *Henry Miller: A Book of Tributes, 1931–1994*, ed. Craig Peter Standish (Orlando, FL, 1994), pp. 321, 324, 325.

13 Robert Young, Jr, 'Regarding Henry: Collecting Henry Miller', *Biblio*, II/1 (February 1997), p. 33.

14 Miller, The *Colossus of Maroussi* (San Francisco, 1941), pp. 112–13.

15 Miller, *Colossus*, pp. 159, 162.

16 Winslow, *Henry Miller: Full of Life*, p. 129; Branko Aleksic, 'The Unpublished Correspondence of Henry Miller and André Breton, the "Steady Rock", 1947–50', *Nexus*, 5 (2008), p. 152; André Breton, *La Clé des champs* (Paris, 1953), p. 125; Anna Balakian, *André Breton: Magus of Surrealism* (New York, 1971), p. 237.

17 Miller, *Frère Jacques*, p. 91; *Wisdom of the Heart*, pp. 32–3, 85.

18 MacNiven, ed., *The Durrell–Miller Letters*, p. 153.

19 *Writers Three: A Literary Exchange on the Works of Claude Houghton* (Ann Arbor, MI, 1995), p. 32; see 'In Memory: Letters of J. D. Salinger' (1967–75), at www.ramakrishna.org/activities/Salinger/Salinger.htm.

20 *Collector's Quest: The Correspondence of Henry Miller and J. Rives Childs, 1947–1965*, ed. Robert Clement Wood (Charlottesville, VA, 1968), p. 14; MacNiven, ed., *The Durrell–Miller Letters*, p. 230.

21 *Of, By and About Henry Miller* (New York, 1947), pp. 32, 33.

22 Miller, *Tropic of Capricorn*, p. 291.

23 Branko Aleksic, 'The Unpublished Correspondence of Henry Miller and André Breton', *Nexus*, 5 (2008), p. 170.

24 Jackson, *Ephemera*, p. 163; MacNiven, ed., *The Durrell–Miller Letters*, p. 162.

25 Beatrice Commenge, *Henry Miller: Ange, Clown, Voyou* (Paris, 1991), p. 273; Gilbert Neiman, 'No Rubbish, No Albatrosses', in *Henry Miller: A Book of Tributes, 1931–1994*, ed. Craig Peter Standish (Orlando, FL, 1994), p. 101.

26 Miller, *Letters to Anaïs Nin*, pp. 316–17; MacNiven, ed., *The Durrell–Miller Letters*, p. 157; Brassaï, *Happy Rock*, p. 150.

27 Brassaï, *Happy Rock*, p. 2.

28 MacNiven, ed., *The Durrell–Miller Letters*, p. 153; Anaïs Nin, *Mirages: The Unexpurgated Diary of Anais Nin, 1939–1947*, ed. Paul Herron (Athens, OH, 2013), pp. 116–18.

29 Winslow, *Henry Miller: Full of Life*, p. 92; Victoria Price, *Vincent Price: A Daughter's Biography* (New York, 1999), pp. 121–2, and Victoria Price, 'Henry Miller in Lotos Land: Paint as you Like, and Die Happy', 3 December 2009, at www.therumpus.net.

30 Jackson, *Ephemera*, p. 164.

31 MacNiven, ed., *The Durrell–Miller Letters*, p. 162.

32 Belmont, *Henry Miller in Conversation*, p. 70.

33 'Prince of Denmark', *New Republic*, CVIII (10 May 1942), p. 642.

34 Henry Miller, *Big Sur and the Oranges of Hieronymus Bosch* (Norfolk, CT, 1957); Jackson, *Ephemera*, p. 179.

35 Winslow, *Henry Miller: Full of Life*, p. 79.

36 J. R. Eyerman, 'Rugged, Romantic, World Apart', *Life* (6 July 1959), p. 57.

37 Nancy Hopkins, *These Are My Flowers: Raising a Family on the Big Sur Coast* (n.p., 2007), pp. 11, 12.

38 *Letters of Henry Miller and Wallace Fowlie*, p. 46; Robert Fink, Preface to his 'A Short Profile of Henry Miller', unpub. MS, Southern Illinois University Special Collections Research Center, pp. i–ii.

39 Brassaï, *Happy Rock*, p. 62.

40 Rogers, *Wise Men Fish Here*, p. 124.

41 *Letters of Henry Miller and Wallace Fowlie, 1943–1972* (New York, 1975), pp. 58, 68; *Henry Miller and James Laughlin: Selected Letters*, ed. George

Wickes (New York, 1996), p. 42; Miriam Cendrars, ed., *Blaise Cendrars–Henry Miller: Correspondence, 1934–1979* (Paris, 1995), p. 371.

42 Mary Dearborn, *The Happiest Man Alive: A Biography of Henry Miller* (New York, 1991), p. 230; Jackson, *Ephemera*, p. 188.

43 James Schevill, *Where to Go, What to Do, When You Are Bern Porter: A Personal Biography* (Gardiner, ME, 1992), p. 81; Linda Hamalian, *Kenneth Rexroth* (New York, 1992), p. 152; Lee Bartlett, *William Everson: The Life of Brother Antoninus* (New York, 1998), p. 97.

44 E. R. Hutchinson *Tropic of Cancer on Trial* (New York, 1968), p. 8.

45 Herbert Read, 'Views and Reviews: Henry Miller', *New English Weekly*, XXVIII (28 December 1944); James Gifford, ed., *The Henry Miller–Herbert Read Letters, 1935–1958* (Ann Arbor, MI, 2007), p. 145.

46 Jackson, *Ephemera*, p. 198.

47 *Letters of Henry Miller and Wallace Fowlie*, p. 154.

48 Ibid., p. 8; Jay Martin, *Always Merry and Bright: The Life of Henry Miller* (Santa Barbara, CA, 1978), pp. 412–13.

49 Wallace Fowlie, *Memory: A Fourth Memoir* (Durham, NC, 1990), pp. 62, 104.

50 *Letters of Henry Miller and Wallace Fowlie*, pp. 7, 8; Wallace Fowlie, *A Journal of Rehearsals* (Durham, NC, 1997), pp. 118, 119.

51 Jackson, *Ephemera*, pp. 198–205.

52 Ibid., p. 198; *Letters of Henry Miller and Wallace Fowlie*, p. 74; *Henry Miller: The Paintings, A Centennial Retrospective* (Carmel, CA, 1991), p. 21.

53 Linda Hamalian, *Kenneth Rexroth* (New York, 1992), p. 134; Martin, *Always Merry and Bright*, p. 414.

54 *Letters of Henry Miller and Wallace Fowlie*, p. 85.

55 Ibid., p. 87.

56 MacNiven, ed., *The Durrell–Miller Letters*, pp. 189, 182.

57 Ibid., p. 190; *Letters of Henry Miller and Wallace Fowlie*, pp. 94–5.

58 Judson Crews, *The Brave Wild Coast: A Year with Henry Miller* (Los Angeles, 1997) p. 76.

59 'Swami Vivekananda was the most powerful influence on me. He was a flaming sword.' T. V. Kunhi Krishnan, 'Miller: Karmayogi or sexualist?', *Hindustani Times* (23 June 1980).

60 John Wain, 'The Great Burroughs Affair', *New Republic* (1 December 1962), p. 22.

61 Henry Miller, *My Bike and Other Friends* (Santa Barbara, CA, 1978), p. 19; MacNiven, ed., *The Durrell–Miller Letters*, p. 192.

62 *Letters of Henry Miller and Wallace Fowlie*, p. 105.

63 Fred Kaplan, *Gore Vidal: A Biography* (New York, 2000), p. 219; Winslow, *Henry Miller: Full of Life*, pp. 144–5; Henry Miller, *Stand Still Like the Hummingbird* (Norfolk, CT, 1962), pp. 111–18.

64 Haniel Long, 'Introduction', in Long, *The Marvelous Adventure of Cabeza de Vaca* (Clearlake, CA, 1992), p. 14.

65 Dearborn, *The Happiest Man Alive*, p. 241.

66 'French Assail U.S. Books: Moral League Sues Publisher of Henry Miller Novels', *New York Times* (17 November 1946).

67 Michel Lecureur, *Raymond Queneau: Biographie* (Paris, 2002), pp. 294–5; Oliver Todd, *Albert Camus: A Life* (New York, 1998), p. 286.

68 Stuart Kendall, *Georges Bataille* (London, 2007), pp. 176–7; Georges Bataille, *Oeuvres Complètes, XI: Articles 1, 1944–1949* (Paris, 1988), pp. 41–55, 107–12.

69 Mildred Brady, 'The New Cult of Sex and Anarchy', *Harpers*, CXCIV (April 1947), pp. 312–22.

70 Personal communication from Joshua Abbuhs and see joshuablubuhs.com; Miller, *Big Sur and the Oranges of Hieronymus Bosch*, p. 167. On Fort, see Jeffrey Kripal, *Authors of the Impossible: The Paranormal and the Sacred* (Chicago, 2012), pp. 93–141.

71 *Circle 7–8* (1946), reprinted in Reginald Moore, ed., *Modern Reading 14* (London, 1947), p. 47.

72 Paul Feyerabend, *The Tyranny of Science* (Cambridge, 2012). Miller, 'Preface', in Alfred Perlès, *My Friend, Henry Miller* (New York, 1962), p. vi.

73 MacNiven, ed., *The Durrell–Miller Letters*, p. 201.

74 Winslow, *Henry Miller: Full of Life*, p. 170.

75 Robert Fink, 'A Short Profile of Henry Miller', unpub. MS, Southern Illinois University Special Collections Research Center, pp. 5, 6, 7.

76 Michael Shelden, *Friends of Promise: Cyril Connolly and the World of Horizon* (London, 1989) pp. 171, 172; MacNiven, ed., *The Durrell–Miller Letters*, p. 203.

77 Winslow, *Henry Miller: Full of Life*, p. x.

78 *Henry Miller: The Paintings, A Centennial Retrospective* (Carmel, CA, 1991), p. 22; On Miller as painter, see Donald Friedman, *The Writer's Brush: Paintings, Drawings, and Sculpture by Writers* (Minneapolis, MN, 2007), pp. 268–9.

79 Dearborn, *The Happiest Man Alive*, p. 246; on Delaney and Miller, see David Leeming, *Amazing Grace: A Life of Beauford Delaney* (New York, 1998).

80 Dearborn, *The Happiest Man Alive*, pp. 242, 244; Martin, *Always Merry and Bright*, p. 423.

81 Anaïs Nin, *The Diaries of Anaïs Nin*, vol. IV: *1944–1947* (New York, 1971), p. 219.

82 Cendrars, ed., *Blaise Cendrars–Henry Miller*, pp. 100, 380; Wallace Fowlie, *Aubade: A Teacher's Notebook* (Durham, NC, 1983), p. 193; Mark Polizzotti, *Revolution of the Mind: The Life of André Breton* (New York, 1997), p. 493; Branko Aleksic, 'Unpublished Correspondence', *Nexus*, 5, pp. 152, 153, 155.

83 *Letters of Henry Miller and Wallace Fowlie*, p. 44; MacNiven, ed., *The Durrell–Miller Letters*, p. 214; Nin, *The Diaries of Anaïs Nin*, vol. IV, p. 61.

84 Winslow, *Henry Miller: Full of Life*, p. 172.

85 *Letters of Henry Miller and Wallace Fowlie*, p. 54.

86 Ibid., pp. 118, 82. Also see Bertrand Mathieu, *Orpheus in Brooklyn: Orphism, Rimbaud, and Henry Miller* (The Hague, 1976).

87 George Wickes, ed., *Henry Miller and James Laughlin: Selected Letters* (New York, 1996), pp. 49, 72; Brassaï, *Happy Rock*, p. 102; Childs, *Collector's Quest*, p. 9.

88 Ralph Freedman, *Hermann Hesse, Pilgrim of Crisis: A Biography* (New York, 1997), p. 9; George Wickes, 'Introduction', Wickes, ed., *Henry Miller and James Laughlin: Selected Letters*, p. xix.

89 *Lawrence Durrell and Henry Miller: A Private Correspondence*, ed. George Wickes (New York, 1963), p. 252.

90 *The Henry Miller Reader*, ed. Lawrence Durrell (New York, 1969), p. 388; F. J. Temple, *Henry Miller* (Paris, 1977), p. 114.

91 *Henry Miller: The Paintings, A Centennial Retrospective*, p. 46.

92 Dearborn, *The Happiest Man Alive*, p. 242; Wickes, *Laurence Durrell and Henry Miller*, p. 228.

93 Kevin Starr, *Coast of Dreams* (New York, 2006), p. 8

94 Henry Miller, *Lettres à Maurice Nadeau, 1947–1978*, ed. Sophie Bogaert (Paris, 2012), p. 85.

95 Ranganath Nandyal, Henry Miller in the Light of Eastern Thought (New Delhi, 1991), p. 54 ff; *Henry Miller: Years of Trial and Triumph, 1962–1964: The Correspondence of Henry Miller and Elmer Gertz*, ed. Elmer Gertz and Felice Flannery Lewis (Carbondale, IL, 1978), p. 23; Miller, 'Signs of Love', *Playboy* (February 1972), p. 107.

96 MacNiven, ed., *The Durrell–Miller Letters*, pp. 232–3.

97 *People* magazine (August 1978), p. 62; *Saturday Review* (5 May 1956); Jackson, *Ephemera*, p. 364.

98 Lawrence Durrell, 'Studies in Genius: Henry Miller', *Horizon* (July 1949), p. 45.

99 Miller, *The Books in My Life*, p. 37; also see 'Is Fiction?', *Occident* (Spring, 1950), p. 7: 'The most fictive of all, possibly, are what are called autobiographies, that is, those which boast of being truthful accounts.'

100 Dearborn, *The Happiest Man Alive*, p. 252; MacNiven, ed., *The Durrell–Miller Letters*, pp. 234, 246.

101 Winslow, *Henry Miller: Full of Life*, p. 253.

102 Henry Miller and John Cowper Powys, *Correspondance Privée* (Paris, 1944), pp. 30, 41.

103 Childs, *Collector's Quest*, p. 37.

104 *Letters of Henry Miller and Wallace Fowlie*, p. 135.

105 Winslow, *Henry Miller: Full of Life*, p. 259; Paul Ferris, ed., *The Collected Letters of Dylan Thomas* (London, 2000), p. 843.

106 Winslow, *Henry Miller: Full of Life*, p. 258; Jean-Charles De Fontbrune, *Henry Miller and Nostradamus: Entretiens sur la fin d'un monde* (Monaco, 1994), p. 59.

107 Edmond Buchet, *Les Auteurs dans ma vie* (Paris, 1969), p. 214.

108 Martin, *Always Merry and Bright*, p. 436; Winslow, *Henry Miller: Full of Life*, p. 270.

109 Fink, *A Short Profile of Henry Miller*, p. 12; Jackson, *Ephemera*, p. 318.

110 *Henry Miller: Years of Trial and Triumph, 1962–1964: The Correspondence*, p. 2; Brassaï, *Happy Rock*, p. 83.

111 Stefan Zweig, *Balzac* (New York, 1946), p. 167.

6 Magus on the Mountain, Tropics Triumphant, 1952–62

1 Kathryn Winslow, *Henry Miller: Full of Life* (Los Angeles, 1986), p. 271; Mary Dearborn, *The Happiest Man Alive: A Biography of Henry Miller* (New York, 1991), p. 257.

2 *Henry Miller, Lettres à Maurice Nadeau, 1947–1978*, ed. Sophie Bogaert (Paris, 2012), pp. 150, 147; Ian S. MacNiven, ed., *The Durrell–Miller Letters, 1935–80* (New York, 1988), p. 261.

3 MacNiven, ed., *The Durrell–Miller Letters*, pp. 262–3; Dearborn, *The Happiest Man Alive*, p. 257.

4 Leslie A. Fiedler, review of *Books in My Life* in *Yale Review*, XLII (March 1953), pp. 455–60.

5 *Lawrence Durrell and Henry Miller: A Private Correspondence*, ed. George Wickes (New York, 1964), pp. 326–7; on 'exaltation', see Henry Miller, *The Books in My Life* (New York, 1969), p. 63. About 25 years later, Miller's praise softened: 'Krishnamurti has one grave fault, I discover – no sense of humor.' See *Dear, Dear Brenda: The Love Letters of Henry Miller to Brenda Venus*, ed. Gerald Seth Sindell (New York, 1986), p. 104.

6 Miller, *The Books in My Life*, p. 52. Also see Holly Hofmann, 'Frederick Carter's Apocalyptic Dragon and D. H. Lawrence's Mystic Heritage to the Villa Seurat', 17 April 1999, www.angelfire.com/pa/Anaïsaigner/Dragon.htm, accessed 20 March 2014.

7 Brassaï, *Henry Miller: Happy Rock* (Chicago, 2002), p. 146; *The Books in My Life*, p. 96; Yasunori Honda, *In Quest of Draco and the Ecliptic: Henry Miller's Interspatial Literature* (Dallas, PA, 2003), p. 15.

8 Frank L. Kersnowski and Alice Hughes, eds, *Conversations with Henry Miller* (Jackson, MS, 1994), p. 225.

9 Brassaï, *Happy Rock*, p. 5.

10 Maurice Nadeau, *Une Vie en littérature* (Brussels, 2002), p. 64.

11 Edmond Buchet, *Les Auteurs dans ma vie* (Paris, 1969), pp. 213–14 (translation mine).

12 Henry Miller, *Frère Jacques: Lettres à Frédéric Jacques Temple, 1948–1980* (Fontenay-le-Comte, 2012), p. 18; *Collector's Quest: The Correspondence of Henry Miller and J. Rives Childs, 1947–1965* (Charlottesville, VA, 1968), p. 126; *The Durrell-Miller Letters, 1935–80*, ed. Ian S. MacNiven (New York, 1988), p. 267.

13 Buchet, *Les Auteurs dans ma vie*, p. 223.

14 Miller, *Frère Jacques*, p. 21; F. J. Temple, 'L'Oncle d'Amerique',
    Syntheses, 249/50 (February–March 1967), p. 33 (translation mine);
    my translation from Frédéric-Jacques Temple, 'Miller Chez Nous',
    La Tour de Feu: Henry Miller ou les mauvaises frequentations, 47
    (Autumn 1955) p. 52 (12 May 1953).

15 Miller, *Frère Jacques*, p. 21.

16 Jean-Charles de Fontbrune, *Henry Miller et Nostradamus* (Monaco,
    1994), p. 17; Stephane Gerson, *Nostradamus* (New York, 2012),
    pp. 249–52, 254, 257; Henry Miller, 'A Few Chaotic Recollections',
    in *From Your Capricorn Friend: Henry Miller and the 'Stroker', 1978–1980*
    (New York, 1984), pp. 36–7.

17 Dearborn, *The Happiest Man Alive*, p. 259; *Lawrence Durrell and Henry
    Miller: A Private Correspondence*, ed. George Wickes (New York, 1963),
    p. 271.

18 Dearborn, *The Happiest Man Alive*, pp. 260–61.

19 *These Are My Flowers: Raising a Family on the Big Sur Coast,
    Letters of Nancy Hopkins*, ed. Heidi Hopkins (Big Sur, CA, 2007),
    pp. 56, 70.

20 *Lawrence Durrell and Henry Miller*, p. 277.

21 James Hoopes, *Van Wyck Brooks* (Amherst, MA, 1977), pp. 284–5.

22 James Knowlson, *Damned to Fame: The Life of Samuel Beckett*
    (New York, 1997), p. 357.

23 Henry Miller, *Plexus* (New York, 1965), p. 631.

24 Ibid., pp. 625, 628.

25 Miller, *Lettres à Maurice Nadeau*, p. 211; Martin, *Always Merry and
    Bright*, p. 442.

26 Allen Ginsberg, *Howl*, ed. Barry Miles (New York, 1995), p. 151; *Jack
    Kerouac and Allen Ginsberg: The Letters*, ed. Bill Morgan and David
    Stanford (New York, 2010), p. 140; for Miller's influence on Ginsberg,
    see Bill Morgan, *I Celebrate Myself*, pp. 218, 225; 'The Struggle Against
    Censorship', *Burroughs Live*, pp. 330–43.

27 Jack Kerouac, *Selected Letters* (New York, 1996), p. 563.

28 Michael Duncan and Kristine McKenna, *Semina Culture: Wallace
    Berman and His Circle* (New York, 2005), p. 327; Ferguson, p. 326;
    William Hjortsberg, *Jubilee Hitchhiker: The Life and Times of Richard
    Brautigan* (Berkeley, CA, 2012), p. 186.

29 Robert Fink, 'A Short Profile of Henry Miller', unpub. MS, Southern Illinois University Special Collections Research Center, p. 23; Robert Ferguson, *Henry Miller: A Life* (New York, 1991), p. 325.

30 Buchet, *Les Auteurs dans ma vie*, p. 213.

31 *Letters of Henry Miller and Wallace Fowlie, 1943–1972* (New York, 1975), p. 148.

32 Miller, *Lettres à Maurice Nadeau*, p. 211.

33 Pierre Assouline, *Simenon: A Biography* (New York, 1997), p. 289.

34 Henry Miller, Joseph Delteil, *Correspondence Privée, 1935–1978*, ed. F. J. Temple (Paris, 1980), p. 77; 'A Day with Henry Miller' in the *Big Sur/Monterey News* (1955), p. 4.

35 Bob Nash, *On My Way* (Carmel, CA, 1996), p. 37; Fink, 'A Short Profile of Henry Miller', p. 33.

36 Miller, *Lettres à Maurice Nadeau*, p. 237.

37 Dearborn, *The Happiest Man Alive*, pp. 265, 266; *Henry Miller: His World of Urania*, p. 31; Anaïs Nin, *The Diaries of Anaïs Nin*, vol. VI: *1955–1966*, ed. Gunther Stuhlmann (New York, 1977), p. 148.

38 Dearborn, *The Happiest Man Alive*, p. 267.

39 Nin, *The Diaries of Anaïs Nin*, vol. VI, p. 314; Dearborn, *The Happiest Man Alive*, p. 267; Jong, *The Devil at Large*, pp. 178–9.

40 Fink, 'A Short Profile of Henry Miller', pp. 73, 74; MacNiven, ed., *The Durrell–Miller Letters*, p. 299.

41 MacNiven, ed., *The Durrell–Miller Letters*, p. 284 (13 February 1957).

42 Childs, *Collector's Quest*, pp. 102, 103.

43 Ibid., pp. 104, 106; MacNiven, ed., *The Durrell–Miller Letters*, p. 292; Katrin Burtschell, 'Anaïs Nin, Henry Miller and Japan: An Endless Fascination', *A Café in Space: The Anaïs Nin Literary Journal*, 3 (2005), pp. 40–63.

44 Henry Miller, *Big Sur and the Oranges of Hieronymus Bosch*, p. 22, quoting p. 104 of Fraenger. For reviews, see Thomas Parkinson, 'The Hilarity of Henry Miller', *The Listener* (19 June 1958), p. 1021; Wallace Fowlie, 'Two American Autobiographies', *Accent*, XVII (Summer 1957), pp. 188–92.

45 Miller, *Big Sur*, p. 23.

46 Lewis Hyde, *The Gift: How the Creative Spirit Transforms the World* (Edinburgh, 1983), p. xiv.

47 On Miller and Esalen, see Jeffrey J. Kripal, *Esalen: America and the Religion of No Religion* (Chicago, 2007), pp. 27, 34, 36–40, 42–3.

48 Miller, *Big Sur*, p. 76.
49 Miller, *The Books in My Life*, p. 16; Miller, Delteil, *Correspondence Privée*, p. 74 (translation mine); Miller, *Lettres à Maurice Nadeau*, pp. 82–3.
50 C. G. Jung, *Flying Saucers: A Modern Myth of Things Seen in the Skies* (Princeton, NJ, 1978), p. 5; Gerhard Wehr, *Jung: A Biography* (Boston, MA, and London, 2001), p. 411.
51 Lawrence Durrell, ed., *The Henry Miller Reader*, p. 371; Charles Rembar, *The End of Obscenity* (New York, 1968), p. 338.
52 Roger Jackson, *Henry Miller: His Life in Ephemera, 1914–1980* (Ann Arbor, MI, 2012), p. 424; the second, longer, letter was published as 'Defense of the Freedom to Read' in the July 1959 *Two Cities*, and then in the *Evergreen Review* (November, 1959).
53 *Henry Miller on Writing*, pp. 190, 195.
54 Jackson, *Ephemera*, pp. 377–9.
55 *Letters of Flannery O'Connor: The Habit of Being*, ed. Sally Fitzgerald (New York, 1980), p. 302.
56 *Lawrence Durrell and Henry Miller*, p. 387.
57 Hopkins, *These Are My Flowers*, p. 128.
58 MacNiven, ed., *The Durrell–Miller Letters*, p. 335 (11 November 1958).
59 Ibid., p. 315 (2 April 1958).
60 Charles Williams, *Arthurian Torso: Containing the Posthumous Fragment of The Figure of Arthur and a Commentary on the Arthurian Poems of Charles Williams by C. S. Lewis* (London, 1952), p. 45.
61 George Steiner, 'Life-Size', *New Yorker* (2 May 1988), pp. 118, 116–19.
62 See David Stephen Calonne, 'Henry Miller: Cosmologist', p. 581.
63 'The Immortal Bard', *A Review of English Literature*, IV (January 1963), p. 24.
64 *Art and Outrage: A Correspondence about Henry Miller between Lawrence Durrell and Alfred Perlès* (New York, 1961), p. 36.
65 Jay Martin, *Always Merry and Bright: The Life of Henry Miller* (Santa Barbara, CA, 1978), p. 447.
66 Miller, *Frère Jacques*, p. 47; on Rosset, see Loren Glass, *Counterculture Colophon: Grove Press, the Evergreen Review and the Incorporation of the Avant Garde* (Stanford, CA, 2013).
67 *Henry Miller Literary Society Newsletter*, 2 (November 1959): Buchet, *Les Auteurs dans ma vie*, p. 259; MacNiven, ed., *The Durrell–Miller Letters*, p. 343; Brassaï, *Happy Rock*, p. 22.

68 Miller, *Frère Jacques*, p. 47; Alister Kershaw and F. J. Temple, eds, *Richard Aldington: An Intimate Portrait* (Carbondale and Edwardsville, IL, 1965), p. 78; letter (29 September 1967) to Rowohlt written from Paris, in *Henry Miller: Le Magazine*, 10 (April 1995).

69 Dearborn, *The Happiest Man Alive*, p. 272; Martin, *Always Merry and Bright*, p. 451; MacNiven, ed., *The Durrell–Miller Letters*, pp. 348, 349.

70 MacNiven, ed., *The Durrell–Miller Letters*, p. 357.

71 'Joseph Delteil and Francois D'Assise', *Two Cities* (15 May 1960), p. 77.

72 *Two Cities*, V (15 December 1959), pp. 25–44, later reprinted in *In Defense of Ignorance*; Italo Calvino, 'My City is New York', in *Hermit in Paris: Autobiographical Writings*, trans. Martin McLaughlin (London, 2003), p. 237.

73 Miller, 'Europe Revisited: Special Letter to the HMLS', *Henry Miller Literary Society Newsletter*, 4 (August 1960), p. 1.

74 Ibid. Al Goldstein, 'Henry Miller, A *Screw* Interview: The Sultan of Twat', *Screw*, 62 (11 May 1970), p. 5.

75 Jackson, *Ephemera*, p. 439.

76 Brassaï, 18 May 1960, *Conversations with Picasso*, p. 320; Brassaï, *Happy Rock*, pp. 85, 134–5.

77 Miller, 'Europe Revisited', pp. 1, 2.

78 Gertz, *Henry Miller: Years of Trial*, p. 250.

79 MacNiven, ed., *The Durrell–Miller Letters*, p. 273.

80 Maria Bloshteyn points out that 'Berdiaev would be the first Russian intellectual to pay serious attention to Miller's own work'. See Bloshteyn, *The Making of a Counter-Culture Icon: Henry Miller's Dostoevsky* (Toronto, 2007), p. 58.

81 *Lettres à Maurice Nadeau*, p. 189; Vincent Birge, 'Travels With Henry: Searching for Shangri-La', in *Henry Miller: A Book of Tributes, 1931–1994*, ed. Craig Peter Standish (Orlando, FL, 1994), p. 522; Buchet, *Les Auteurs dans ma vie*, p. 275.

82 Assouline, *Simenon: A Biography*, p. 331.

83 Georges Simenon, *When I Was Old* (New York, 1971), p. 127.

84 Birge, 'Travels With Henry', p. 522.

85 MacNiven, ed., *The Durrell–Miller Letters*, pp. 380–81.

86 Brassaï, *Happy Rock*, p. 102; H. M. Ledig-Rowohlt, 'Vorwort', *Henry Miller: A Book of Tributes, 1931–1994*, ed. Craig Peter Standish (Orlando, FL, 1994), pp. 527, 528.

87 Jackson, *Ephemera*, p. 444.

88 Elie Faure, *La Danse sur le feu et l'eau* (Paris, 1920), p. 113.

89 *Rhinozeros*, III (1961), p. 3.

90 Miller, letter to Rosset, 14 July 1960, quoted in Martin, *Always Merry and Bright*, p. 463; E. R. Hutchinson, *Tropic of Cancer on Trial*, p. 50; Dearborn, *The Happiest Man Alive*, p. 277. On the *Tropic of Cancer* trial and obscenity, see Felice Flanery Lewis, *Literature, Obscenity, and Law* (Carbondale, IL, 1976), pp. 208–13.

91 Birge, 'Travels With Henry', p. 522; Miller, *Frère Jacques*, pp. 60, 62.

92 Birge, 'Travels With Henry', p. 523; MacNiven, ed., *The Durrell–Miller Letters*, p. 386.

93 Brassaï, *Happy Rock*, p. 104; Miller, *Frère Jacques*, p. 96; Dearborn, *The Happiest Man Alive*, p. 280.

94 Hutchinson, *Tropic of Cancer on Trial*, p. 53; Martin, *Always Merry and Bright*, p. 464.

95 See 'Renate and the Astrologer', in Henry Miller, *Joey: A Loving Portrait of Alfred Perlès Together with Some Bizarre Episodes Relating to the Other Sex* – vol. III: *A Book of Friends* (Santa Barbara, CA, 1979), pp. 117–21; on Vincent Birge, *My Bike and Other Friends: Volume II, Book of Friends*, pp. 33–40.

96 Dearborn, *The Happiest Man Alive*, p. 280; Ferguson, *Henry Miller: A Life*, p. 351; Martin, *Always Merry and Bright*, pp. 466, 467; MacNiven, ed., *The Durrell–Miller Letters*, p. 387.

97 Hutchinson, *Tropic of Cancer on Trial*, pp. 1, 2; Arthur Marwick, *The Sixties* (Oxford, 1998), p. 147; Winslow, *Henry Miller: Full of Life*, p. 308.

98 Winslow, *Henry Miller: Full of Life*, pp. 310, 312, 313.

99 Saskia Hamilton, ed., *The Letters of Robert Lowell* (New York, 2005), p. 408.

100 George Wickes, ed., *Henry Miller and James Laughlin: Selected Letters* (New York, 1996), pp. 197, 198; Winslow, *Henry Miller: Full of Life*, p. 316.

101 Jackson, *Ephemera*, p. 482.

102 Winslow, *Henry Miller: Full of Life*, pp. 316–17.

103 Buchet, *Les Auteurs dans ma vie*, p. 288; Miller, *Frère Jacques*, p. 67.

104 Jackson, *Ephemera*, p. 496; Gertz, ed., *Henry Miller: Years of Trial*, p. 83.

105 Dearborn, *The Happiest Man Alive*, p. 282.

106 John Calder, 'Introduction', *A Henry Miller Reader* (London, 1985), p. 18.

107 Victor Bockris, *With William Burroughs: A Report from the Bunker* (New York, 1996), p. 127; Anthony Blond, 'Unshockable Edinburgh', *Books and Bookmen* (October 1962), p. 27.

108 Hildegard Knef, *The Gift Horse* (New York, 1971), pp. 373–4; *L'Herne 3: Louis-Ferdinand Céline*; Miller letter dated 1 October 1962, 'Percha-Bei-Starnberg (obb.) Allemagne'; reprinted in original English as 'A Letter on Céline', *Paris Review*, VIII/31 (Winter–Spring 1964), p. 137.

109 Brassaï, *Happy Rock*, pp. 105, 106.

110 Gertz, ed., *Henry Miller: Years of Trial*, pp. 119, 120.

111 Rembar, *The End of Obscenity*, pp. 209, 210, 215.

112 Winslow, *Henry Miller: Full of Life*, pp. 324, 325.

113 Gertz, ed., *Henry Miller: Years of Trial*, pp. 140, 142.

114 Jackson, *Ephemera*, p. 504; Gertz, ed., *Henry Miller: Years of Trial*, pp. 58–9.

115 Nin, *The Diaries of Anaïs Nin*, vol. VI, pp. 307, 308.

116 Gertz, ed., *Henry Miller: Years of Trial*, p. 133.

117 Ibid., pp. 139, 145.

7 Fame and Insomnia in Pacific Palisades, 1963–71

1 Ian S. MacNiven, ed., *The Durrell–Miller Letters, 1935–80* (New York, 1988), p. 392; Frank L. Kersnowski and Alice Hughes, eds, *Conversations with Henry Miller* (Jackson, MS, 1994), p. 66; Kathryn Winslow, *Henry Miller: Full of Life* (Los Angeles, 1986), p. 322; Frawley Becker, *And the Stars Spoke Back* (Lanham, MD, 1994), p. 214; *Dear, Dear Brenda: The Love Letters of Henry Miller to Brenda Venus* (New York, 1986), pp. 31, 32; Noel Young, 'Remembering Henry Miller', n.p.

2 Susan Kidder Herr, 'Henry and Me', *Nexus*, 3 (2006), p. 119; Bern Porter, interviewed by Phil Nurenberg, *Vagabond White Paper #5* (Ellensburg, VA, 1983), n.p.

3 Anthony Heilbut, *Exiled in Paradise: German Refugee Artists and Intellectuals in America from the 1930s to the Present* (Berkeley, CA, 1997).

4 Brassaï, *Henry Miller: Happy Rock* (Chicago, 2002), pp. 160, 167;
    Conversations with Belmont, p. 64; Harry Kiakis, 'A Birthday Party for
    Henry', *Nexus*, 7 (2010), p. 99; Becker, *And the Stars Spoke Back*, p. 214.

5 MacNiven, ed., *The Durrell–Miller Letters*, p. xiv.

6 *Henry Miller: Years of Trial and Triumph, The Correspondence of Henry
    Miller and Elmer Gertz*, ed. Elmer Gertz and Felice Flanery Lewis
    (Carbondale, IL, 1978), p. 149.

7 'Introduction' to Henry Miller, *Just Wild About Harry* (Norfolk, CT,
    1963), p. 10.

8 Winslow, *Henry Miller: Full of Life*, p. 323.

9 MacNiven, ed., *The Durrell–Miller Letters*, p. 398; Roger Jackson, *Henry
    Miller: His Life in Ephemera, 1914–1980* (Ann Arbor, MI, 2012), p. 545.

10 *Conversations with Henry Miller*, ed. Frank L. Kersnowski and Alice
    Hughes (Jackson, MS, 1994), p. 66.

11 *Henry Miller: Years of Trial*, p. 249; *Lawrence Durrell and Henry Miller:
    A Private Correspondence* (New York, 1964), p. 397.

12 *Conversations with Henry Miller*, p. 194.

13 Bob Dylan, *Tarantula* (New York, 1971), pp. 130–31; *Bob Dylan,
    The Essential Interviews*, ed. Jonathan Cott (New York, 2006), p. 214.

14 Cott, *Bob Dylan, The Essential Interviews*, p. 224; *Sexus*, pp. 24–25;
    Joyce Howard, ed., *Letters by Henry Miller to Hoki Tokuda Miller*
    (New York, 1986), p. 112.

15 *Henry Miller: Years of Trial*, pp. 213, 231; Henry Miller, *Nexus*
    (New York, 1965), p. 307.

16 Madeleine Chapsal, *Quinze Ecrivains: entretiens* (Paris, 1963), p. 112
    (translation mine).

17 *Henry Miller: Years of Trial*, pp. 222, 257, 284.

18 Ibid., pp. 263, 270.

19 Ibid., p. 275.

20 Florian Steiner, *More! 1994–1996, The Companion Volume to Henry
    Miller: A Book of Tributes*, ed. Craig Peter Standish (Orlando, FL, 1997),
    p. 46; Jackson, *Ephemera*, pp. 526, 654, 734; Miller, *From Your
    Capricorn Friend*, pp. 26, 46.

21 *Henry Miller: Years of Trial*, pp. 316, 318; Jackson, *Ephemera*, p. 555.

22 *Collector's Quest: The Correspondence of Henry Miller and J. Rives Childs,
    1947–1965*, ed. Richard Clement Wood (Charlottesville, VA, 1968),
    p. 161; Gertz, ed., *Henry Miller: Years of Trial*, p. 293; *People Magazine*

(21 August 1978), interview with Patricia Burstein, p. 62; Brassaï, *Happy Rock*, pp. 161, 140.

23 Buchet, *Les Auteurs de Ma Vie*, p. 337.

24 Gertz, ed., *Henry Miller: Years of Trial*, pp. 234, 313.

25 Gail Gerber, *Trippin' with Terry Southern* (Jefferson, NC, 2009), pp. 5, 20; Brassaï, *Happy Rock*, p. 161; *Dear, Dear Brenda*, p. 91; *Letters . . . to Hoki Tokuda Miller*, p. 54.

26 Gertz, ed., *Henry Miller: Years of Trial*, p. 317.

27 *Letters of Henry Miller and Wallace Fowlie* (New York, 1965), p. 152.

28 William Webb, *Henry and Friends: The California Years, 1946–1977* (Santa Barbara, CA, 1991), p. 60; Henry Miller, *Flashback*, pp. 22–3.

29 MacNiven, ed., *The Durrell–Miller Letters*, p. 404.

30 Miller, 'Revolt in the Desert', *Cavalier*, XV (January 1965), pp. 30, 31, 32.

31 Jackson, *Ephemera*, p. 558.

32 *Letters . . . to Hoki Tokuda Miller*, pp. 3, 10; Webb, *Henry and Friends*, p. 86.

33 *Letters . . . to Hoki Tokudo Miller*, p. 23.

34 Ibid., pp. 25, 26, 27, 29, 32, 33, 47; on graphology see Stephen J. Gertz, 'The Hands (and Notebooks and Little Black Book) of Henry Miller', 10 March 2010, at www.booktryst.com.

35 On Miller and Bukowski, see David Stephen Calonne, *Charles Bukowski* (London, 2012), pp. 76–7, 193–4, n.90.

36 George Steiner, 'Books: Mondo Freudo', *New Yorker* (21 January 1967).

37 Jackson, *Ephemera*, p. 583.

38 Ibid., p. 585; *New York Times* (8 September 1967).

39 Jackson, *Ephemera*, p. 584; Hoki Tokuda, *Mrs Henry Miller's Nightmare* (Ann Arbor, MI, 1995), pp. 21, 33; Mary Dearborn, *The Happiest Man Alive: A Biography of Henry Miller* (New York, 1991), p. 294.

40 'Odd Couple', *New Yorker* (28 June 1993), p. 33; *Henry Miller and Elmer Gertz: Selected Letters 1964–1975* (Ann Arbor, MI, 1998), pp. 68, 69.

41 MacNiven, ed., *The Durrell–Miller Letters*, p. 421; *Letters . . . to Hoki Tokuda Miller*, p. 139.

42 Dearborn, *The Happiest Man Alive*, pp. 294–5.

43 Ian S. MacNiven, *Lawrence Durrell: A Biography* (London, 1998), p. 565; Tokuda, *Nightmare*, p. 21.

44 MacNiven, ed., *The Durrell–Miller Letters*, pp. 426, 432; Jackson, *Ephemera*, p. 585.

45 Winslow, *Henry Miller: Full of Life*, p. 329.

46 Allen Edwardes and R.E.L. Masters, *The Cradle of Erotica* (New York, 1977), pp. 64, 300, 301; *Letters . . . to Hoki Tokuda Miller*, p. 61.

47 Jackson, *Ephemera*, p. 644; *Letters . . . to Hoki Tokuda Miller*, p. 89. Dates (u.s. style) of watercolours in order of book appearance: (1) 9/6/66; (2) 5/8/67; (3) 8/3/66; (4) 11/7/66; (5) 'Anno d'amore 1966'; (6) 11/9/66; (7) 9/15/66; (8) 8/22/66; (9) 9/27/69; (10) 12/24/66; (11) 11/28/66; (12) 11/23/66.

48 MacNiven, ed., *The Durrell–Miller Letters*, p. 428; *New York Review of Books* (15 February 1968), full-page ad, p. 9.

49 'Bonnie and Clyde: A Toccata for Half-Wits', in *From Your Capricorn Friend*, pp. 87–92.

50 *Durrell–Miller Letters*, p. 429.

51 Robert Snyder, 'Henry Miller: A Reminiscence', in *Critical Essays on Henry Miller*, ed. Ronald Gottesman, p. 391.

52 Jackson, *Ephemera*, p. 583.

53 Pauline Kael, *New Yorker* (7 March 1970), p. 95.

54 *My Life and Times*, p. 46; 'Introduction: The Red Herring and the Diamond–backed Terrapin', *Art in Cinema: A Symposium on the Avant-garde Film*, ed. Frank Stauffacher (San Francisco, 1947), p. 5; Brassaï, *Happy Rock*, p. 30.

55 MacNiven, ed., *The Durrell–Miller Letters*, p. 437.

56 Roger Jackson, 'Henry Miller: A Tribute in Numbers', in *Henry Miller: A Book of Tributes, 1931–1994*, ed. Craig Peter Standish (Orlando, FL, 1994), p. 542; Jackson, *Ephemera*, p. 644.

57 Harry Kiakis, 'To Paris, Via Montreal, June 22–23, 1969', *Nexus*, 9 (2012), p. 145; letter to Noel Young, Lilly Library; Miller, On the Sins of Omissions', *New York Times* (2 January 1972).

58 MacNiven, ed., *The Durrell–Miller Letters*, p. 438.

59 Jackson, *Ephemera*, p. 642.

60 Evelyn J. Hinz, ed., *Anaïs Nin: A Woman Speaks* (Chicago, 1975), pp. 100–101.

61 Gore Vidal, 'In Another Country', *New York Review of Books* (22 July 1971); see also Norris Church Mailer, *A Ticket to the Circus* (New York, 2010), p. 237; Fred Kaplan, *Gore Vidal: A Biography* (New York, 2000), p. 640.

62 Gore Vidal, *United States: Essays, 1952–1992* (New York, 1995), p. 584; Camille Paglia, 'Feminists Must Begin to Fulfill Their Noble, Animating Ideal', *Chronicle of Higher Education* (25 July 1997), p. B4; and Camille Paglia's 'Tournament of Modern Personae: D. H. Lawrence's *Women in Love*', in her *Vamps and Tramps: New Essays* (New York, 1995), p. 329.

63 MacNiven, *Lawrence Durrell: A Biography*, p. 587; MacNiven, ed., *The Durrell–Miller Letters*, p. 446; *Letters of Henry Miller and Wallace Fowlie, 1943–1972* (New York, 1975), p. 159; David Stephen Calonne, 'Henry Miller: Cosmologist', in *Henry Miller: A Book of Tributes, 1931–1994*, ed. Craig Peter Standish (Orlando, FL, 1994); Bertrand Mathieu, 'Le Chemin interieur', in *L'Arc: Henry Miller*, ed. Marc Saporta (Paris, 1985), p. 89; Mircea Eliade, 'The Occult and the Modern World', in *Occultism, Witchcraft and Cultural Fashions* (Chicago, 1976), pp. 52–3.

64 Milton O. Percival, *William Blake's Circle of Destiny* (New York, 1977), p. 242.

65 Percival, *Blake's Circle of Destiny*, p. 3; Barbara Kraft, 'The Last Days of Henry Miller', *Ping-Pong: Journal of the Henry Miller Library*, 1/1 (1994), pp. 1–2. Also see, Robert Mc L. Wilson, 'Gnosticism', in *The Oxford Companion to the Bible* (New York, 1993), p. 256.

66 See the review of *My Life and Times* by Anthony Burgess in *New York Times* (2 November 1972), p. 189.

67 MacNiven, ed., *The Durrell–Miller Letters*, pp. 449, 450; Jackson, *Ephemera*, p. 675.

68 'Knut Hamsun, *Mysteries*', *New York Times*, LXXVI/34 (22 August 1971), pp. 1, 30.

69 MacNiven, *Lawrence Durrell: A Biography*, p. 589.

8 On the Way to Devachan, 1972–80

1 See Miguel Serrano, *C. G. Jung and Hermann Hesse: A Record of Two Friendships* (New York, 1975), p. 8.

2 Miller, *Reflections on the Death of Mishima* (Santa Barbara, CA, 1972), pp. 33, 35, 36.

3 Roger Jackson, *Henry Miller: His Life in Ephemera, 1914–1980* (Ann Arbor, MI, 2012), p. 671; Ian S. MacNiven, ed., *The Durrell–Miller Letters, 1935–80* (New York, 1988), pp. 444, 456–7, 482.

4 MacNiven, ed., *The Durrell–Miller Letters*, pp. 459, 479; *Lettres à Maurice Nadeau*, p. 328.

5 *Letters of Henry Miller and Wallace Fowlie, 1943–1972* (New York, 1975), p. 158; *On Turning Eighty* (Santa Barbara, CA, 1972), pp. 7, 13, 17.

6 See Marcel Marceau letter, 'Marceau, Marcel. [Henry Miller]. Autographed & Illustrated Letter Signed. [Smile at the Foot of the Ladder]', at www.tbclrarebooks.com, accessed 20 March 2014.

7 Reprinted as the 'Introduction' to Norma Lee Browning, *Omarr: Astrology and the Man* (New York, 1977), pp. 11–15.

8 Browning, *Omarr*, p. 307.

9 S. Omarr, *Henry Miller: His World of Urania* (London, 1960), p. 55.

10 Harry Kiakis, 'To Paris, Via Montreal June 22–23, 1969', *Nexus*, 9 (1969), p. 146.

11 MacNiven, ed., *The Durrell–Miller Letters*, p. 465; David Stephen Calonne, *The Colossus of Armenia: G. I. Gurdjieff and Henry Miller, with Five Unpublished Letters to Pham Cong Thien* (Ann Arbor, MI, 1997).

12 *Lettres à Maurice Nadeau*, pp. 325–6.

13 MacNiven, ed., *The Durrell–Miller Letters*, pp. 456, 479.

14 *Lettres à Maurice Nadeau*, p. 321.

15 Beaton, *Waiting for the Angel: A Biography of George Seferis*, pp. 176–7.

16 'First Impressions of Greece', in *Sextet* (Santa Barbara, CA, 1977), p. 58.

17 Ibid., p. 85.

18 Ibid., p. 84.

19 *Henry Miller and Elmer Gertz: Selected Letters, 1964–1975* (Ann Arbor, MI, 1998), p. 80.

20 Kathryn Winslow, *Henry Miller: Full of Life* (Los Angeles, 1986), p. 332; Noel Young, *Remembering Henry Miller*, n.p.; MacNiven, ed., *The Durrell–Miller Letters*, p. 467; Thiebaud, *What Doncha Know About Henry Miller?*, p. 23.

21 *The Waters Reglitterized*, p. 52.

22 Miller, 'Two Writers in Praise of Rabelais and Each Other', *New York Times* (7 September 1974).

23 Erica Jong, *The Devil at Large: Erica Jong on Henry Miller*, pp. 259, 295.

24 Loren Glass, *Counterculture Colophon: Grove Press, the 'Evergreen Review', and the Incorporation of the Avant-Garde* (Stanford, CA, 2013), p. 51; Phillip Roth on Henry Miller, at www.webofstories.com, accessed 20 March 2014.

25 Jim Harrison, *Wolf: A False Memoir* (New York, 1971), p. 156; *Conversations with Jim Harrison*, ed. Robert DeMott (Jackson, MS, 2002), p. 178.

26 John Updike on Miller, see *Picked-Up Pieces* (New York, 1976), pp. 441–2, 505; Vladimir Nabokov, *Ada, or Ardor: A Family Chronicle* (New York, 1969), pp. 136, 596. See also Philippe Sollers in 'Liberte de Henry Miller', *Cahiers Henry Miller 1* (Perigueux, 1994), p. 9.

27 MacNiven, ed., *The Durrell–Miller Letters*, pp. 474–7.

28 Joyce Howard, ed., *Letters by Henry Miller to Hoki Tokuda Miller* (New York, 1986), p. 61.

29 Miller, 'A Letter to Gaston Criel', in *Stroker 11, The Theatre and Other Pieces*, p. 14.

30 Lawrence J. Shifreen and Roger Jackson, eds, *Henry Miller: A Bibliography of Primary Sources* (Ann Arbor, MI, 1993), p. 442.

31 Wallace Fowlie, *Rimbaud and Jim Morrison* (Durham, NC, 1993), p. 98.

32 Tom Schiller, director, *Henry Miller Asleep & Awake* [1975] (DVD, 2007).

33 Gordon, *Writer and Critic*, p. 45.

34 MacNiven, ed., *The Durrell–Miller Letters*, p. 375.

35 Frank L. Kersnowski and Alice Hughes, eds, *Conversations with Henry Miller* (Jackson, MS, 1994), p. 192; Jackson, *Ephemera*, p. 763.

36 Susan Kidder Herr, 'Henry and Me', *Nexus*, 3 (2006), p. 122; Frawley Becker, *And the Stars Spoke Back* (Lanham, MD, 1994), p. 215.

37 MacNiven, ed., *The Durrell–Miller Letters*, p. 481; Winslow, *Henry Miller: Full of Life*, p. 331.

38 Robert Kirsch, *Lives, Works and Transformations*, ed. Linda Rolens (Santa Barbara, CA, 1978), p. 67.

39 On writers and their bicycles, see James E. Starrs, ed., *The Noiseless Tenor: The Bicycle in Literature* (New York, 1982); Miller, *Flashback*, pp. 44–5; *He Said – She Said: Henry Miller and Sevasty Koutsaftis* (Ann Arbor, MI, 1998).

40 Jay Martin, *Always Merry and Bright: The Life of Henry Miller* (Santa Barbara, CA, 1978), p. 490.

41 *Dear, Dear Brenda: The Love Letters of Henry Miller to Brenda Venus*, ed. Gerald Seth Sindell (New York, 1986), pp. 13, 17, 19

42 Ibid., pp. 87, 250.

43 Plato, *The Republic,* trans. Desmond Lee (Harmondsworth, 1975), I, 329C, p. 63.

44 *Dear, Dear Brenda,* p. 41.

45 Suzanne Brogger, *To My Danish Sheherazade: A Visit and Correspondence from Henry Miller* (Ann Arbor, MI, 1998), p. 16.

46 Miller, *J'suis pas plus con qu'un autre,* p. 23.

47 *Genius and Lust,* reviewed by Frederick Crews in 'Stuttering Giant', *New York Review of Books,* XXIV (3 March 1977), reprinted as 'Kinetic Art', in *Skeptical Engagements* (New York, 1986), pp. 187–94; Michael Lennon, *Norman Mailer: A Double Life* (New York, 2013), pp. 486, 591; *The Book of Lists* (1977), p. 227.

48 David Stephen Calonne, 'Samadhi All the Time: Henry Miller and Buddhism', *Stroker,* 67, pp. 9–19; Miller, 'Preface' to Pandelis Prevelakis, *The Sun of Death* (New York, 1964), p. 9.

49 'A Nation of Lunatics', in *Four Visions of America,* p. 113.

50 Thomas Ayck, *Gegen die u.s. Gesellschaft: Gespraeche mit Henry Miller und James Baldwin* (Bad Homburg, 1977), p. 17 (translation mine).

51 John Cowper Powys, *Autobiography* (New York, 1934), pp. 449, 451.

52 Jackson, *Ephemera,* p. 759.

53 Barbara Kraft, 'A Conversation with Henry Miller', *Michigan Quarterly Review,* XX/2 (Spring 1981), p. 55.

54 Italo Calvino, *Letters, 1941–1985,* ed. Michael Wood (Princeton, NJ, 2013), p. 476.

55 *Henry Miller, Joseph Delteil: Correspondance privée, 1935–1978,* ed. F.-J. Temple (Paris, 1980), p. 185.

56 Twinka Thiebaud, *What Doncha Know about Henry Miller?* (Belvedere, CA, 2011), 'Dear Reader', p. 3; Barbara Kraft, 'The Last Days of Henry Miller', *Ping-Pong,* I/1 (1994), p. 5.

57 Elmer Gertz, *To Life: The Story of a Chicago Lawyer* (Carbondale, IL, 1990), pp. 257, 259, 260; MacNiven, ed., *The Durrell–Miller Letters,* p. 506; Clifford Terry, 'Dirty Old Henry Miller at 86', *Chicago Herald Tribune* (12 February 1978), p. 34; Kraft, 'The Last Days of Henry Miller', pp. 1, 2–3.

58 *In Touch: The Letters of Paul Bowles* (New York, 1994), p. 488; also see Bowles's letter to Miller of 7 September 1979, p. 489.

59 Miller, *From Your Capricorn Friend,* p. 60.

60 Pascal Vrebos, *444 Ocampo Drive,* ed. Karl Orend (Ann Arbor, MI, 2003), p. 56.

61 Nguyen Huu Hieu, 'Hail to the Cosmological Writer', in *Henry Miller: A Book of Tributes, 1931–1994*, ed. Craig Peter Standish (Orlando, FL, 1994), pp. 505–11.

62 Irving Stettner, 'Henry and the Music of the Spheres', 'Preface' to *In Quest of Draco and the Ecliptic*, pp. 5, 6 ; Henry Miller, 'An Open Letter to *Stroker!*', in Miller, *From Your Capricorn Friend*, p. 9.

63 Stettner, 'Henry and the Music of the Spheres', p. 7.

64 MacNiven, ed., *The Durrell–Miller Letters*, p. 507; Jackson, *Ephemera*, pp. 347, 787–8.

65 MacNiven, ed., *The Durrell–Miller Letters*, p. 510; *Stroker Anthology, 1974–1994*, p. 163.

66 Miller, *From Your Capricorn Friend*, p. 99.

67 Einer Moos, 'Memories and Dreams Unearthed', *Stroker*, 26–27, double issue (1983), p. 48.

68 Perlès, 'Henry Miller – Dead?', p. 32.

69 Kraft, 'The Last Days of Henry Miller', p. 18.

70 Ibid., pp. 8, 16; Deborah Johansen, 'Paint as you Like and Die Happy', *Ping-Pong*, 1/1 (1994), p. 36.

71 Miller, *Frère Jacques*, p. 129.

72 Kathryn Winslow, *Henry Miller: Full of Life* (Los Angeles, 1986), p. 339; 'Playing Ping Pong With Henry Miller', BBC Radio 4, 25 August 2013, at www.bbc.co.uk.

Select Bibliography

Works by Henry Miller

Tropic of Cancer (Paris, 1934)
What Are You Going To Do About Alf? (Paris, 1935)
Aller retour New York (Paris, 1935)
Black Spring (Paris, 1936)
Scenario (A Film with Sound) (Paris, 1937)
Money and How it Gets that Way (Paris, 1938)
Max and the White Phagocytes (Paris, 1938)
Tropic of Capricorn (Paris, 1939)
Hamlet, Volume I (Paris, 1939)
The Cosmological Eye (Norfolk, CT, 1939)
Hamlet, Volume II (Mexico City, 1941)
The World of Sex (Chicago, 1941)
The Colossus of Maroussi (San Francisco, 1941)
The Wisdom of the Heart (Norfolk, CT, 1941)
The Angel is My Watermark (Fullerton, CA, 1944)
Sunday After the War (Norfolk, CT, 1944)
Murder the Murderer (Berkeley, CA, 1944)
The Plight of the Creative Artist in the United States of America (Berkeley, CA, 1944)
Semblance of a Devoted Past (Berkeley, CA, 1945)
A Henry Miller Miscellanea (Berkeley, CA, 1945)
Obscenity and the Law of Reflection (Yonkers, NY, 1945)
Why Abstract? (Norfolk, CT, 1945)
The Air-Conditioned Nightmare (Norfolk, CT, 1945)
Maurizius Forever (San Francisco, 1946)
Patchen: Man of Anger and Light (New York, 1946)

Into the Night Life (Berkeley, CA, 1947)

Of, By and About Henry Miller (New York, 1947)

Varda, The Master Builder (Berkeley, CA, 1947)

Remember to Remember (Norfolk, CT, 1947)

The Smile at the Foot of the Ladder (New York, 1948)

Sexus (Paris, 1949)

The Waters Reglitterized (Sacramento, CA, 1950)

The Books in My Life (Norfolk, CT, 1952)

Plexus (Paris, 1953)

Nights of Love and Laughter (New York, 1955)

Devil in Paradise (New York, 1956)

Quiet Days in Clichy (Paris, 1956)

The Time of the Assassins (Norfolk, CT, 1956)

Big Sur and the Oranges of Hieronymus Bosch (Norfolk, CT, 1957)

The Red Notebook (Highlands, NC, 1958)

Art and Outrage (New York, 1959)

The Henry Miller Reader (Norfolk, CT, 1959)

Nexus (Paris, 1960)

To Paint is to Love Again (Alhambra, CA, 1960)

Tropic of Cancer (New York, 1961)

Tropic of Capricorn (New York, 1962)

Stand Still Like the Hummingbird (Norfolk, CT, 1962)

Just Wild about Harry (Norfolk, CT, 1963)

Black Spring (New York, 1963)

Henry Miller on Writing (Norfolk, CT, 1964)

Sexus (New York, 1965)

Plexus (New York, 1965)

Nexus (New York, 1965)

Order and Chaos Chez Hans Reichel (New Orleans, LA, 1966)

Insomnia; or, The Devil at Large (Albuquerque, NM, 1960)

My Life and Times (Chicago, 1972)

Reflections on the Death of Mishima (Santa Barbara, CA, 1972)

On Turning Eighty (Santa Barbara, CA, 1972)

First Impressions of Greece (Santa Barbara, CA, 1973)

This is Henry, Henry Miller from Brooklyn (Los Angeles, CA, 1974)

The Nightmare Notebook (New York, 1975)

Henry Miller's Book of Friends (Santa Barbara, CA, 1976)

J'suis pas plus con qu'un autre (Paris, 1976)
Genius and Lust (New York, 1976)
Gliding into the Everglades (Lake Oswego, OR, 1977)
Mother, China, and the World Beyond (Santa Barbara, CA, 1977)
Sextet (Santa Barbara, CA, 1977)
My Bike and Other Friends (Santa Barbara, CA, 1978)
*Joey: A Loving Portrait of Alfred Perlès Together with Some Bizarre Episodes
    Relating to the Other Sex* (Santa Barbara, CA, 1979)
The World of Lawrence: A Passionate Appreciation (Santa Barbara, CA, 1980)
Henry and June: From the Unexpurgated Diary of Anaïs Nin (New York,
    1986)

Select Correspondence

Blaise Cendrars–Henry Miller: Correspondance, 1934–1979: 45 ans d'amitié,
    ed. Miriam Cendrars (Paris, 1995)
*Collector's Quest: The Correspondence of Henry Miller and J. Rives Childs,
    1947–1965*, ed. Richard Clement Wood (Charlottesville, VA, 1968)
Dear, Dear Brenda: The Love Letters of Henry Miller to Brenda Venus, ed.
    Gerald Seth Sindell (New York, 1986)
Henry Miller and Elmer Gertz: Selected Letters, 1964–1975 (Ann Arbor, MI,
    1998)
Henry Miller and James Laughlin: Selected Letters, ed. George Wickes
    (New York, 1996)
Henry Miller, John Cowper Powys: Correspondence privée, ed. Nordine
    Haddad (Paris, 1994)
Henry Miller, Joseph Delteil: Correspondence privée, 1935–1978, ed. F.-J.
    Temple (Paris, 1980)
The Henry Miller–Herbert Read Letters, 1935–1958, ed. James Gifford
    (Ann Arbor, MI, 2007)
Henry Miller: Letters to Anaïs Nin, ed. Gunther Stuhlmann (New York, 1965)
Henry Miller: Letters to Emil, ed. George Wickes (New York, 1989)
*Henry Miller: Years of Trial and Triumph, the Correspondence of Henry Miller
    and Elmer Gertz*, ed. Elmer Gertz and Felice Flannery Lewis
    (Carbondale and Edwardsville, IL, 1978)
Lawrence Durrell and Henry Miller: A Private Correspondence, ed. George
    Wickes (New York, 1963)

Lettres à Maurice Nadeau, 1947-1978, ed. Sophie Bogaert (Paris, 2012)
Letters by Henry Miller to Hoki Tokuda Miller, ed. Joyce Howard (New York, 1986)
Letters of Henry Miller and Wallace Fowlie (New York, 1965)
A Literate Passion: Letters of Anaïs Nin and Henry Miller, 1932–1953, ed. and intro. Gunther Stuhlmann (New York, 1987)
The Durrell–Miller Letters, 1935–80, ed. Ian S. MacNiven (New York, 1988)
Writer and Critic: A Correspondence with Henry Miller, ed. William A. Gordon (Baton Rouge, LA, 1968)

Critical Literature

Ayck, Thomas, *Gegen die U.S.–Gesellschaft: Gesprache mit Henry Miller and James Baldwin* (Bad Homburg, 1977)
Bataille, Georges, 'La Morale de Miller' and 'L'Inculpation d'Henry Miller', in *Oeuvres Complètes, XI: Articles 1, 1944–1949* (Paris, 1988)
Blanchot, Maurice, 'From Lautréamont to Miller', in *The Work of Fire*, trans. Charlotte Mandell (Stanford, CA, 1995)
Bloshteyn, Maria, *The Making of a Countercultural Icon: Henry Miller's Dostoyevsky* (Toronto, 2007)
Bolckmans, Alex, 'Henry Miller's *Tropic of Cancer* and Knut Hamsun's *Sult*', *Scandinavica*, 14 (1975)
Calonne, David Stephen, 'Anaïs Nin, Henry Miller and Psychoanalysis', in *Anaïs: A Book of Mirrors* (Huntington Woods, MI, 1996)
——, *Charles Bukowski: Critical Lives* (London, 2012)
——, ed., *Charles Bukowski: Sunlight Here I Am / Interviews & Encounters* (Northville, MI, 2003)
——, *The Colossus of Armenia: G. I. Gurdjieff and Henry Miller* (Ann Arbor, MI, 1997)
——, 'The Discovery of Yourself: Lawrence Durrell and Gostan Zarian in Greece', in Anna Lillios, ed., *Lawrence Durrell and the Greek World* (London, 2004)
——, 'Euphoria in Paris: D. H. Lawrence and Henry Miller', *Library Chronicle of the University of Texas at Austin*, 34 (1986)
——, 'Foreword', *Henry Miller: Letters to 'The Black Cat'* (Ann Arbor, MI, 1996)
——, 'Henry Miller: Cosmologist', in *Henry Miller: A Book of Tributes, 1931–1994*, ed. Craig Peter Standish (Orlando, FL, 1994)

——, 'Henry Miller, Ernest Hemingway and Smyrna 1922' in *Armenian Smyrna/Izmir: The Aegean Communities* (Costa Mesa, CA, 2012)

——, 'Henry Miller and Tibet', *Stroker* 68, ed. Irving Stettner (2000)

——, 'Henry Miller, William Saroyan and *The Booster*', *Stroker* 65 and 66, ed. Irving Stettner (1999)

——, 'Samadhi All the Time: Henry Miller and Buddhism', *Stroker* 67, ed. Irving Stettner (2000)

——, *William Saroyan: My Real Work is Being* (London and Chapel Hill, NC, 1983)

Cendrars, Miriam, *Blaise Cendrars* (Paris, 1993)

Chapsal, Madeleine, *Quinze Ecrivains: Entretiens* (Paris, 1963)

Dearborn, Mary, *The Happiest Man Alive: A Biography of Henry Miller* (New York, 1991)

De Grazia, Edward, *Girls Lean Back Everywhere: The Law of Obscenity and the Assault on Genius* (New York, 1993)

Fontbrune, Jean-Charles de, *Henry Miller et Nostradamus* (Monaco, 1994)

Hoffman, Daniel, ed., *The Harvard Guide to Contemporary American Writing* (Cambridge, MA, 1979)

Hutchinson, E. R., *'Tropic of Cancer' on Trial: A Case History of Censorship* (New York, 1968)

Jackson, Roger and Lawrence Shifreen, *Henry Miller: A Bibliography of Primary Sources* (Ann Arbor, MI, 1993)

——, *Henry Miller: His Life in Ephemera, 1914–1980* (Ann Arbor, MI, 2012)

Jünger, Ernst, *Uber die Linie,* in *Werke,* vol. 5: *Essays 1: Bertrachtungen zur Zeit* (Stuttgart, 1960)

Keeley, Edmund, *Inventing Paradise: The Greek Journey, 1937–47* (New York, 1999)

Kendall, Stuart, *Georges Bataille* (London, 2007)

Krissdottir, Morine, *Descents of Memory: The Life of John Cowper Powys* (New York, 2007)

Lennon, J. Michael, *Conversations with Norman Mailer* (Jackson, MS, 1988)

——, *Norman Mailer: A Double Life* (New York, 2013)

MacNiven, Ian, *Lawrence Durrell: A Biography* (London, 1998)

Mathieu, Bertrand, *Orpheus in Brooklyn: Orphism, Rimbaud, and Henry Miller,* Preface by Wallace Fowlie (The Hague and Paris, 1976)

Nesbit, Thomas, *Henry Miller and Religion* (New York, 2007)

Orwell, George, 'The End of Henry Miller,' *London Tribune* (4 December 1942), pp. 18–19

——, 'English Writing in Total War', *New Republic* (14 July 1941)

Perlès, Alfred, *My Friend Henry Miller* (London, 1973)

Porter, Bern, ed., *The Happy Rock: A Book About Henry Miller* (Berkeley, CA, 1945)

Pound, Ezra, *Selected Letters 1907–1941*, ed. D. D. Paige (New York, 1971)

Queneau, Raymond, 'Tropic of Cancer; Black Spring', *La Nouvelle Revue Française*, XXV (1 December 1936), pp. 1083–4

Read, Forrest, ed., *Pound/Joyce: The Letters of Ezra Pound to James Joyce* (New York, 1967)

Rembar, Charles, *The End of Obscenity: The Trials of Lady Chatterley, Tropic of Cancer and Fanny Hill* (New York, 1986)

Schevill, James, *Where to Go, What to Do, When You Are Bern Porter: A Personal Biography* (Gardiner, ME, 1992)

Schmidt, Henning, *Der Mythos Henry Miller* (Heidelberg, 1977)

Shapiro, Karl, 'The Greatest Living Author', in *In Defense of Ignorance* (New York, 1960)

——, 'Henry Miller and Myself', *Carleton Miscellany*, V (Summer 1964)

——, 'Poets of the Cosmic Consciousness', in *In Defense of Ignorance* (New York, 1960)

Singer, Isaac Bashevis, *Conversations with Isaac Bashevis Singer*, ed. Richard Burgin (New York, 1985)

Strausbaugh, John, *The Village, 400 Years of Beats and Bohemians, Radicals and Rogues: A History of Greenwich Village* (New York, 2013)

Weddle, Jeff, *Bohemian New Orleans: The Story of the Outsider and Loujon Press* (Jackson, MS, 2007)

Wickes, George, *Henry Miller* (Minneapolis, MI, 1996)

Williams, Linda, 'Critical Warfare in Henry Miller's *Tropic of Cancer*', in *Feminist Criticism: Theory and Practice*, ed. Susan Sellers (Toronto, 1991)

Winslow, Kathryn, *Henry Miller: Full of Life* (Los Angeles, 1986)

Journals and Websites

Nexus: An International Henry Miller Journal (10 annual issues published since 2004)

www.cosmotc.blogspot.co.uk (Cosmodemonic Telegraph Company: A Henry Miller Blog)

www.henrymiller.org (Henry Miller Memorial Library)

Acknowledgements

I would like to thank Valentine and Tony Miller for their permission to use material from the Henry Miller Estate. Thanks to Roger Jackson, bibliographer and publisher *extraordinaire*, who has helped me immeasurably. I am particularly grateful for his recent gargantuan 832-page masterwork, *Henry Miller: His Life in Ephemera, 1914–1980* (2012) which was a treasure-trove of formerly either unknown or inaccessible information. Thanks to Roderick Beaton, Alison Bechdel, Paul Herron, Gary Koeppel, Barbara Kraft, Jacques Meny, Paul Lorenz, Ian MacNiven, Lauren Macmillan, Gail Mezey Morris and Twinka Thiebaud. Special thanks to Matt Zacharias. Thanks as always for everything to Maria Beye. I would like to thank Vivian Constantinopoulos and Aimee Selby at Reaktion Books for their professional expertise. Again as ever, gratitude to my constant companion, J. S. Bach.

Permissions

Excerpt from 'Les Anges sont blanc', translated by Edmund Keeley, p. 259 in *George Seferis: Collected Poems*, copyright © 1969, 1981, 1995 the Estate of George Seferis and Princeton University Press.

Excerpts from *Henry Miller, Years of Trial and Triumph, 1962–1964: The Correspondence of Henry Miller and Elmer Gertz*, copyright © 1978 Southern Illinois University Press.

Excerpts from *Crazy Cock* by Henry Miller, copyright © 1991 by Estate of Henry Miller. Foreword copyright © 1991 by Erica Jong. Introduction copyright © 1991 by Mary V. Dearborn. Excerpts from *Moloch* by Henry Miller, copyright © 1992 by Estate of Henry Miller. Introduction copyright © 1992 by Mary V. Dearborn. Excerpts from *Nexus* by Henry Miller,

Photo Acknowledgements

AKG Images: pp. 111, 113 (Denise Bellon); Alison Bechdel, © 2013, reproduced by permission: pp. 150, 151; Karl Bissinger: p. 117; Columbia University, New York, Rare Book and Manuscript Library, Hubert Harrison Papers: p. 31; Association des Amis de Jean Giono: p. 71 (Manosque / Jacques Meny); © Peter Gowland: p. 134; Courtesy The Lilly Library, Indiana University, Bloomington, Indiana: p. 132; The Library of Congress, Washington, DC, Carl Van Vechten Photographic Collection: p. 99; Valentine and Tony Miller: pp. 80, 81 (The Henry Miller Estate / Grove Press), 88 (The Henry Miller Estate); © Gail Mezey Morris: pp. 159, 171; Anaïs Nin Trust, all rights reserved: pp. 39, 53; Schweizerische Nationalbibliothek NB, Bern, Switzerland: p. 51; George Seferis Photographic Archive / National Bank of Greece Cultural Foundation, © Anna Lontou: p. 77; Smithsonian, Washington, DC, National Portrait Gallery / Art Resource: p. 6; UCLA Library Special Collections: pp. 11, 17, 56, 68; University of Washington Libraries, Special Collections, Mary Randlett UW 36125 and UW 36124: pp. 103, 105; Yale University / Beinecke Library Rare Book and Manuscript Library: p. 19.